G000153996

The Kosovo crisis and the
of post-Cold War European security

MANCHESTER
UNIVERSITY PRESS

The Kosovo crisis and the evolution of post-Cold War European security

Paul Latawski
Martin A. Smith

Manchester University Press
Manchester and New York

published exclusively in the USA by Palgrave

Copyright © Paul Latawski and Martin A. Smith 2003

The right of Paul Latawski and Martin A. Smith to be identified
as the authors of this work has been asserted by them in accordance
with the Copyright, Designs and Patents Act 1988.

Published by
Manchester University Press
Oxford Road, Manchester M13 9NR, UK
and Room 400, 175 Fifth Avenue, New York, NY 10010, USA
www.manchesteruniversitypress.co.uk

Distributed exclusively in the USA by
Palgrave, 175 Fifth Avenue, New York,
NY 10010, USA

Distributed exclusively in Canada by
UBC Press, University of British Columbia, 2029 West Mall
Vancouver, BC, Canada V6T 1Z2

British Library Cataloguing-in-Publication Data
A catalogue record for this book is available from the British Library

Library of Congress Cataloging-in-Publication Data applied for

ISBN 0 7190 5979 8 *hardback*
     0 7190 5980 1 *paperback*

First published 2003

11 10 09 08 07 06 05 04 03   10 9 8 7 6 5 4 3 2 1

Typeset by Helen Skelton, Brighton, UK
Printed in Great Britain
by Bookcraft (Bath) Ltd, Midsomer Norton

Contents

Preface

The origins of this book are rooted during *Operation Allied Force* in 1999. Even as that conflict raged, the two authors debated the issues and decided that a book was necessary in order to examine a number of the fascinating and important questions spawned by the Kosovo crisis. After considerable deliberation, the present structure was adopted for considering the crisis within the continuum of developments in post-Cold War European security.

The book has been greatly assisted by the inputs of a number of people who deserve special mention and our thanks. Dr Christopher Donnelly, the Special Advisor to the Secretary-General of NATO, kindly arranged a series of very valuable interviews with NATO officials. These greatly illuminated a number of issues examined here. Similarly, Mrs Anne Aldis and other members of the Conflict Studies Research Centre at Camberley assisted the authors in the preparation of our material. An expression of well-deserved appreciation is necessary to Andrew Orgill and his team at the Royal Military Academy Sandhurst library. They were very helpful in addressing our bibliographic requests and pointing us in the direction of books, articles and other material useful for coming to grips with the complicated issues raised by the Kosovo crisis. Finally, family and friends gave considerable encouragement and support and they receive our heartfelt thanks – particularly Dorina Latawska who patiently endured much 'shop talk' from the authors during the gestation of this book!

The final task to be performed here is to note that the analysis, opinions and conclusions expressed or implied in this book are those of the authors alone. They do not necessarily represent the views of the Royal Military Academy Sandhurst, the UK Ministry of Defence or any other government agency.

Paul Latawski, Martin A. Smith

Notes on the authors

Paul Latawski is Senior Lecturer in Defence and International Affairs at the Royal Military Academy Sandhurst. He is also an Associate Fellow at the Royal United Services Institute in London. His principal research interests include contemporary Poland and security in Central and South East Europe. Recent publications in these areas include *The Transformation of the Polish Armed Forces: Preparing for NATO* (RUSI, 1999) and *Britain, NATO, and the Lessons of the Balkan Conflicts 1991–1999*, co-edited with Stephen Badsey (Frank Cass, 2003).

Martin A. Smith is Senior Lecturer in Defence and International Affairs at the Royal Military Academy Sandhurst. His main research interests are in the fields of international and European security. Recent books include *NATO in the First Decade after the Cold War* (Kluwer, 2000) and *Uncertain Europe*, co-edited with Graham Timmins (Routledge, 2001). He is currently collaborating on book projects on the European Union, NATO and Russia, and an introduction to the theory and practice of European security.

List of abbreviations

AFOR	Albania Force
CFSP	Common Foreign and Security Policy
CJTF	Combined Joint Task Force
EAA	Euro-Atlantic Area
EAPC	Euro-Atlantic Partnership Council
EC	European Community
EDC	European Defence Community
EEC	European Economic Community
ESDP	European Security and Defence Policy
EU	European Union
FRG	Federal Republic of Germany
FRY	Federal Republic of Yugoslavia
G8	Group of Eight
ICG	International Crisis Group
IFOR	Implementation Force
KFOR	Kosovo Force
KLA	Kosovo Liberation Army (UCK in Albanian)
KVM	Kosovo Verification Mission
NAC	North Atlantic Council
NATO	North Atlantic Treaty Organisation
NOD	Non Offensive Defence
NRC	NATO-Russia Council
OSCE	Organisation for Security and Co-operation in Europe
PfP	Partnership for Peace
PJC	Permanent Joint Council (NATO-Russia)
RNAC	Russia-North Atlantic Council
SACEUR	Supreme Allied Commander Europe

SFOR	Stabilisation Force
TEU	*Treaty on European Union*
UK	United Kingdom
UN	United Nations
UNHCR	United Nations High Commissioner for Refugees
UNMIK	United Nations Interim Administration Mission in Kosovo
UNPROFOR	United Nations Protection Force
UNSC	United Nations Security Council
US	United States
USAF	United States Air Force
USEUCOM	United States European Command
WEU	Western European Union
XFOR	Extraction Force

Introduction

The structure and purpose of this book

This volume does not seek to offer a detailed account of the background to and course of the Kosovo crisis, which reached its peak of intensity in 1998–99. A number of highly competent such studies have already been published.[1] Nor are the discussions that follow framed principally as a 'lessons learned' analysis. The main objective here, rather, is to examine and assess the impact of the Kosovo crisis on the continuing evolution and development of key issues relating to post-Cold War European security overall.

In measuring this impact the discussions begin, logically, with the North Atlantic Treaty Organisation (NATO). This was the chosen instrument through which its member states sought to achieve their objective of compelling the government of President Slobodan Milosevic in the Federal Republic of Yugoslavia (FRY) to cease and desist from what the former considered to be unacceptable activities in Kosovo province. Further, the FRY was also compelled effectively to cede authority over Kosovo to an international protectorate. NATO thus sits at the nexus of a number of important debates. Perhaps the most controversial concern the nature of its intervention and the circumstances in which such interventions in international affairs may be considered justifiable and legitimate. Reflecting their importance in most assessments of the Kosovo crisis, these issues are examined here in Chapter 1.

Chapter 2 considers structural issues and looks at the impact of the conduct of *Operation Allied Force* – the NATO bombing campaign of March–June 1999 – on both the internal workings of NATO and the expansion of its geographical areas of interest and remit within Europe.

This is followed, in Chapter 3, by an assessment of the premises, assumptions and ultimate prospects for success of western-led attempts, through NATO and other international institutions, to bring about social, political and economic reconstruction in South East Europe.[2] Such efforts are being undertaken on the basis of trying to transplant western norms and values relating to, for example, liberal democracy and an inclusive – or 'civic' – national identity.

Relations between NATO and its members, on the one hand, and Russia on the other, represent arguably the single most important set of links in contemporary European security affairs. The Kosovo crisis can be described as a watershed event in the development of Russia–NATO relations in the period since Russia re-emerged as an independent state in December 1991. Chapter 4 of this volume thus offers a detailed account of the difficult, occasionally tortuous, but ultimately essential diplomatic co-operation between the Russians and NATO members which accompanied the ongoing air campaign in the spring and early summer of 1999. The impact of the crisis, and of this co-operation, on the relationship since that time is also considered here.

One of the favourite 'lessons of Kosovo' drawn by commentators and observers since 1999 has been to do with the extent to which *Operation Allied Force* painted up a military 'capabilities cap' between the European members of NATO and the United States. As a direct result of this, it is often argued, the member states of the European Union (EU) resolved to develop an autonomous collective military capability in order to enable them hopefully to avoid such an embarrassing degree of operational dependence on the US in Europe in the future. The discussions in Chapter 5 argue that the impact of the Kosovo crisis in this area has, in reality, been relatively marginal and certainly less significant than the view sketched out above suggests. To be sure, the intra-EU debates on the issue did get going at the same time as Kosovo was reaching crisis point. However, the prime movers in these debates – France and the United Kingdom – were motivated principally by other concerns.

The discussions in Chapter 6, finally, are concerned with the issue of why NATO and its members took such an interest in Kosovo when they appeared to have few if any conventional strategic or economic interests tied up there. The answer, it is suggested here, lies in considering the enduring importance of the post-Second World War 'Atlantic Community' that has developed amongst the NATO members, and the *de facto* extension of its boundaries since the end of the Cold War.

Serb activities in Kosovo, it is argued, represented not a territorial threat to NATO but rather a challenge to the core values for which it claimed to stand. A response was thus deemed essential in order not only to defeat this challenge but, in doing so, to uphold the credibility of the institution itself.

Before embarking on these discussions, a brief recap on the background to and the course of the crisis in Kosovo may be useful. As indicated above, it is not our intention to describe or assess them in detail; that task has been ably accomplished elsewhere. The objective here is to provide a sufficient degree of background information in one convenient place at the outset so as to spare both authors and readers the necessity of having to digress in the main chapters with background material.

Kosovo and the crisis

Kosovo was, for a long time, at the margins of European affairs. The problems relating to it that leapt onto the front pages in 1998–99 were, for many, a 'quarrel in a far-away country between people of whom we know nothing' to quote the now infamous words of British Prime Minister Neville Chamberlain in 1938.[3] The crisis in Kosovo may have been, amongst other things, an indictment of the western public's knowledge and understanding of South East Europe's history, politics and geography, but it was far from being a peripheral matter in the evolution of post-Cold War European security. As Roland Dannreuther has observed, the importance of the Kosovo crisis has been that it has acted as a 'prism through which some of the most contentious and unresolved questions of contemporary international politics have been debated'.[4]

The historical background

It is safe to say that Kosovo is a land that has not been greatly frequented in the past by outside travellers, or in more recent times by tourists on package holidays. Its inaccessibility, however, is less due to challenging topographical features than a political geography characterised by disorder and violence that has made this corner of South East Europe, in periods of its history, a place best avoided. As Ger Duijzings has observed, 'Kosovo is an example of a poor, peripheral and conflict-ridden society, where the central authority of the state has been nominal for much of its modern history'.[5]

The physical geography of Kosovo is easy to understand. The mountains ringing Kosovo make it a natural geographical unit. On its southern rim are the *Šar* mountains – the highest range – bordering Albania. On the western side are the *Prokletije* (Accursed) mountains, so called because of the difficulty in crossing them. On Kosovo's eastern side stand the *Skopska Crna Gora* and, in the northern reaches, the *Kopaonik* mountains form the border with Serbia proper. The interior of Kosovo is a kind of high plain divided into two roughly equal parts by a range of hills running from east to west. The rivers in Kosovo either flow north or south from this line of hills. The largest city and administrative capital is Pristina in the northern part of the territory.[6]

As a political unit, Kosovo formed part of the medieval Serb Kingdom. By the second half of the fifteenth century, it had become part of the Ottoman Empire's conquests in the region. It remained in the Ottoman Empire until the First and Second Balkan Wars of 1912 and 1913, when it became, once again, a province of Serbia. Apart from the period of the Second World War, Kosovo remained in Serbia's 'successor', Communist Yugoslavia.[7] Whether as part of the Ottoman Empire, Serbia or Yugoslavia, Kosovo was one of the poorer regions of those states. Apart from some mineral wealth, agriculture was the mainstay of economic activity.[8]

Ethnic composition of Kosovo

From the nineteenth century onwards, the competing national movements of the Albanian and Serb inhabitants of the province increasingly shaped the story of Kosovo. For each group, the province was associated with historical events seen as central to the development of their national identities. The Serbs have historically seen Kosovo as the cradle of their medieval Serb Kingdom; a land of monasteries, castles and the resting place of great kings. In terms of Serb national mythologies, there is no more important event than the Battle of Kosovo (*Kosovo Polje*), fought between the Serb Kingdom and the Ottomans in 1389. Less a defeat than a draw, *Kosovo Polje*, however, marked the beginning of the end of medieval Serbia. The legends and myths associated with Prince Lazar, the Serb leader at *Kosovo Polje*, provided an important link between the medieval kingdom and the emergence of a modern Serb national consciousness from the nine-teenth century onwards.[9] Regardless of its ethnographic composition (discussed below), Kosovo was regarded as a key part of the Serb national patrimony.

For the Albanians, Kosovo also occupies an important place in the development of Albanian nationalism. In one of its southern cities, Prizren, the development of the Albanian national identity received a powerful boost. In Prizren, during one of the innumerable crises of South East Europe that involved the European great powers, the Albanians formed a political organisation called the 'League of Prizren' in 1878 to support the Ottoman Empire's control of the Albanian inhabited parts of the region. One of the leading figures in the League was Abdul Frasheri, who inspired united political action amongst the Albanians of the Ottoman Empire. The aim of the League was to try to prevent the dismemberment of the Ottoman Empire by the great powers; particularly the Albanian inhabited territories of South East Europe. Although supporting the Ottoman government, the League of Prizren would eventually be suppressed by Ottoman forces because of its nationalist tendencies. The League, however, marked an impor-tant moment in the awakening of an Albanian national identity.[10]

With Kosovo thus important to both the Serb and Albanian national identity, it was almost certain to be a contested piece of territory. In nationalist conflicts of this kind, demography plays an important role in formulating claim and counter-claim. The ethno-graphic composition of Kosovo and its evolution since the nineteenth century, form an important backdrop to the contemporary conflicts between Albanian and Serb for control of it. By the last quarter of the nineteenth century, the population of Kosovo had an Albanian majority, with the Serbs as a sizeable minority.[11] Although statistical data must be treated with some caution in these situations, it is clear that, even allowing for political distortion, the Serb community was diminishing in terms of its overall numbers. After Kosovo became part of Serbia in the twentieth century, colonisation programmes did little to arrest the trend of a growing Albanian majority. During the period of Communist Yugoslavia, the Albanian majority continued to grow as illustrated in Table Intro.1.

On the eve of the 1999 conflict, the Serb minority was estimated as forming about 10 per cent of the population. In the wake of the Serb exodus following the June 1999 withdrawal of FRY military and police forces, the number of Serbs living in Kosovo may have been cut by as much as three-quarters of its pre-conflict total.[12]

Table Intro.1   *Ethnic composition of Kosovo, the censuses of 1961, 1971
                   and 1981 (%)*

	1961	*1971*	*1981*
Albanians	67.1	73.7	77.5
Serbs	23.5	18.3	13.2

Source: M. Vickers, *Between Serb and Albanian: A History of Kosovo* (London, Hurst and Co., 1998), p. 318.

Kosovo 1989–99: conflict, diplomacy and conflict

The proximate background to the Kosovo conflict of March–June 1999 was the mounting Albanian–Serb tension and violence of the previous decade. The Albanians, who had enjoyed a measure of autonomy in Communist Yugoslavia; controlling such things as local administration and education, saw this swept away from the late 1980s. This happened in the face of resurgent Serb nationalism and, more particularly, the policies of President Milosevic who exploited it to strengthen his political position in Serbia. The Albanian response was initially non-violent. A semi-clandestine parallel society and political life developed in Kosovo despite intermittent pressure from the Serb authorities.

By the late 1990s, however, non-violent protest began to give way to armed Albanian resistance to what was seen as Serb oppression. This manifested itself in the emergence of the Kosovo Liberation Army (KLA) which, by the late 1990s, was gaining support within Kosovo and international attention, even if its military achievements against the FRY security forces were modest.[13] As the dispute became violent, it led increasingly to deaths, displacement of Albanians and destruction of property.

Although some outside observers had become concerned about the growing tensions in Kosovo, the initially relatively low level of violence, as compared with that seen in Bosnia in the first half of the 1990s, meant that these did not register high up on the agendas of European security organisations such as NATO. In 1998, however, as fighting intensified between FRY security forces and the KLA, Kosovo did move up the political agenda of a NATO determined to stop the crisis escalating to a level of violence seen earlier in Croatia and, especially, Bosnia.

By autumn 1998, the violence in Kosovo had resulted in a situation where an estimated 250,000 Kosovar Albanians had been ousted from their homes; roughly one fifth of their number lacking proper shelter. In the context of this situation, the United Nations Security Council (UNSC) passed Resolution 1199 in September 1998, calling for a cease-fire, withdrawal of most FRY security forces and talks between the parties in conflict. It also issued a warning about a looming 'humanitarian catastrophe' resulting from the fighting.[14] In an effort to increase pressure on the Milosevic government in Belgrade, NATO threatened airstrikes in order to induce his compliance with the terms of the UN Resolution.

A combination of diplomacy and this military pressure persuaded the FRY President to agree to comply in October. An agreement with Milosevic was brokered by US Assistant Secretary of State, Richard Holbrooke. He was the man widely credited with successfully bringing about the negotiation of the Dayton agreement, which had ended the Bosnian civil war three years previously. FRY compliance with the Holbrooke-Milosevic agreement was to be verified by the Organisation for Security and Co-operation in Europe (OSCE). This was the only outside monitoring agency that Milosevic was prepared to accept in Kosovo. The OSCE created an unarmed, civilian 'Kosovo Verification Mission' (KVM), which began operating in November 1998. A small, French-led NATO military 'Extraction Force' was deployed to neighbouring Macedonia in case the KVM required emergency evacuation.

By the beginning of 1999, the Holbrooke-Milosevic agreement was beginning to unravel. The FRY authorities began to move forces back into Kosovo claiming, not entirely unreasonably, that their efforts to comply with the UN Resolution had done little but give the KLA a breathing space in which to regroup and occupy positions formerly held by FRY forces. On the Albanian side, allegations were made of fresh killings and atrocities being committed by the FRY forces.

In the face of this deterioration, a final diplomatic effort began in January 1999 when the parties in conflict were summoned to Rambouillet outside Paris. These high-level negotiations sought a general settlement in the manner of the Dayton process for Bosnia. The 'Contact Group', consisting of France, the Federal Republic of Germany, Italy, the United Kingdom, Russia and the United States, aimed for a settlement that NATO was prepared to underwrite with a major peace support force in Kosovo. The proposals at Rambouillet offered substantial autonomy for the Kosovar Albanians and held out the eventual prospect of a referendum that might lead to independence. The Kosovar Albanians, with some reservations, eventually accepted the formula, but the FRY delegation walked away from the draft proposals.[15] The FRY's refusal to sign, and the deteriorating situation inside Kosovo, led to the withdrawal of the KVM in March and, within a week, NATO's decision to finally use coercive airpower.

Operation Allied Force, March–June 1999

When NATO launched *Operation Allied Force* on 24 March 1999, its members and planners expected air operations to be successfully concluded within a few days. In the event, NATO's military effort lasted for over two months. In this exercise in military coercion, the United States publicly ruled out, at the start, the idea of committing forces to a land invasion of Kosovo. When the FRY refused to be cowed by the air onslaught, this thus called into question NATO's strategy of what some had called 'immaculate coercion'.[16]

As in most modern armed conflicts, the media was an important factor, with the protagonists fighting a second battle across the airwaves.[17] NATO's well-publicised targeting mistakes, such as the accidental bombing of Albanian refugees and the Chinese Embassy in Belgrade,[18] illustrated the importance of effective media management in modern conflict and the consequences when this proved difficult or impossible.

As the operation dragged on, NATO increased the numbers of aircraft and widened the targeting list to strike at the heart of the FRY's infrastructure, government and media apparatus. By June 1999, it was increasingly clear that NATO would use whatever level of force was necessary for it to prevail. The use of ground forces was, at last, being seriously considered. There was also mounting evidence that the air attacks were causing serious damage and that unrest was beginning to surface inside Serbia. By then also, NATO's diplomatic pressure was being actively supported by Russia.

In early June, President Milosevic indicated his acceptance of the international demands, compliance with which was necessary to end the bombing.[19] After brief negotiations with NATO, represented by Lieutenant General Sir Michael Jackson, the FRY leadership agreed to withdraw its security forces and accept a NATO-led peacekeeping force and a UN international administration mission in Kosovo. These points were incorporated into Security Council Resolution 1244, which was passed shortly thereafter. On the question of the future status of Kosovo, the Resolution was deliberately ambiguous. Unlike in the Rambouillet drafts, there was no clear signal that a referendum on eventual independence would be organised.[20] Kosovo's future thus remained uncertain.

Notes

1 The best are I. Daalder and M. O'Hanlon, *Winning Ugly: NATO's War to Save Kosovo* (Washington DC, Brookings, 2000) and T. Judah, *Kosovo: War and Revenge* (New Haven, Yale University Press, 2000).

2 In this volume, the geographical descriptor 'South East Europe' is preferred to the loaded designation 'the Balkans'. It covers the successor states to the Cold War Communist Yugoslavia: Bosnia and Herzegovina, Croatia, Macedonia, Slovenia and the Federal Republic of Yugoslavia, which embraces Serbia and Montenegro. It also covers their immediate neighbours: Albania, Bulgaria, Greece, Hungary and Romania. On the problems of using the term 'the Balkans' see J. Gow, 'A region of eternal conflict? The Balkans – semantics and security', in W. Park and G. W. Rees (eds), *Rethinking Security in Post-Cold War Europe* (London, Longman, 1998), pp. 155–8.

3 BBC Radio Broadcast, 27 September 1938.

4 R. Dannreuther, 'War in Kosovo: history, development and aftermath', in M. Buckley and S. Cummings (eds), *Kosovo: Perceptions of War and Its Aftermath* (London, Continuum, 2001), p. 13.

5 G. Duijzings, *Religion and the Politics of Identity in Kosovo* (London, Hurst and Co., 2000), p. 5.

6 For full geographical descriptions of Kosovo see N. Malcolm, *Kosovo: A Short History* (Basingstoke, Papermac, 1998), pp. 1–21 and R. Osborne, *East Central Europe* (New York, Praeger, 1967), p. 205ff.

7 For detailed accounts of Kosovo's history see Malcolm, *Kosovo: A Short History* and M. Vickers, *Between Serb and Albanian: A History of Kosovo* (London, Hurst and Co., 1998).

8 Malcolm, *Kosovo: A Short History*, pp. 4–5.

9 B. Anzulovic, *Heavenly Serbia: From Myth to Genocide* (London, Hurst and Co., 1999), pp. 11–31; T. Judah, *The Serbs: History, Myth and the Destruction of Yugoslavia* (New Haven, Yale University Press, 1997), pp. 29–47 and S. Ramet, 'The Kingdom of God or the Kingdom of Ends: Kosovo in Serbian perception', in Buckley and Cummings, *Kosovo: Perceptions of War and Its Aftermath*, pp. 30–3.

10 T. Zavalani, 'Albanian nationalism', in P. Sugar and I. Lederer (eds), *Nationalism in Eastern Europe* (Seattle, University of Washington Press, 1973), pp. 61–6.

11 Malcolm, *Kosovo: A Short History*, pp. 193–5.

12 E. Cody, 'Out of work and hope, Serbs evacuate Kosovo', *Washington Post* (17 February 2000).

13 For a comprehensive study of the KLA see A. Heinemann-Gruder and W-C. Paes, *Wag the Dog: The Mobilisation and Demobilisation of the Kosovo Liberation Army (Brief 20)* (Bonn, International Center for Conversion, 2001).

14 *Resolution 1199 (1998)*. Website reference www.un.org/Docs/scres/1998/sres1199.htm.

15 On the Rambouillet negotiations see M. Weller, 'The Rambouillet conference on Kosovo', *International Affairs*, 75:2 (1999), 211–51.

16 For a highly detailed account of NATO military operations see A. Cordesman, *The Lessons and Non-Lessons of the Air and Missile Campaign in Kosovo* (Westport, Praeger, 2001).

17 See P. Hammond and E. Herman (eds), *Degraded Capability: The Media and the Kosovo Crisis* (London, Pluto Press, 2000).

18 D. Priest, 'NATO concedes its bombs likely killed refugees', *Washington Post* (20 April 1999) and D. Williams, 'Missiles hit Chinese Embassy', *Washington Post* (8 May 1999).

19 The nature and evolution of these demands is discussed here in Chapter 4, pp. 100–3.

20 *Resolution 1244 (1999)*. Website reference www.un.org/Docs/scres/1999/99sc1244.htm.

Chapter 1

NATO, Kosovo and 'humanitarian intervention'

NATO's employment of military power against the government of Slobodan Milosevic over Kosovo has been among the most controversial aspects of the Alliance's involvement in South East Europe since the end of the Cold War. The air operations between March and June 1999 have been variously described as war, 'humanitarian war', 'virtual war', intervention and 'humanitarian intervention' by the conflict's many commentators and critics. Key features of the debates over NATO's employment of military power have been concerned with its legality and legitimacy (i.e. the role of the UN and international law), its ethical basis and its impact on the doctrine of non-intervention in the domestic affairs of states. The conceptual debates that have raged over these issues are important not only within the context of European security but more generally for their impact on the international system as a whole. This chapter examines these issues by focusing on three broad questions. Why did NATO undertake military action over Kosovo? What kind of armed conflict did it engage in? Can such a resort to force be justified?

'Dirty Harry' or 'a knight in shining armour'? NATO's decision to use military force over Kosovo

An implicit UN mandate?

NATO members first declared a willingness to use force over Kosovo in autumn 1998. The pivotal event at this time was the Holbrooke-Milosevic agreement, reached in October. Holbrooke had been explicitly dispatched to Belgrade by then American Secretary of State Madeleine Albright to 'underscore [to President Milosevic] the clear requirements of UN Security Council Resolution 1199 and to emphasize the need for prompt and full compliance'.[1] Further, his mission to Belgrade was announced on the day after publication of a report to the Security Council by UN Secretary-General Kofi Annan dealing with the FRY's lack of compliance with previous UNSC Resolutions. In this report Annan 'appealed to the international community to undertake urgent steps in order to prevent a humanitarian disaster' in Kosovo during the winter.[2] The close proximity of timing suggests that this call provided both a spur and justification for the Holbrooke mission. The UN, via Resolution 1199, was, therefore, centrally if indirectly involved in the framing of the terms of reference for the Holbrooke mission, the accompanying NATO airstrike threat and, later, NATO's military action between March and June 1999.

It can also be argued that the UN Secretary-General gave a *de facto* green light to military action on a visit to NATO headquarters in January 1999. In his public remarks before meeting the North Atlantic Council, NATO's top decision-making body, Annan said that 'the bloody wars of the last decade ... have [not] left us with any illusions about the need to use force, when all other means have failed. We may be reaching that limit, once again, in the former Yugoslavia'.[3] According to Bruno Simma, he also told a press conference that '*normally* a UN Security Council Resolution is required' [emphasis in the original] to authorise military action by UN member states; suggesting, perhaps, that one might not be with regard to Kosovo.[4] Indeed, Tomás Valásek has claimed that NATO members purposely 'sought and obtained an indirect endorsement' of the right to use force over Kosovo from Kofi Annan in January 1999, two months before *Operation Allied Force* was launched.[5]

The launch of *Operation Allied Force* was, nevertheless, accompanied by a major international controversy over the fact that NATO members had not obtained, or sought, an *explicit* mandate in the form of a UNSC Resolution. During the course of the operation, NATO members spent a good deal of time and effort justifying it, usually within a frame of reference to the UN.[6] Reference was made to NATO's role in helping maintain the Dayton peace regime in Bosnia (where it was operating under a UN mandate), that could be threatened by uncontrolled violence in Kosovo. Further, it was asserted that NATO had received the implicit authorisation of the Security Council for military action on account of its support for the Holbrooke-

Milosevic agreement, which had, as noted, been concluded with the threat of airstrikes in the background.

An especially commonly cited argument was that NATO was acting 'in the spirit' of the UN Charter in attempting to compel the Milosevic government to cease and desist its repressive activities in Kosovo. The then NATO Secretary-General, Javier Solana, encapsulated this argument at his first press conference after *Operation Allied Force* got underway. He declared that 'the NATO countries think that this action is perfectly legitimate and it is within the logic of the UN Security Council [sic] ... we are engaged in this operation in order not to wage war against anybody but to try to stop the war'.[7] This line of argument was bolstered by reference to key UNSC Resolutions. The first UN Kosovo Resolution – 1160 – had been passed by the Security Council in March 1998. It spoke of 'the serious political and human rights issues in Kosovo'.[8] In September, Resolution 1199 used stronger language. It spoke of the need to 'avert the impending humanitarian catastrophe' in the province.[9] In addition, as noted above, the UN Secretary-General had called upon member states to take action to prevent a 'humanitarian disaster' in Kosovo. Given the inclusion of such phrases, there is some basis for the NATO claim to have been acting in the spirit of the Resolutions and of the UN Charter more generally.

The *de facto* blessing of the UN Secretary-General, although welcome for NATO, had limited value. Kofi Annan's views were, at best, privately encouraging whilst he publicly upheld the principles of the UN Charter. His public position with regard to Kosovo was confirmed in the widely quoted remarks that he made to the press on the day that *Operation Allied Force* was launched:

> It is indeed tragic that diplomacy has failed, but there are times when the use of force may be legitimate in the pursuit of peace. In helping maintain international peace and security, Chapter 7 of the United Nations Charter assigns an important role to regional organisations. But as Secretary-General, I have many times pointed out, not just in relation to Kosovo, that under the Charter, the Security Council has primary responsibility for maintaining international peace and security, and this is explicitly acknowledged in the North Atlantic Treaty. Therefore, the Council should be involved in any decision to resort to force.[10]

The UN Secretary-General could not, in any event, have bestowed international legitimacy on *Operation Allied Force* even if he had been so minded. He only has the right, under Article 99 of the UN Charter, to 'bring to the attention of the Security Council any matter which in his opinion may threaten the maintenance of international peace and security'. He cannot, however, give authorisation on behalf of the Security Council or force its members to do so.

The lack of explicit UN authorisation provoked serious opposition to NATO's military action, not least among two of the permanent members of the Security Council; China and Russia. The Chinese Ambassador to the UN, Qin Huasun, described NATO's military operations as a 'blatant violation of the UN Charter, as well as the accepted norms in international law'.[11] He was categorical in express-ing the view that 'the Chinese Government strongly opposes such an act'. Russian condemnation was even more forthright. President Boris Yeltsin called NATO's operation 'nothing other than an open aggression'. It had, in the Russian government's view, 'created a dangerous precedent' that 'threatened international law and order'.[12] Forthright criticism was not only limited to those that predictably took a strong view on the sanctity of state sovereignty. The Rio Group of Latin American states similarly expressed its 'anxiety' over the use of force in 'contravention of the provisions of Article 53' of the UN Charter.[13] Clearly therefore, important components of the interna-tional community did not accept notions of an implicit mandate for NATO's action.

Humanitarian and strategic imperatives?

Apart from justifying its action within the context of previous UN decisions, NATO presented another set of arguments based on humanitarian and regional stability considerations. In a press statement on 23 March 1999, Solana outlined the reasons behind the decision to begin airstrikes against Yugoslavia. He stated that NATO action resulted from the fact that 'all efforts to achieve a negotiated, political solution to the Kosovo crisis having failed, no alternative is open but to take military action'. He made clear that 'NATO is not waging war against Yugoslavia' but instead military action had been initiated to 'support the political aims of the international community'. In supporting these aims, Solana emphasised that NATO's action was intended to 'avert a humanitarian catastrophe' and 'prevent more human suffering and more repression and violence against the civilian population of Kosovo'.

This was a point Solana stressed on three occasions in his state-ment. He also indicated that NATO wanted to see the end of human suffering embodied in a 'political settlement' with an 'international military presence' to underwrite it. A further overarching aim of NATO was to 'prevent instability spreading in the region'.[14]

In another press release issued on 23 March, NATO echoed the themes in Solana's remarks. This additional statement, however, placed more of an accent on the Alliance endeavouring to support the aims of the international community to find a political solution:

> NATO's overall political objectives remain to help achieve a peaceful solution to the crisis in Kosovo by contributing to the response of the international community. More particularly, the Alliance made it clear in its statement of 30th January 1999 that its strategy was to halt the violence and support the completion of negotiations on an interim solution ... Alliance military action is intended to support its political aims. To do so, NATO's military action will be directed towards halting the violent attacks being committed by the VJ [Yugoslav Army] and MUP [Interior Ministry Forces] and disrupting their ability to conduct future attacks against the population of Kosovo, thereby supporting international efforts to secure FRY agreement to an interim political settlement.[15]

The most definitive statement of NATO's initial war aims was issued as air operations continued in early April 1999. In forthright terms, NATO made clear that military action was driven by compelling humanitarian reasons and in support of the political aims of the international community:

> The Federal Republic of Yugoslavia (FRY) has repeatedly violated United Nations Security Council resolutions. The unrestrained assault by Yugoslav military, police and paramilitary forces, under the direction of President Milosevic, on Kosovar civilians has created a massive humanitarian catastrophe which also threatens to destabilise the surrounding region. Hundreds of thousands of people have been expelled ruthlessly from Kosovo by the FRY authorities. We condemn these appalling violations of human rights and the indiscriminate use of force by the Yugoslav government. These extreme and criminally irresponsible policies, which cannot be defended on any grounds, have made necessary and justify the military action by NATO ... NATO's military action against the FRY supports the political aims of the international community: a peaceful, multi-ethnic and democratic Kosovo in which all its people can live in security and enjoy universal human rights and freedoms on an equal basis.[16]

The major powers within the Alliance, in their individual public statements, echoed the NATO line. President Bill Clinton, in a television address on 24 March, maintained that military action came only 'after extensive and repeated efforts to obtain a peaceful solution to the crisis in Kosovo'. 'Only firmness now', Clinton declared, 'can prevent greater catastrophe later'.[17] British Prime Minister Tony Blair, in a statement to the House of Commons, said that, for the Kosovar Albanians driven out of the province, <u>'we have in our power the means to help them secure justice and we have a duty to see that justice is now done'</u>.[18] French President Jacques Chirac asserted that what was at stake was 'peace in Europe' and 'human rights'.[19] German Chancellor Gerhard Schröder argued that the 'Alliance wants to stop serious, systematic human rights violations and prevent a humanitarian catastrophe in Kosovo'.[20]

In providing a rationale for military action, NATO and its member states made clear that exhaustion of all diplomatic avenues, urgent humanitarian considerations and a desire to support the political aims of the international community justified the decision to employ military power. Furthermore, the desire to avoid a spillover of the conflict into neighbouring states, with the consequential destabilisation of the region, was an important consideration.[21] Finally, there was an underlying sense that Serb actions in Kosovo represented an unacceptable violation of the core norms and values embodied in the contemporary 'Atlantic Community'. This latter dimension will be explored further in Chapter 6.

Because NATO undertook military action without the explicit authorisation of the UN Security Council, but with a number of compelling humanitarian and strategic justifications, the basis of the operation was bound to generate a great deal of controversy. The controversies were not all political. Just as the action pushed the envelope of international politics and legality, it also opened up important military conceptual debates.

Was Kosovo a 'war'?

General Wesley Clark, Supreme Allied Commander Europe (SACEUR) – the highest ranking military officer in NATO and leader of the Alliance's military operations during the 1999 conflict – has commented in his memoirs that 'we were never allowed to call [this] a war. But it was, of course'.[22]

Probing further into Clark's memoirs gives a fuller picture of his analysis of the nature of the conflict:

> Operation Allied Force was modern war – limited, carefully constrained in
> geography, scope, weaponry, and effects. Every measure of escalation was
> excruciatingly weighed. Diplomatic intercourse with neutral countries,
> with those opposed to NATO's actions, and even with the actual adver-
> sary continued during and around the conflict. Confidence-building
> measures and other conflict prevention initiatives derived from the Cold
> War were brought into play. The highest possible technology was in use,
> but only in carefully restrained ways. There was extraordinary concern for
> military losses, on all sides. Even accidental damage to civilian property
> was carefully considered. And 'victory' was carefully defined.[23]

Such eminent academic figures as Professor Sir Adam Roberts have
echoed Clark's view. Roberts has written that 'NATO leaders were
reluctant to call their action "war". However, it was war – albeit war of
a peculiarly asymmetric kind. It indisputably involved large-scale and
opposed use of force against a foreign state and its armed forces'.[24] The
commentator Michael Ignatieff called the Kosovo conflict a 'virtual
war', one in which NATO 'obtained its objectives without sacrificing
a single Allied life'.[25] Ignatieff went on to argue that Kosovo was a
'paradigm of ... [a] paradoxical form of warfare: where technological
omnipotence is vested in the hands of risk-averse political cultures'.[26]
Others called the conflict a 'humanitarian war'.[27] From Charles
Krauthammer's point of view, 'humanitarian war requires means that
are inherently inadequate to its ends'.[28] Given this spectrum of
opinion, can NATO's military action over Kosovo be accurately
termed a 'war' at all?

War has been defined as the 'systematic application of organised
violence by one state to another to accomplish adjustments in political,
economic, cultural, or military relations'.[29] *The Penguin Dictionary of
International Relations* defines war as 'direct, somatic violence
between state actors'.[30] These broad definitions, on first reflection,
seem to describe the armed conflict over Kosovo but they only really
scratch the surface of the concept of war. In Carl von Clausewitz's
'ideal' type of 'total' or 'absolute' war, there is an enemy against whom
war is to be waged employing all available resources until the 'terms of
victory' can be dictated.[31] Given NATO's relatively limited aims (not
'regime change' in Belgrade, for example, but to compel Milosevic to
come to terms over Kosovo) and its self-imposed constraints on the use
of force, the Kosovo conflict did not match these classical criteria.

General Clark's analysis, however, does classify the armed conflict
over Kosovo as a 'modern' *limited* war. The idea of limited war is not
new. As Robert Osgood, one of the Cold War period's principal
analysts of the idea noted, 'the concept and practice of limited war are

as old as war itself'.[32] During the Cold War, the idea of limited war was the subject of considerable interest, particularly in the United States.[33] Osgood, one of the major contributors to the discussion, defined it in the following way:

LIMITED
WAR

> A limited war is one in which the belligerents restrict the purposes for which they fight to concrete, well-defined objectives that do not demand the utmost military effort of which the belligerents are capable and that can be accommodated in a negotiated settlement.[34]

Expanding on Osgood's definition, these types of conflicts can be limited geographically, are fought over limited objectives, use limited means (weaponry) and have limitations regarding the targets that can be subjected to attack.[35] A more contemporary analysis of the characteristics of limited war suggests that another limitation needs to be added – to prevail with a minimum cost in lives. As one analyst has written: 'casualties may soon represent a dominant, perhaps the dominant measurement of success or failure in wars of limited ends and means such as Operation Allied Force in Kosovo'.[36] In short, limited war means 'that either the ends or means or both, are limited in the conflict'.[37]

It is recognised that one of the problems of waging a limited war is that those asked to fight it are often inculcated with an *absolutist* perspective of war that works against limitations on the use of force.[38] Much analysis, moreover, narrowly places the accent on the nature of the military conduct of conflict rather than fully integrating its political dimension. Yet, as Clausewitz has long reminded us, 'war is the continuation of politics by other means'.[39] This suggests that the concept of limited war is of use in reference to the Kosovo conflict only in the most generic sense of helping us to understand the limitations placed by politicians on the military conduct of operations, rather than fully capturing the nature of the conflict itself.

A further constraint on seeing the Kosovo conflict as a limited war in classical terms is the strong contemporary association of the concept with the Cold War. Although of long lineage, limited war thinking today is very much rooted in the experience of the Cold War, particularly that of the 1950s and 1960s. Thinking regarding limited war became linked to the need to avoid a total war that would entail the large-scale employment of nuclear weapons by the two superpowers. As a consequence of this, John Garnett has argued, 'only conflicts that contain the potentiality for becoming total can be described as limited'.[40] This legacy of Cold War thinking on the limited war concept suggests that it is not applicable to the conflict over Kosovo.

It seems clear that the Kosovo conflict is better described metaphorically rather than conceptually as a 'war' or 'limited war'.[41] As for constructions such as 'humanitarian war' or 'virtual war', they are labels bereft of any real conceptual meaning. If, therefore, the Kosovo conflict cannot be conceptually best understood as a form of war, how can it be conceived?

The intervention and non-intervention debates

The military operations conducted by NATO in 1999 have been described as an 'intervention' by many commentators and governments. The idea of intervention is well-trodden ground in terms of the international relations discourse. As a concept, however, it has spawned a variety of permutations; from 'collective' to 'humanitarian' intervention.[42] Moreover, intervention is often viewed critically against the backdrop of the doctrine of non-intervention in the affairs of states. Richard Little represented this view well when he wrote that 'in the international arena intervention is generally seen to be a violation of sovereignty, and a threat to world order'.[43] Others, however, see intervention as a 'ubiquitous feature' of the international system. Hedley Bull has argued that 'no serious student can fail to feel that intervention is sometimes justifiable' and that there are 'exceptions to the rule of non-intervention'.[44] Whichever of these views one may subscribe to, it is clear that intervention in the affairs of another state raises a number of questions regarding the ethics, legality and ultimately the legitimacy of the intervention. The contested issues of intervention and non-intervention are not new in terms of the international system. Since the end of the Cold War, however, the debates have been reinvigorated, not least as a result of the Kosovo crisis and conflict. The crisis, and NATO's response, represents one of the key watersheds in the post-Cold War debates on the question of intervention.

The doctrine of non-intervention

The doctrine of non-intervention in the affairs of sovereign states is a well-understood facet of the international system. It is grounded in the principle of sovereignty – what many consider to be the *grundnorm* of the state-centred international order. Sovereignty is the default setting of the Westphalian state system that emerged after 1648. Simply expressed, sovereignty means the independence of a territorially defined state that also, within its boundaries, enjoys the right to order its internal affairs as it sees fit.[45] Following on from the central tenet of a state's right of domestic jurisdiction is the idea that a state should be free from outside interference. This corollary forms the substance of the doctrine of non-intervention.

This doctrine of non-intervention is well established in the fabric of the international system. The UN Charter, in Article 2 paragraph 7, famously reflects the degree to which non-intervention is ensconced as a guiding concept. It states that 'Nothing in the present Charter shall authorise the United Nations to intervene in matters which are essentially within the domestic jurisdiction of any state or shall require the Members to submit such matters to settlement under the present Charter'.[46]

The strength of support for the idea of non-interference is undoubtedly very strong within the international community. Further proof can be seen in two UN General Assembly Resolutions on the 'Inadmissibility of Intervention in the Domestic Affairs of States', passed in December 1965 and in an updated version in December 1981. The latter document declared that 'No State or group of States has the right to intervene or interfere in any form or for any reason whatsoever in the internal and external affairs of other States'.[47] The 1981 Resolution elaborated on the 'rights and duties' entailed under the doctrine of non-intervention, categorically stating that it is:

> the duty of a State to refrain from armed intervention, subversion, military occupation or any other form of intervention and interference, overt or covert, directed at another State or group of States, or any act of military, political or economic interference in the internal affairs of another State, including acts of reprisal involving the use of force.[48]

Despite its status as a *grundnorm*, the integrity of the doctrine of non-intervention has never been unchallenged in application. The underpinning concept of sovereignty, as Alan James has argued, has a dual meaning. It encompasses an understanding of sovereignty both as status and rights. James argues that 'the link between sovereignty as status and sovereignty as rights is that, although the second sense of sovereignty is intimately associated with the first, it is not a concomitant but a consequence of it. Sovereign rights attach to those entities that enjoy sovereign status'.[49]

We must qualify if a state is sovereign or not before considering intervention.

In the age of the 'failed state', what constitutes 'sovereign status' is a question with important implications for the doctrine of non-intervention. When a country ceases to have a functioning and effective central government, and contains an anarchical condition within its borders, it is difficult to sustain the idea of the doctrine of non-intervention in either a *de facto* or *de jure* sense. As Fowler and Bunck have argued, 'it is ultimately the international community that determines whether a particular political entity qualifies as a sovereign state'.[50] Moreover, the boundary line between sovereignty and intervention is a shifting one conditioned by 'what it means to be a state at a particular place and time'.[51]

The idea that a universal norm of human rights applies to all individuals and transcends notions of sovereignty also has implications regarding statehood. It suggests that the criteria of legitimate statehood include respect for human rights. When this is viewed against the background of the development of international human rights norms, it points to more perforations in the doctrine of non-intervention and provides opportunity, if not intent, for intervention.[52]

Intervention *– defining*

Defining intervention is a difficult business because of the number of forms it can take. As Thomas Otte has observed, 'there is no precise and generally acknowledged concept of intervention'.[53] The multifaceted quality of intervention is often reflected in standard definitions. Indeed, one dictionary of international relations describes it as 'a portmanteau term which covers a wide variety of situations where one actor intervenes in the affairs of another'.[54] Hedley Bull has called it a 'dictatorial or coercive interference, by an outside or outside parties, in the sphere of jurisdiction of a sovereign state'.[55] This definition implies a range of modes of intervention that could embrace political, economic or even normative ones through institutions acting on behalf of the international community. It also suggests that, in the light of the doctrine of non-intervention, it can be perceived as a negative phenomenon. John Vincent has defined it in a similar manner to Bull, but attaches a more neutral proviso – that intervention is 'not necessarily lawful or unlawful, but it does break a conventional pattern of international relations'.[56] These broad definitions do not, by themselves, offer much precision or utility for considering NATO's military action over Kosovo. What they do highlight is the need to consider the ways and means of intervention.

Interventions can be classified in a number of categories; such as the employment of political, economic or military power. In the international system, military force continues to be 'the most widely available instrument' for intervening in a country's domestic affairs.[57] According to Thomas Otte, 'military intervention is the planned limited use of force for a transitory period by a state (or group of states) against a weaker state in order to change or maintain the target state's domestic structure or to change its external policies'.[58] Contemplating military intervention, however, produces its own admixture of challenging political and military decisions.[59] Typically, military intervention means embarking on a conflict where there is an asymmetry in military power. The intervener almost invariably enjoys considerable military advantages over the target state. Such supremacy, however, cannot be taken for granted as military interventions risk becoming protracted and leading to escalation.[60] It is more often than not the case that it is easier to become enmeshed in a military intervention than to find a viable exit strategy. Such risks mean that the intervener must practice 'selectivity' before undertaking military intervention.[61]

Otte's definition of military intervention is certainly useful in characterising NATO's action over Kosovo. Nevertheless, as in the case of the consideration of ideas of limited war discussed earlier, such a conceptualisation does not adequately take into account the political reasons for the military intervention. Stanley Hoffmann's observation that 'the purpose of intervention is the same as that of all other forms of foreign policy; it is to make you do what I want you to do, whether or not you wish to do it'[62] indicates the underlying generic purpose of military intervention. It does not, however, adequately reveal *why* a state or group of states launches a military intervention. In particular it omits those crucial initial factors of political motivation or aims that triggered military intervention in the first place and subsequently shape its ethical qualities, legality and legitimacy.

For that icon of the realist school of international relations, Hans Morgenthau, the rationale for military intervention was clear: 'all nations will continue to be guided in their decisions to intervene and their choice of intervention by what they regard as their respective national interests'. According to Morgenthau, the doctrine of non-intervention was something political leaders 'never ceased to pay lip service to'. Moreover, he was dismissive of the prospect of international norms supplanting national interest when it came to justifying a military intervention. 'It is futile to search', argued Morgenthau, 'for an abstract principle which would allow us to distinguish in a concrete case between legitimate and illegitimate intervention'.[63]

Others, such as Freeman, have taken a broader view; that other, systemic, factors contribute to military intervention even if ultimately national self-interest lies at the foundation of the decision to intervene:

> A state or society that descends into civil strife or anarchy is a cancer on the international body politic that endangers its neighbours and its region. Segments of its population may destabilise neighboring states by seeking refuge there. Its domestic violence may spill over its borders. Such internal disorder is a threat to international order and the interests of other states. It invokes the logic of reason of system ... Direct or indirect intervention by states in the internal proceedings of others is never disinterested. States carry out such intervention as a matter of self-interest, the interest of the international state system, or both. Of these motives, the most compelling is self-interest.[64]

Universal norms – role in outcome

The idea that universal norms could provide legitimacy to military intervention and override the doctrine of non-intervention moves the intervention debate, in political terms, beyond the paradigm of national interest guiding the intervener. Writing in 1984, Hedley Bull envisaged circumstances where the norms of international society could lead to intervention:

> It is clear that the growing legal and moral recognition of human rights on a world-wide scale, the expression in the normative area of the growing interconnectedness of societies with one another, has as one of its consequences that many forms of involvement by one state or society in the affairs of another, which at one time would have been regarded as illegitimate interference, will be treated as justifiable.[65]

It is on this question – whether or not military intervention can be driven by norms such as human rights – that NATO's military action over Kosovo has been most debated. It has been the most significant source of dispute amongst the conflict's many interpreters. This type of intervention, a humanitarian one, is among the most contentious as its claim to legitimacy can arguably supersede both national sovereignty and the authority of the UN or any other legitimating international organisation. From the point of view of contemporary European and international security, therefore, the crucial issue is whether or not a right to humanitarian intervention actually exists.

Humanitarian Intervention = most contentious

'Humanitarian intervention'

James Mayall has observed that 'the concept of humanitarian intervention occupies an ambiguous place in the theory and practice of
international society'.[66] Humanitarian intervention not only occupies
an ambiguous place but is also a concept steeped in controversy. Most
of the controversy centres on its ethics and legitimacy. In terms of
defining the concept, there is not yet a consensus on its meaning but
one factor seems to predominate, the issue of violation of human
rights. One of the most succinct definitions, in focusing on this *raison
d'être* of humanitarian intervention, is that of Sean Murphy, who has
defined it as being:

> The threat or use of force by a state, group of states, or international
> organisation primarily for the purpose of protecting the nationals of the
> target state from widespread deprivations of internationally recognized
> human rights.[67]

Francis Abiew has defined humanitarian intervention in a way akin
to that of Murphy: 'humanitarian intervention, understood in the
classical sense, involves forcible self-help by a state or group of states to
protect human rights'.[68] Pressing this line of argument to its limits,
Mervyn Frost maintains that 'humanitarian intervention must be
understood as directed at maintaining civil society – the global society
of rights holders which has no borders'.[69]

Not everyone, however, accepts the narrow rationale of just
protecting human rights. According to Oliver Ramsbotham, 'humanitarian intervention means cross-border action by the international
community in response to human suffering' more broadly.[70]
Ramsbotham identifies various forms of humanitarian intervention
including 'coercive' and 'non-coercive governmental humanitarian
intervention' as well as 'transnational, intergovernmental and non-
governmental humanitarian intervention'.[71] Implicit in all of these
are drivers of humanitarian intervention that go beyond upholding
human rights.

These broader considerations are also sometimes evident where
the concept of humanitarian intervention has made its way into the
lexicon of policy-makers. For example, a Finnish security and defence
policy paper published in June 2001 defined humanitarian intervention in a way that embraces a broader perspective:

> Humanitarian intervention means military intervention by the interna-
> tional community or some other actor in an internal or international

conflict, if necessary without the consent of the country in question, in order to save human lives, protect human rights and to ensure that humanitarian aid reaches its target.[72]

The Finnish definition incorporates the related concept of 'military-civilian humanitarianism'. It suggests that the need to alleviate human suffering resulting from natural disaster, famine or conflict provides still more reasons for humanitarian intervention than simply thwarting human rights abuses.[73] Overall, the heart of the matter lies in how one defines 'humanitarianism' and how one addresses the important paradox presented by lethal armed force being applied in the name of saving life.[74]

The ethics of humanitarian intervention: the problem of criteria

Establishing a set of criteria to guide humanitarian intervention presents a difficult problem. Although analysts had long been willing to provide criteria, politicians holding the reins of power and responsibility had been more reticent, at least until the time of the NATO intervention over Kosovo. In this context, it is worth exploring the British example of an official and public discussion of criteria for humanitarian intervention.

The Kosovo crisis and the ongoing NATO air operations provided the impetus and the spur for a key speech given by Tony Blair in Chicago in April 1999. Here, he declared that 'the most pressing foreign policy problem we face is to identify the circumstances in which we should get actively involved in other people's conflicts'. In addressing this question, Blair suggested that there were ethical considerations that took precedence over established norms of non-intervention. In particular he argued that:

> The principle of non-interference must be qualified in important respects. Acts of genocide can never be a purely internal matter. When oppression produces massive flows of refugees which unsettle neighbouring countries, then they can properly be described as 'threats to international peace and security'.

Blair went on to outline a possible test, consisting of a series of questions, to determine the appropriateness of an intervention:

- First, are we sure of our case? *Blair's criteria for intervention*

- Second, have we exhausted all diplomatic options?
- Third, on the basis of a practical assessment of the situation, are there military operations we can sensibly and prudently undertake?
- And finally, do we have national interests involved?[75]

The 'Blair Doctrine' was further elaborated nearly a year later by Robin Cook, then Foreign Secretary. Cook raised what is the central question concerning the ethics and criteria of humanitarian intervention – 'how can the international community avert crimes against humanity while at the same time respecting the rule of international law and the sovereignty of nation states?'. Cook's speech was clearly designed to contribute to the debate regarding this question. In particular he offered some 'guidelines for intervention in response to massive violations of humanitarian law and crimes against humanity'. These were:

- First, any intervention, by definition, is an admission of failure of prevention.
- Second, we should maintain the principle that armed force should only be used as a last resort.
- Third, the immediate responsibility for halting violence rests with the state in which it occurs.
- Fourth, when faced with an overwhelming humanitarian catastrophe, which a government has shown it is unwilling or unable to prevent or is actively promoting, the international community should intervene ... It must be objectively clear that there is no practicable alternative to the use of force to save lives.
- Fifth, any use of force should be proportionate to achieving the humanitarian purpose and carried out in accordance with international law.
- Sixth, any use of force should be collective. No individual country can reserve to itself the right to act on behalf of the international community.[76]

Proving massive human rights violations or genocide to the point of initiating a humanitarian intervention is a daunting problem for policy makers, however elaborate the early warning mechanisms that can be put into place.[77] Obtaining incontrovertible evidence is a difficult enough issue for individual governments, let alone amorphous bodies such as the international community. Moreover, the conduct of military interventions since the Cold War has generated a number of dilemmas for the intervener, particularly ones in response to massive human rights violations. One of these significant intervention dilemmas is the contradictory desire of the populations of democratic states to see human rights norms enforced whilst being unwilling to pay a price, either in lives or treasure.[78]

Yet, against all the hurdles, the option of doing nothing, for those governments and international institutions capable of undertaking humanitarian intervention, does not seem credible. The legacy of the terrible bloodletting of the twentieth century points to a higher moral *grundnorm* that no civilised state or community of states can lightly cast aside. Although it was certainly not the only factor, there was undoubtedly a sense of this motivating NATO leaders in 1998 and 1999 towards the view that 'something had to be done' about the humanitarian situation in Kosovo.

Establishing criteria for humanitarian intervention is centrally about the problem of applying morality to politics and conflict. This is certainly nothing new, as illustrated by the long-standing existence of well-articulated principles of a 'just war' doctrine. These principles are organised around *jus ad bellum* and *jus in bello*; meaning justice in going to war and justice in the conduct of war.[79] The criteria of just war can be summarised as shown in Table 1.1 (p. 28).

What is striking about the criteria for humanitarian intervention outlined by Blair and Cook, against the backdrop of the Kosovo crisis and its aftermath, is the way in which they follow the principles of the just war. The ideas propounded in Blair's and Cook's speeches emphasising last resort, proportionality and the legitimacy of the case, reflect criteria of the just war doctrine. Because the just war doctrine is, centrally, concerned with establishing moral criteria governing the use of force, its applicability to the problem of establishing criteria for humanitarian intervention should be readily apparent. Mona Fixdal and Dan Smith, writing on 'Humanitarian intervention and just war', emphasise that 'in seeking a framework that is simultaneously both ethical and political for discussing decisions to resort to force, the Just War tradition seems a self-evident path to explore'.[80] Taking a broader view of the application of the just war doctrine to the post-Cold War security environment, J. Bryan Hehir has stressed the factors that make it relevant:

> The post-Cold War setting for intervention is shaped by two realities: the erosion of sovereignty and intensifying interdependence. These two distinct features of international politics promise an increase in the kinds of intervention and its incidence. To assess the moral character of intervention will require an emphasis on the political aspects of the just war ethic.[81]

Table 1.1   *Just war criteria*

	Jus ad Bellum – *Justice in Recourse to War*
Legitimate or Right Authority	Only legitimate governments or supranational authority can lawfully engage in war
Just Cause	Defence against a violent, unwarranted aggression against the state
Just Intention	Goals must be just; restore peace to all parties engaged in conflict
Last Resort	Military force can only be employed after all other options exhausted
Proportionality	Means of war must be proportional to the offence; recourse to war must lead to more good than harm
Reasonable Hope	The recourse to war must stand a reasonable chance of success and not be undertaken in the absence of such reasonable hope
Comparative Justice	No state possesses absolute justice in pursuit of aims

	Jus in Bello – *Justice in the Conduct of War*
Discrimination	Non-combatants protected from direct or intentional attack
Proportionality	Military actions limited by necessity to achieve goals and to avoid unnecessary suffering of non-combatants

Sources: A. Coates, *The Ethics of War* (Manchester, Manchester University Press, 1997), pp. 123–272; Major General The Rev. I. Durie, 'Just War in an Unjust World', unpublished paper for the International Symposium in Military Ethics, Royal Norwegian Air Force Academy, Trondheim, November 1999; M. Fixdal and D. Smith, 'Humanitarian intervention and just war', *Mershon International Studies Review* (1998), 4.

Not everyone, however, agrees that the just war doctrine provides criteria to guide humanitarian intervention. Mervyn Frost argues that 'humanitarian intervention is not best understood as an action which fits into theories of just warfare, as they involve war between states. The concerns of just war theory about proper authority, just cause and just means are not readily applicable to humanitarian intervention'.[82] Despite this caveat, just war doctrine has occupied a central place in the debates on establishing criteria for humanitarian intervention.[83] What is more, analysts seeking to establish such criteria draw on the just war doctrine whether or not they make an explicit link between it and their criteria.[84]

Not all criteria in the humanitarian intervention debate draw on the just war doctrine.[85] What is, however, characteristic of the strands of the debate over criteria for humanitarian intervention is the desire to establish an ethical basis for taking action. The fact that there is a need to articulate ethical criteria highlights questions about the legality of humanitarian intervention (in terms of international law) and the difficult political choices that humanitarian intervention presents to members of the international community. Ultimately, the quest to articulate ethical criteria for humanitarian intervention is a debate born out of the contested legality and legitimacy of the phenomenon.

The UN, NATO and the legality and legitimacy of intervention

NATO's military intervention over Kosovo brought into bold prominence, as noted earlier, ongoing debates about the legality and legitimacy of the Alliance's action.[86] One side of this debate has been largely critical of NATO's action, arguing that it lacked the legal basis necessary to give it legitimacy. 'NATO countries – ', wrote *The Economist*, 'albeit with the best of motives – have put themselves, like Mr Milosevic, outside the law'.[87] Similarly, Mark Littman QC, in a critique of the legality of NATO's action, concluded that 'given the weight of opinion and legal authority against the NATO position ... it is difficult to avoid the conclusion that the NATO action was illegal'.[88] In his detailed analysis of humanitarian intervention and international law, Simon Chesterman takes the view that 'there is no "right" of humanitarian intervention in either the UN Charter or customary international law'.[89] Friedrich Kratochwil generally takes a similar line, coming to the conclusion that no right of humanitarian intervention exists save in the cases of the 'institution of the protection of nations' or authorised under Chapter VII of the UN Charter.[90] As noted earlier, major states such as China and Russia opposed NATO's Kosovo operation over questions essentially related to its legality. The arguments were not entirely one-sided. Other commentators maintained that NATO's action could in fact be justified under international law.[91] On balance, however, the debate on the legality of NATO's action over Kosovo for the most part supports the view that *Operation Allied Force* lacked a firm grounding in international law.

At the nexus of this debate stands the United Nations, the international organisation charged with 'the maintenance of international

peace and security'. The absence of a formal UN mandate for the
NATO air operation was problematic in this respect as the UN, with
its global remit and broad security and humanitarian roles, is widely
regarded as being the principal (some would say sole) international
legitimising agency for military action.

The UN's Charter stresses, as noted, the principle of non-
intervention and its legal superstructure is optimised for dealing with
interstate aggression rather than intervention in the affairs of a state.[92]
Indeed, some critics of the UN argue that these attributes of the
Charter make it less relevant to the current international security
environment characterised, as it has been, by intrastate violence and
attendant human rights abuses.[93] The UN Charter, however, does
emphasise the importance of human rights, even if the document does
not make upholding them an explicit function of the UN. This does
not necessarily mean that the UN and, in particular, its Security
Council is powerless to act in the face of massive human rights abuses
within states. A number of analysts have argued that, under Article 39
of the Charter, the UNSC could sanction intervention in the affairs of
a state on the strength of it posing a 'threat to the peace'.[94] Not all
agree with this view of the Security Council's powers, arguing that
such an interpretation 'is expanding the scope of its authority beyond
that originally envisioned'.[95] Overall it may be said that, on the issue of
human rights, the UN is strong on norm articulation but weaker on
the instruments to ensure adherence to those norms.

Ironically, perhaps, NATO members seemed to reaffirm the need
not to give up on the UN at the very moment that they were acting
without its explicit authority *vis-à-vis* Kosovo in the spring of 1999. At
the NATO Washington summit, held when *Operation Allied Force* was
in full swing in April, a deliberate effort seemed to have been made to
build UN-friendly language into the key declarations. Both the
Washington Summit Communiqué and the new NATO *Strategic
Concept* included affirmations that, 'as stated in the Washington Treaty
[i.e. NATO's founding treaty], we recognise the primary responsibility
of the United Nations Security Council for the maintenance of
international peace and security'. The *Strategic Concept*, in formally
setting out a new (in *de jure* terms) role for NATO of being prepared
to engage in 'crisis management [and] crisis response operations',
stipulated that these would be undertaken 'in conformity with Article
7 of the Washington Treaty'.[96] This states that the treaty 'does not
affect, and shall not be interpreted as affecting in any way the rights
and obligations under the Charter of the Parties which are members of

the United Nations, or the primary responsibility of the Security Council for the maintenance of international peace and security'.[97]

Various causal factors have been suggested in explanation of the inclusion of what seemed, at first sight, to be a clear statement of intent in Washington to ensure that NATO does not undertake military action without UN authorisation again. It has been argued that the UN-friendly language was included at French insistence, with the US acquiescing in order to preserve allied unity in the midst of the pressing crisis.[98] Others have suggested that the failure of *Operation Allied Force* to coerce Milosevic into backing down by the time of the Washington summit had 'tempered the interventionist urge consid-erably' amongst NATO members generally.[99]

Historically, however, NATO's view of itself has been that of a free-standing regional organisation not hierarchically subordinate to the UNSC. Sure enough, voices have since been heard arguing that the overall tone of the 1999 Washington documents does *not* suggest that NATO and its members will feel, in future, bound by acceptance of UN primacy. Dick Leurdijk and Dick Zandee have drawn attention to passages in the *Washington Summit Communiqué* and *Strategic Concept* where NATO is described as 'an Alliance of nations committed to the Washington Treaty and the United Nations Charter'. This form of words seems innocuous but, according to Leurdijk and Zandee:

> By thus binding itself once more to both documents, NATO appears to give itself an equal position to the UN and not a subservient one ... Thereby NATO assures itself of an autonomous freedom of action, also in those cases where an explicit consent by the Security Council would be impossible. From a legal point of view it comes down to a lessening of the importance of the UN as compared to that of NATO.[100]

In sum, the wording of the 1999 summit statements is ambiguous and capable of being interpreted in different ways. As with many diplomatic documents, such ambiguity is almost certainly intentional – if only to satisfy the differing agendas of NATO member states. In considering their response to future cases where military intervention might be required, it is unlikely that NATO members – or at least the more powerful among them – would regard their hands as being tied by statements agreed to under the pressure of a major and ongoing crisis in the spring of 1999.

Conclusions

NATO's intervention in Kosovo during 1999 was undertaken with humanitarian reasons being among several factors driving the armed action. Although the UN did not authorise the intervention in a *de jure* sense, NATO's action derived *some* legitimacy from prior UNSC Resolutions. It gained more from the fact that it was clear to nearly all outside observers that FRY forces had been responsible for serious abuses of the human rights of the Albanian population in Kosovo.

It was the moral and ethical dimension underpinning NATO's action, coupled with the employment of military coercion that led to it being labelled a 'humanitarian intervention'. The descriptor thus gained a new currency as a result of the events of spring 1999. Kosovo was, arguably, the first such action in Europe. The descriptor was not widely used at the time of the UN-sponsored international relief efforts in Bosnia between 1992 and 1995. Also, it can be argued that these efforts did not qualify as 'intervention' in the sense in which the term has been defined here. The UN did not seek at the time to compel the various warring factions and their state sponsors to alter the behaviour (i.e. the civil war) which had produced the humanitarian crisis.

The NATO action in Kosovo gave significant impetus to debates about the nature, justification and relevance of such activities in the post-Cold War European security environment. Interventions driven by ethical considerations reveal important contradictions in the international system. On one level, as Nicholas Wheeler has observed, 'humanitarian intervention exposes the conflict between order and justice at its starkest'.[101] NATO members' efforts to justify their Kosovo intervention also reflected the contradictions and frustrations of attempting to uphold some norms (regarding human rights) while seemingly violating others (relating to the legality or otherwise of the use of armed force).

The difficulties and contradictions have helped to ensure that, in the minds of many analysts and commentators, the Kosovo crisis offers a dubious precedent for future international intervention in Europe or elsewhere. Adam Roberts has suggested that, at most, NATO's military response to the crisis 'may occupy a modest place as one halting step in a developing but still contested practice of using force in defence of international norms'.[102] Whatever one's views of its merits or otherwise, the controversies surrounding NATO's action over Kosovo are likely to help ensure that it continues to stand less as a precedent for future such interventions than as an exceptional response to violence, human suffering and the perceived need to restore security and stability in a particularly volatile region of Europe.

Notes

1 *Ambassador Holbrooke Travel to Brussels and Belgrade.* Website reference http://secretary.state.gov/www/briefings/statements/.
2 *Report of the Secretary-General Prepared Pursuant to Resolutions 1160 (1998) and 1199 (1998) of the Security Council.* Website reference www.un.org/Docs/sc/reports/1998/s1998912.htm.
3 Statement by Kofi Annan, Secretary General of the United Nations. Website reference www.nato.int/docu/speech/1999/s990128a.htm.
4 B. Simma, 'NATO, the UN and the use of force: legal aspects', *European Journal of International Law*, 10:1 (1999). Website reference www.ejil.org/journal/Vol10/No1/ab1-1.html.
5 T. Valásek, 'NATO at 50', *Foreign Policy in Focus*, 4:11 (1999). Website reference www.foreignpolicy-infocus.org/briefs/vol4/v4n11nato_body.html.
6 For more detail see M. A. Smith, 'Kosovo, NATO and the United Nations', in S. Badsey and P. Latawski (eds), *Britain, NATO and the Lessons of the Balkan Conflicts* (London, Frank Cass, forthcoming).
7 Press conference by Secretary-General, Dr Javier Solana and SACEUR, Gen. Wesley Clark. Website reference www.nato.int/kosovo/press/p990325a.htm.
8 *Resolution 1160 (1998)* (New York, United Nations, 1998).
9 *Resolution 1199 (1998).* Website reference www.un.org/Docs/scres/1998/sres1199.htm.
10 'UN Sec-Gen Kofi Annan on NATO Air Strikes March 24 1999' (Washington DC, US Information Service, 1999).
11 'Statement by the Chinese Ambassador to the UN, 24 March 1999', in P. Auerswald and D. Auerswald (eds), *The Kosovo Conflict: A Diplomatic History Through Documents* (Cambridge, Kluwer Law International, 2000), p. 727. Hereafter referred to as *Kosovo Documents*. The Chinese government's strict view of sovereignty is being challenged by Beijing's greater international engagement. See B. Gill and J. Reilly, 'Sovereignty, intervention and peacekeeping: the view from Beijing', *Survival*, 42:3 (2000), 41–59.
12 'Statement by the Russian President, 24 March 1999', *Kosovo Documents*, p. 725.
13 'Communiqué of the Rio Group, 25 March 1999', *Kosovo Documents*, p. 737.
14 Press statement by Dr. Javier Solana, Secretary General of NATO, 23 March 1999 (Press Release (1999)040). Website reference www.nato.int/docu/pr/1999/p99-0402.htm.

15 *Political and Military Objectives of NATO Action with Regard to the Crisis in Kosovo, 23 March 1999* (*Press Release (1999)043*). Website reference http://www.nato.int/docu/pr/1999/p99-043e.htm.

16 Statement issued by the North Atlantic Council, 12 April 1999. Website reference www.fco.gov.uk/text_only/news/newstext.asp?2250&print Version=yes.

17 'Statement by the President, 24 March 1999', *Kosovo Documents*, pp. 719–20.

18 'Statement by Prime Minister Blair, 24 March 1999', *Kosovo Documents*, p. 720.

19 'Statement by President Jacques Chirac, 24 March 1999', *Kosovo Documents*, p. 722.

20 'Statement by Chancellor Gerhard Schroeder, 24 March 1999', *Kosovo Documents*, p. 723.

21 Some have even argued that the NATO action might have been justified as collective self-defence under Article 51 of the UN Charter. See P. Egan, 'The Kosovo intervention and collective self-defence', *International Peacekeeping*, 8:3 (2001), 39–58.

22 Gen. W. Clark, *Waging Modern War* (New York, PublicAffairs, 2001), p. xxiii. The very title of Clark's memoirs gives away his thinking on how the conflict should be conceptually understood.

23 *Ibid.*, p. xxiv.

24 A. Roberts, 'NATO's "humanitarian war" over Kosovo', *Survival*, 41:3 (1999), 102.

25 M. Ignatieff, *Virtual War: Kosovo and Beyond* (London, Chatto and Windus, 2000), p. 162.

26 *Ibid.*, p. 163.

27 C. Krauthammer, 'The short, unhappy life of humanitarian war', *The National Interest*, (Autumn 1999), 5–8 and Roberts, 'NATO's "humanitarian war" over Kosovo'.

28 Krauthammer, 'The short, unhappy life of humanitarian war', p. 6.

29 C. Freeman, *Arts of Power: Statecraft and Diplomacy* (Washington DC, United States Institute of Peace Press, 1997), p. 61.

30 G. Evans and J. Newnham, *The Penguin Dictionary of International Relations* (London, Penguin Books, 1998), p. 565.

31 M. Handel, *Masters of War: Classical Strategic Thought (3rd edition)* (London, Frank Cass, 2001), p. 24. See also his third chapter on the definition of war.

32 R. Osgood, *The Reappraisal of Limited War* (Adelphi Paper 54) (London, Institute for Strategic Studies, 1969), p. 41. For in-depth analysis of limited war by significant strategic thinkers see Handel, *Masters of War*, pp. 287–95.

33 For a very good summary of the evolution of limited war thinking see C. Gacek, *The Logic of Force: The Dilemma of Limited War in American Foreign Policy* (New York, Columbia University Press, 1994).

34 R. Osgood, *Limited War: The Challenge to American Strategy* (Chicago, University of Chicago Press, 1957), pp. 1–2.

35 J. Garnett, 'Limited war', in J. Baylis *et al.* (eds), *Contemporary Strategy: Theories and Concepts* (London, Croom Helm, 1987), pp. 191–2.

36 Maj. Gen. R. Scales, 'From Korea to Kosovo: America's army learns to fight limited wars in the age of precision strikes', *Armed Forces Journal International* (December 1999), p. 36.

37 Gacek, *The Logic of Force*, p. 16.

38 Garnett, 'Limited war', p. 201.

39 As quoted in Handel, *Masters of War*, p. 38.

40 Garnett, 'Limited war', p. 192.

41 J. Black, *War: Past, Present and Future* (New York, St. Martin's Press, 2000), pp. 272–97.

42 See H. Bull (ed.), *Intervention in World Politics* (Oxford, Clarendon Press, 1984).

43 R. Little, 'Recent literature on intervention and non-intervention', in I. Forbes and M. Hoffman (eds), *Political Theory, International Relations, and the Ethics of Intervention* (London, St. Martin's Press, 1993), p. 13.

44 Bull, *Intervention in World Politics*, p. 2 and p. 190.

45 For useful discussions of the concept of sovereignty see, *inter alia*, A. James, 'The concept of sovereignty revisited', in A. Schnabel and R. Thakur (eds), *Kosovo and the Challenge of Humanitarian Intervention: Selective Indignation, Collective Action and International Citizenship* (Tokyo, United Nations University Press, 2000), pp. 334–43 and F. Kratochwil, 'Sovereignty as *dominium*: is there a right of humanitarian intervention?', in G. Lyons and M. Mastanduno (eds), *Beyond Westphalia? State Sovereignty and Humanitarian Intervention* (Baltimore, Johns Hopkins University Press, 1995), pp. 21–42.

46 *United Nations Charter*. Website reference www.un.org/aboutun/charter/.

47 *General Assembly Resolution A/RES/36/103 (1981)*. Website reference www.un.org/documents/ga/res/36/a36r103.htm. See also the earlier version, *General Assembly Resolution A/RES/2131 (1965)*. Website reference www.un.org/Dept/dhl/reguide/resins.htm.

48 *General Assembly Resolution A/RES/36/103*.

49 James, 'The concept of sovereignty revisited', p. 336.

50 M. Fowler and J. Bunck, 'What constitutes the sovereign state?', *Review of International Studies*, 22:4 (1996), 404.

51 C. Weber, 'Reconsidering statehood: examining the sovereignty/statehood boundary', *Review of International Studies*, 18:3 (1992), 215.

52 C. Reus-Smit, 'Human rights and the social construction of sovereignty', *Review of International Studies*, 27:4 (2001), 536–8.

53 T. Otte, 'On intervention: some introductory remarks', in A. Dorman and T. Otte (eds), *Military Intervention: From Gunboat Diplomacy to Humanitarian Intervention* (Aldershot, Dartmouth, 1995), p. 3.

54 Evans and Newnham, *The Penguin Dictionary of International Relations*, p. 278.

55 Bull, *Intervention in World Politics*, p. 1.

56 R. J. Vincent, *Non-Intervention and International Order* (Princeton, Princeton University Press, 1974), p. 13.

57 Evans and Newnham, *The Penguin Dictionary of International Relations*, p. 279.

58 Otte, 'On intervention: some introductory remarks', p. 10.

59 See C. Kupchan, 'Getting in: the initial stage of military intervention', in
    A. Levite *et al.* (eds), *Foreign Military Intervention* (New York, Columbia
    University Press, 1992), pp. 243–60.
60 Otte, 'On intervention: some introductory remarks', pp. 6–10.
61 H. Morgenthau, 'To intervene or not to intervene', *Foreign Affairs*, 45:3
    (1967), 436.
62 Bull, *Intervention in World Politics*, p. 9.
63 Morgenthau, 'To intervene or not to intervene', p. 425 and p. 430.
64 Freeman, *Arts of Power*, p. 55.
65 Bull, *Intervention in World Politics*, p. 193.
66 Schnabel and Thakur, *Kosovo and the Challenge of Humanitarian
    Intervention*, p. 321.
67 S. Murphy, *Humanitarian Intervention: The United Nations in an
    Evolving World Order* (Philadelphia, University of Pennsylvania Press,
    1996), pp. 11–12.
68 F. Abiew, *The Evolution of the Doctrine and Practice of Humanitarian
    Intervention* (The Hague, Kluwer Law International, 1999), p. 18. For
    a thorough review of the literature on the concept of humanitarian
    intervention see P. Simons, 'Humanitarian intervention: a review of liter-
    ature', *Project Ploughshares Working Paper* (September 2001). Website
    reference   www.ploughshares.ca/content/WORKING%20PAPERS/
    wp012.html.
69 M. Frost, 'The ethics of humanitarian intervention: protecting civilians to
    make democratic citizenship possible', in K. Smith and M. Light (eds),
    Ethics and Foreign Policy (Cambridge, Cambridge University Press,
    2001), p. 52.
70 O. Ramsbotham, 'Humanitarian intervention 1990–5: a need to recon-
    ceptualize?', *Review of International Studies*, 23:4 (1997), 456–7. A
    similarly broad view is taken in C. Greenwood, 'Is there a right of human-
    itarian intervention?', *The World Today*, 49:2 (1993), 34.
71 Ramsbotham, 'Humanitarian intervention 1990–5', p. 457.
72 *Finnish Security and Defence Policy 2001*. Website reference www.vn.fi/
    plm/report.htm.
73 T. Weiss, *Military-Civilian Interactions: Intervening in Humanitarian
    Crises* (Lanham, Rowman and Littlefield, 1999), p. 3 defines military-
    civilian humanitarianism as 'the coming together of military forces
    and civilian agencies to deal with the human suffering from complex
    emergencies'.
74 See H. Slim, 'Violence and humanitarianism: moral paradox and the
    protection of civilians', *Security Dialogue*, 32:3 (2001), 325–39.
75 Speech by Prime Minister Tony Blair, 'Doctrine of the International
    Community'. Website reference www.fco.gov.uk/text_only/news/
    speechtext.asp?2316&printVersion=yes.
76 Speech by the Foreign Secretary, Robin Cook, 'Guiding Humanitarian
    Intervention'. Website reference www.fco.gov.uk/text_only/news/
    speechtext.asp?3989&printVersion=yes.
77 See J. Heidenrich, *How to Prevent Genocide: A Guide for Policymakers,
    Scholars, and the Concerned Citizen* (Westport, Praeger, 2001), pp. 73–92
    and D. Carment and F. Harvey, *Using Force to Prevent Ethnic Violence:*

An Evaluation of Theory and Evidence (Westport, Praeger, 2001), pp. 13–24.

78 B. Blechman, 'The intervention dilemma', *Washington Quarterly*, 18:3 (1995), 65.

79 Two recent books discussing just war are A. Coates, *The Ethics of War* (Manchester, Manchester University Press, 1997) and R. Regan, *Just War: Principles and Causes* (Washington DC, The Catholic University of America Press, 1996).

80 M. Fixdal and D. Smith, 'Humanitarian intervention and just war', *Mershon International Studies Review*, (1998), 22.

81 J. B. Hehir, 'Just war theory in a post-Cold War world', *Journal of Religious Studies*, (Fall 1992), 254.

82 Frost, 'The ethics of humanitarian intervention', p. 52.

83 Gen. Sir H. Beach and R. Isbister, 'Old wine, new bottle: the just war tradition and humanitarian intervention', *ISIS Briefing on Humanitarian Intervention*, 3 (2000). Website reference www.isisuk.demon.co.uk/0811/isis/uk/hiproject/no3_paper.html and B. Orend, 'Crisis in Kosovo: a just use of force?', *Politics*, 19:3 (1999), 125–30.

84 For examples of criteria see, *inter alia*, R. Johansen, 'Limits and opportunities in humanitarian intervention', in S. Hoffmann *et al.* (eds), *The Ethics and Politics of Humanitarian Intervention* (Notre Dame, University of Notre Dame Press, 1996), pp. 68–83; R. Phillips and D. Cady, *Humanitarian Intervention: Just War vs. Pacifism* (London, Rowman and Littlefield, 1996) and O. Ramsbotham and T. Woodhouse, *Humanitarian Intervention in Contemporary Conflict* (Cambridge, Polity Press, 1996), pp. 225–31.

85 See S. Solarz and M. O'Hanlon, 'Humanitarian intervention: when is force justified?', *Washington Quarterly*, 20:4 (1997), 3–14 and 'Why and when to go in', *The Economist* (6 January 2001), pp. 21–4.

86 N. Wheeler, 'Reflections on the legality and legitimacy of NATO's intervention in Kosovo', in K. Booth (ed.), *The Kosovo Tragedy: The Human Rights Dimensions* (London, Frank Cass, 2001), pp. 147–52.

87 'Law and right: when they don't fit together', *The Economist* (3 April 1999), p. 20.

88 M. Littman, *Kosovo: Law and Diplomacy* (London, Centre for Policy Studies, 1999), p. 7.

89 S. Chesterman, *Just War or Just Peace? Humanitarian Intervention and International Law* (Oxford, Oxford University Press, 2001), p. 226.

90 Kratochwil, 'Sovereignty as *dominium*', p. 42.

91 See P. Thornberry, '"Come, friendly bombs ...": international law in Kosovo', in M. Waller *et al.* (eds), *Kosovo: The Politics of Delusion* (London, Frank Cass, 2001), p. 48.

92 M. Glennon, *Limits of Law, Prerogatives of Power: Interventionism After Kosovo* (Basingstoke, Palgrave, 2001), pp. 17–19 and Murphy, *Humanitarian Intervention*, pp. 68–82.

93 M. Glennon, 'The new interventionism: the search for a just international law', *Foreign Affairs*, 78:3 (1999), 2–3.

94 C. Ero and S. Long, 'Humanitarian intervention: a new role for the

United Nations?', *International Peacekeeping*, 2:2 (1995), 153 and Simma, 'NATO, the UN and the use of force'.

95 Murphy, *Humanitarian Intervention*, p. 392.

96 *Washington Summit Communiqué (Press Release NAC-S(99)64)*. Website reference www.nato.int/docu/pr/1999/p99-064e.htm; *The Alliance's Strategic Concept (Press Release NAC-S(99)65)*. Website reference www.nato.int/docu/pr/1999/p99-065e.htm.

97 *The North Atlantic Treaty Organisation: Facts and Figures* (Brussels, NATO, 1989), p. 377.

98 N. Butler, 'NATO at 50: papering over the cracks', *Disarmament Diplomacy*, 38 (1999). Website reference www.acronym.org.uk/38nato.htm.

99 B. Møller, *The UN, the USA and NATO: Humanitarian Intervention in the Light of Kosovo (Working Paper 23)* (Copenhagen, Copenhagen Peace Research Institute, 1999), pp. 6–7.

100 D. Leurdijk and D. Zandee, *Kosovo: From Crisis to Crisis* (Aldershot, Ashgate, 2001), p. 50.

101 N. Wheeler, *Saving Strangers: Humanitarian Intervention in International Society* (Oxford, Oxford University Press, 2000), p. 11.

102 Roberts, 'NATO's "humanitarian war" over Kosovo', p. 120.

Chapter 2

Kosovo and NATO's post-Cold War adaptation

Since the end of the Cold War, NATO has been significantly reoriented and retooled across the board. This process of change has been captured under two main labels. *Internal adaptation* is NATO-speak for looking at how the institution works, and whether it can be made to work better and more effectively. The process has embraced the possibility of creating procedures and structures whereby European member states might undertake military operations without the front-line participation of US forces. This aspect of the internal adaptation will be discussed in Chapter 5. Under consideration here is a second major element – the effectiveness of NATO's integrated military command and planning structures. Their performance during *Operation Allied Force* will be examined in the first section.

The *external adaptation* of NATO is a term that refers, fairly obviously, to the evolution of relations between NATO and its members, and non-member states in Europe. The most important and controversial element of the external adaptation has been the NATO enlargement process. Other elements include 'outreach' programmes such as Partnership for Peace (PfP). The discussions in the second section here assess the impact of the Kosovo crisis on NATO's external adaptation, with particular reference to its implications for enlargement.

The internal dimension: military command and political decision-making during the Kosovo crisis

During the Cold War years the integrated military command and planning structures of NATO were frequently lauded as constituting a significant part of the core strengths of the institution. Typical in this respect were the remarks made by then Secretary-General Manfred Wörner in London in November 1990. He declared that 'one of NATO's unique historical achievements has been the integrated defence structure', adding that, without this, 'the security guarantees of the Alliance would sooner or later be seen to be illusory'. This was, he claimed, 'not simply because that structure maintains the nuts and bolts of a functioning defence capability. Nations that merge their defence signal their wish to act together in a common unity of purpose'.[1]

The discussions in this section address the issue of how effective the NATO military structures proved to be during *Operation Allied Force*. A glance through official 'lessons learned' reports, scholarly studies and media accounts since the spring of 1999 reveals that there were some significant problems. Allegations were made by senior military officers about the extent of 'political interference' in operational decisions, especially over targeting issues during the bombing campaign. A related controversy developed over the use of the so-called national 'red card' by member governments. Finally, there was the issue of the extent to which the US ran a parallel national command and control structure separate from the multinational NATO one during the course of operations.

The political–military decision-making interface

Undoubtedly, leading allied military officers were frustrated at the degree of political interference, as they saw it. Two of them were particularly outspoken in their criticisms. The then Chairman of the NATO Military Committee, German General Klaus Naumann, went so far as to give public expression to his concerns while still serving and during the course of operations. This was an almost unheard of way for a senior officer to express his views. In May 1999, Naumann was quoted as saying that:

> We need to find a way to reconcile the conditions of coalition war with the principle of the use of surprise and the overwhelming use of force. We did not apply either in Operation Allied Force and this cost time and effort and potentially additional casualties. The net result is that the campaign has been undoubtedly prolonged.[2]

Later, in retirement, Naumann elaborated upon his criticisms. He reportedly blamed lack of political consensus amongst the nineteen

NATO member states for preventing the military from striking more widely at targets in Serbia from the start of the campaign (phase one of *Operation Allied Force* was restricted specifically to the suppression of enemy air defences). He also criticised their general refusal to countenance ground force options at the beginning.[3]

The first criticism echoed comments made by US Air Force (USAF) Lieutenant General Michael Short. As chief of NATO's Southern Europe Air Command, Short had run *Operation Allied Force* under SACEUR, General Clark. In the autumn of 1999, Short was widely quoted as assessing the air operation thus:

> As an airman I would have done this differently. It would not be an incremental air campaign or slow build-up but we would go downtown from the first night so that on the first morning the influential citizens of Belgrade gathered around Milosevic would have awakened to significant destruction and a clear signal that we were taking the gloves off. If you wake up in the morning and you have no power to your house and no gas to your stove and the bridge you take to work is down and will be lying in the Danube for the next 20 years I think you begin to ask 'hey, Slobo, what's all this about?'.[4]

The implication behind the comments of Generals Naumann and Short is that politicians prevented *Operation Allied Force* from being run in a militarily optimal fashion. First, by requiring the bombing campaign to commence with only limited strikes, and second by shaping and constraining target selection throughout. To what extent were these criticisms justified?

During the earliest phase of the operation, in late March 1999, there does seem to have been tight political control. Decisions, even over individual targets, required the approval of all nineteen NATO members in the North Atlantic Council (NAC). Apart from the brief experience of *Operation Deliberate Force* in Bosnia three-and-a-half years previously,[5] member governments had no experience of running a significant coercive military campaign through NATO structures. Under these circumstances it was probably to be expected that they would start with the assumption that everybody would be closely involved. Then US Secretary of Defense William Cohen publicly admitted as much. In testimony to the House of Representatives Committee on Armed Services in mid-April 1999, he said that 'because this is ... the first type of operation NATO has conducted in this fashion, I think initially there was some ... confusion in terms of how this is going to operate, in terms of whether or not individual Members had to approve or disapprove'.[6]

Politicians taking military decisions (an area in which they have _no_ experience)

Later in the same hearings, Cohen stated that 'we went through some initial phases where perhaps there was too much delay in approval and the process wasn't working right. I think we have squared that away now, where Wes Clark feels he has what he needs'.[7] It is significant that Cohen was talking in these terms less than one month into the operation. Although the political element of NATO decision-making *was* too cumbersome right at the start, with all nineteen members expecting their say, it seems to have been quickly realised that a more responsive and streamlined system was required. On 3 April 1999, less than ten days into the operation, *The Times* in London reported that NATO political leaders had decided to 'cast aside some of the bureaucratic shackles that have limited NATO's flexibility'. Specifically they had reportedly decided that SACEUR 'will now be subject to political control by the leaders of America, Britain, France, Germany and Italy and will no longer have to consult all 19 Nato ambassadors about every decision'.[8]

Thereafter, political oversight on a day-to-day basis was exercised by these major powers acting through what was called the 'Quints' group.[9] The significance of the political concession made by the fourteen NATO governments not represented in the Quints should not be underestimated. Despite being relegated to a back-seat role, they were, nevertheless, still expected to maintain NATO-wide political consensus and solidarity behind the objectives of the bombing campaign.

It is likely that there was a *de facto* trade-off involving participation in the Quints and the level of a country's contribution to the operation. The Quints between them provided over 80 per cent of the almost 1,000 aircraft which were involved in its latter stages. The US, UK and France reportedly functioned as an elite within this elite, based on their operational contributions.[10] A limited degree of involvement in the day-to-day supervision of operations may also have suited some NATO members politically. This was especially so in the case of Greece and two out of the three new members (the Czech Republic and Hungary), where public and political opinion was less solidly behind the objectives of the campaign than in the other NATO states.[11]

On occasion, the full NATO membership in the NAC may simply not have been asked for a decision. The British House of Commons Select Committee on Defence concluded that this had been the case with regard to at least one key issue. 'We were told', a report noted:

> that the [NATO] Secretary General authorised the transition from Phase 1 to Phase 2 on 27th March. To have moved to Phase 3[12] would have required the full consent of the NAC. There is some ambiguity about the

nature of the post-Phase 2 stage of operations ... our informal discussions would suggest that the *formal* decision to move to strategic bombing of Serbia was never put directly, in quite those terms, to the NAC. Rather, an extension of the delegation to the Secretary General was made on or around 30 March [emphasis in the original].

The Defence Committee report also quoted the candid General Naumann subsequently admitting that 'phase three could have been seen as an all-out war against Yugoslavia and ... not all NATO nations, were prepared to go as far ... and for that reason *we never took the risk to ask the question* knowing that we may run into some problems'[emphasis added].[13]

Another mechanism for simplifying and, so the military and Quints members hoped, making more effective the political decision-making within NATO was the formal delegation of authority by the NAC, in advance, to Secretary-General Solana. When giving evidence to the House of Commons Defence Committee in May 2000, Sir John Goulden, the UK's then Permanent Representative on the NAC, was asked whether NATO's decision-making machinery had proved sufficiently responsive to the pace of events. His reply was:

> Yes ... mainly because of what I described as the delegation to Solana. Having agreed a plan we did not then constantly update it in the Council. We gave it to the military and Solana helped with the interpretation of the plan. He was completely up to date with the military. When they needed fine tuning or a political issue needed clarification, they would come to us and get it done on the day because the Council functioned daily ... The consultation was very intense. That helps to explain the speed with which we were able to go from launching the campaign to going to phase two, to going to the final targeting decision on 29 March. By 29 March we had authorised all the powers that the military needed for the campaign, within six days of starting.[14]

A picture is beginning to emerge. It is of a process, which got underway in the first days of the operation, informally to streamline NATO's decision-making structures and processes. Partly this was done via the activation of the Quints group and partly via delegation of authority to the Secretary-General, who was granted an important degree of flexibility in determining whether and how to intensify the air operations.

NATO political and military decision-making worked, to a significant extent, *informally* during the period March–June 1999. As members of the House of Commons Defence Committee concluded, when reflecting on a visit to NATO headquarters during 2000:

We formed the distinct impression that the idealised wiring diagrams and flow charts reflecting NATO's command and control arrangements, and its associated staff procedures, had rapidly been thrown aside under the pressures of a real operation, and that this was an operation in which the element of political discretion was far higher than had ever been envisaged within the mindset of the Cold War in which NATO had grown up.[15]

The limits of NATO authority: use of the 'red card'

The concept of the NATO 'red card' was something that, before the Kosovo crisis, had been familiar only to the *cognoscenti*. Consequently, when it attracted media coverage during and after *Operation Allied Force*, it may have appeared to the untutored eye as if something new and debilitating had suddenly been introduced.

In fact the extent of NATO 'military integration' had never been as profound or significant as many had assumed. At no point in its history had NATO been granted a formal supranational dimension by its member states. Members who have assigned forces to actual or potential NATO missions have been careful about the degree of authority that they have been prepared to delegate. In military parlance, they have not been willing to delegate operational *command* to NATO. Rather, allied commanders have been granted operational *control*. The essential difference has been succinctly summarised by the House of Commons Defence Committee:

> Operational Command gives a commander authority to do virtually what he likes with the forces under his command, whereas Operational Control only gives him authority to use those forces for the missions or tasks for which they have been specifically assigned by contributing nations. The effect of this is that if commanders with Operational Control wish to use their forces for tasks different to those for which they were assigned, they have to seek national approval.[16]

This requirement for national approval is what gives NATO members red card – i.e. veto – rights. *Operation Allied Force* was the first occasion on which the media and interested publics became aware of the existence of this veto power. Within NATO, however, it was nothing new and its use was dealt with in a more matter-of-fact way than contemporary press coverage suggested.

This is not to say that it did not become a contentious issue from time to time. Tensions arose when people sought to make political mileage out of it. This was most clearly seen in a post-operation spat between the US and France. In October 1999, the controversial General Short was quoted in the press as singling out the French for criticism on the grounds that they had allegedly played a major role in constraining NATO targeting strategy during the later stages of *Operation Allied Force*, by vetoing particular targets in Serbia.[17] French officials soon replied, again through the press, with counter-accusations that the US had conducted the operation in large part outside NATO command structures.[18]

Long-standing Franco–US animosities over NATO made these disputes appear more serious than they probably were. Besides the French, other Quints group members had exercised vetoes over particular targets without attracting US criticism, at least in public. It is known, for example, that the UK sometimes brandished the red card in this area. The then Chief of Defence Staff, General Sir Charles Guthrie, confirmed it to the House of Commons Defence Committee in the spring of 2000.[19]

The limitations imposed by NATO members' reluctance to go beyond giving operational control to allied commanders could be, nevertheless, a source of frustration. Lieutenant General Sir Michael Jackson, the first commander of NATO's Kosovo Force (KFOR), reflected upon the problems that could result, from the perspective of military command and planning, when looking back on the build-up of NATO ground forces in neighbouring Macedonia early in 1999. Jackson asserted that, 'because transfer of authority to NATO command only goes so far', the national deployments to Macedonia were somewhat chaotic and disorganised. What this meant on the ground was that:

> The great land grab [was] on … who's going to get the best patch and accommodation and workshops, and it can come down to who out-bids whom. It's not a very good way, but the militarily efficient way of doing it is nobody enters the rear-area, in a period such as we are going through now, and nobody takes a contract, without Headquarters … approval. But that means that they would have to be under command, and once again, without an Activation Order it can't be done, because that is the constitutional position of NATO.[20]

Jackson was centrally involved in the best-known red card incident of the entire NATO Kosovo campaign. This came right at the end of *Operation Allied Force*, just as the deployment of KFOR was about to commence. Jackson was ordered by SACEUR to deploy a force to confront Russian troops who had made a 'dash' to the airport in Pristina.[21] He demurred and referred the matter to the British government, which consulted the US government. The US, in turn, overruled SACEUR. Jackson's basis for refusing to carry out the order was that SACEUR was exceeding his operational control in attempting to task NATO forces with a mission that no member government had agreed to. The US, in common with other NATO members, had not delegated operational *command* to any NATO officer.[22] The incident has subsequently been confirmed in Clark's memoir of the crisis.[23]

For a time it appeared as if this incident had the potential to develop into a major controversy. There were some in the US who tried to ensure that it did. In the autumn of 1999, Senator John Warner, Chairman of the Senate Armed Services Committee, was quoted as saying that 'we can't have second-guessing at every level of command in a military organisation if it is to be effective', and threatening to hold Senate hearings on the matter.[24] Subsequently, though, the controversy petered out. Jackson himself made light of the matter. He later wrote of 'a little sideplay by the Russian contingent which had us all amused. Especially the chain of command', adding that Pristina airport 'formed no part of our initial plans ... the whole thing frankly was very much hyped up by the press'.[25]

The US and NATO: parallel structures

There is no doubt that the United States had run a parallel national command and planning structure alongside the multinational NATO one during *Operation Allied Force*. In its *After-Action Report* on the operation, published in January 2000, the Department of Defense described both structures in detail with accompanying wiring diagrams![26] The key link at the top was General Clark. Since the appointment of Dwight Eisenhower as the first SACEUR in 1951, the post – always held by an American – has been double-hatted. This meant that in addition to serving as SACEUR, Clark, in common with his predecessors, also served as Commander-in-Chief of US European Command (USEUCOM); a national appointment.

The US government also operated a strict requirement for political oversight of military decisions, based on the President's constitutional position as Commander-in-Chief. Other heads of government would sometimes have a direct input into targeting decisions. Tony

Blair, for example, did get 'involved in targeting ... but very seldom' according to his Chief of Defence Staff.[27] As for the French, they reportedly 'did exercise some restraining power on NATO planners, particularly after the first couple of weeks ... but the net effect was generally to push back the bombing of some specific targets at most a few days'.[28] In the US case, *all* suggested targets generated by NATO planners and hence sent up to SACEUR were passed on by General Clark – wearing his USEUCOM hat – to the Pentagon which, in turn, generally passed them all the way up to the President.[29]

It has also been claimed that the US refused to release key military assets, even nominally, to NATO command. Richard Connaughton has written that 'the conventional fighter effort was controlled by NATO HQ. Bomber operations, B-52s from Fairford, Gloucestershire and B-2s from Missouri, and Stealth fighter operations were not made available for NATO tasking but tasked directly from the Pentagon'.[30]

James Thomas has noted one particularly important way in which the existence of parallel military processes complicated matters for NATO. As *Operation Allied Force* progressed, target *selection* was increasingly being carried out by the US alone. Target *approval*, on the other hand, remained a multilateral activity amongst the Quints. According to Thomas, this dual approach was almost bound to cause friction and delay, because 'European countries found it difficult to approve quickly targets which they had no hand in selecting, and where they had to rely on US estimates of collateral damage'.[31]

Notwithstanding the existence of the parallel structures, and the consequent extent to which the US could run a national dimension to the operations, the degree of US control evidently did not go far enough for some. In April 1999, Congressman Steven Kuykendall told Secretary of Defense Cohen that 'we are actually the hammer in NATO, the rest of them [i.e. the European members] just come along for the ride ... we are the leader and we need to act like the leader. We are not doing that in NATO right now'.[32] Speaking in similar vein later in the same month was Eliot Cohen, a respected American defence academic. He told the House Armed Services Committee that 'the challenge really is for the United States, which is the leader of this operation, which is probably now supplying something like three-quarters or more of the effort, to really dominate it'.[33] Reviewing the course of operations early in 2000, General Short said that the US should have told its NATO allies that 'we will take the alliance to war and we will win this thing for you, but the price to be paid is we call the tune'.[34]

On the other hand, there were some powerful American voices raised in support of the view that the existence of parallel military structures during *Operation Allied Force* had complicated efforts to attain unity of command – a key goal of the military in any operation. Speaking to the Brookings Institution, a leading think tank, in June 2000, General Clark conceded this point. Having put up a wiring diagram of the parallel structures, he stated that:

> When you hear a lot of different opinions about this from military people, and you hear people say well, they weren't quite sure what was happening, why was this done, why was that done, it should not surprise anyone. This is about as complex a command structure as anyone would ever fear to see. But we had it and we worked it.[35]

The Pentagon's *After-Action Report* also conceded the point in stating that 'parallel US and NATO command-and-control structures complicated operational planning and unity of command. These structures are well defined but had not been used previously to plan and conduct sustained combat operations'. The report suggested that the US and its NATO allies should, in future, 'develop an overarching command-and-control policy and agree on procedures for the policy's implementation'.[36] This could, of course, mean trying to get Europeans to agree that the US should command 'NATO' operations unhindered, as suggested by General Short and others.

NATO as a 'degraded' institution?

Speaking before the House Armed Services Committee in April 1999, retired USAF General Charles Link said, discussing NATO's decision-making and command arrangements during Kosovo operations:

> I think the key thing to remember here is that this is an arrangement that would have worked well when NATO was under attack because one could assume a community of interests among all the then 16 nations. When we use NATO in the way that it is being used now, that particular command construct really gets blurred because, as we have seen, each of the member nations may have, since they are not concerned about their own security in a direct way, they may have other economic, political or social interests that color their views towards the central theme of action.[37]

NATO's taking on of missions not directly connected with the defence of its member states' territory (which had been its exclusive Cold War role) thus carried the seeds of a potential degrading of the institution's effectiveness. This could happen as agreement and consensus on controversial issues become more difficult to achieve. It is a danger which NATO members seemed aware of during the Kosovo crisis. Hence the premium which was placed on 'solidarity', 'unity' and 'cohesion' at the time. This meant that member states accepted constraints on their individual attitudes and behaviour.

Tim Judah has recounted a story that nearly illustrates the practical impact of these considerations during the air operation:

> NATO commanders wanted to destroy the Podgorica air base. But first, they had to get past France's opposition to bombing Montenegro. At a morning intelligence briefing, Clark was informed that Yugoslav artillery in Montenegro was shelling northern Albania. 'Forget the French!' Clark thundered, according to the participants. 'No, no, no, wait! Hold off on that', he said. 'I'll get French permission. I'll get it'. Within hours, Clark and three of the Clinton administration's top players – [Secretary of State Madeleine] Albright, national security adviser Samuel R. 'Sandy' Berger and defense secretary William S. Cohen – dialed their counterparts in Paris. By the next morning, Clark had political approval for the strike.[38]

Whether or not this story is literally true in all its details, it *is* plausible. It illustrates two important things. First, US reluctance to act unilaterally when a row with a major NATO ally threatened. At the same time, it illustrates the reluctance of the French to persist in blocking an airstrike when to do so might have fractured NATO cohesion.

In their report on the *Lessons of Kosovo*, the House of Commons Defence Committee wrote about a 'paradox ... at the heart of the lessons to be learned' and placed this part of their text in bold print for special emphasis:

> Although Alliance unity was only one factor amongst those which eventually enabled NATO to prevail, it was a necessary condition for the others to have effect. Unity was, in the end, the Alliance's greatest strength. At the same time it was NATO's weakest point ... the maintenance of its unity was the factor which most significantly restricted the military options open to the Alliance to pursue an efficient and successful coercive strategy against Milosevic.[39]

It is almost certain that the Milosevic government had calculated that, if they could ride out the early waves of airstrikes, NATO's cohesion would begin to fray and ultimately crumble. This did not happen during the more than two months that the bombing campaign ultimately had to be prosecuted. The decision-making and military command procedures during the operation were both fraught and messy, but they ultimately 'worked' in that no member state broke ranks and nobody dropped out. Milosevic was thus, eventually, the one who conceded defeat.

The external dimension:
security assurances in South East Europe

The term 'NATO enlargement by stealth' can be used to describe a situation whereby countries that have not legally acceded to its treaty nevertheless evolve a set of enduring political, operational and institutional links with NATO. These develop to the extent that key aspects of their practical relations with it are, to all intents and purposes, as significant and well established as those of the formal members. The discussions in this section ask whether such a process has been hastened in South East Europe by the Kosovo crisis.

Formal NATO enlargement entails new members signing the Washington Treaty and so acquiring the security guarantees contained in its Article 5 ('an attack on one member state shall be considered an attack on them all'). The official position of existing members has been that such guarantees are available only to countries that have been through a constitutional accession process. Fear that the guarantees might be diluted led member states to ring-fence them by refusing to consider suggestions for formal 'associate membership' of NATO.[40] As the officially endorsed *Study on NATO Enlargement* put it in September 1995, 'there must be no security guarantees given or members within the Alliance that are "second tier" and no modifications of the Washington Treaty for those who join'.[41]

It could be argued, at least before 11 September 2001, that, with the end of the Cold War, the Article 5 guarantees of joint territorial defence of members were no longer very important. Yet, as Paul Cornish has asserted, 'it is not easy to conceive of a military alliance of sovereign states being, at bottom, anything other than collective and territorial. Residual and symbolic it may be, but if the 'Three Musketeers' collective defence commitment were to be removed, the Alliance could collapse politically and militarily'.[42] Notwithstanding the ending of the Cold War that first brought it into being, the Article 5 foundation thus remains essential if NATO is to continue in business.

Notwithstanding the stated intention of current NATO members not to permit any association arrangements, the distinctions between members and non-members have become increasingly blurred, most especially in the South East European region. There are a number of reasons for this. Some of them pre-date the Kosovo crisis, whilst others are a direct consequence of it.

The impact and influence of Partnership for Peace

The NATO PfP programme was developed primarily by then US Defense Secretary Les Aspin during 1993 and formally adopted at a NATO summit in Brussels in January 1994. As outlined in the official summit documents, the objectives of PfP have been to 'promote closer military cooperation and interoperability' between NATO and 'partner' states. This would be achieved through joint training and exercising, with a particular focus on potential peacekeeping and related operations, together with the 'facilitation of transparency in national defence planning and budgeting processes'. As a further, crucial, incentive to prospective partner countries to sign up, the NATO members also declared that 'active participation in Partnership for Peace will play an important role in the evolutionary process of the expansion of NATO'.[43] By 2002, twenty-seven non-NATO European countries were participating.

Istvan Szonyi has argued persuasively that, as it has developed, the attitudes and behaviour of both NATO members and non-member partners have been increasingly 'socialised' by their participation in PfP:

> Socialization in this context means that the various participants in PfP [have] engaged in a process of thorough and mutual adaptation. The process of adaptation was manifold because it involved all the partners concerned in PfP. The important point in this respect is that it was not only the 'Eastern' countries which adapted to 'NATO' requirements but NATO states also adapted to the needs and concerns of the former.[44]

Szonyi supports his contention by arguing that NATO member states have supported the PfP financially, through hosting military exercises and, perhaps most importantly, by 'involving the Partners in the process of consultation, planning and review'.[45] Partner countries, meanwhile have adapted through hosting exercises, developing military co-operation amongst themselves within the overall PfP framework and becoming 'familiarized with NATO standards and procedures even beyond the scope of peacekeeping'.[46] It is on the basis of this ongoing process of mutual socialisation that the importance of the role of PfP in South East Europe begins to emerge.

The PfP has played a particularly important role in the evolution of NATO involvement in Albania. This hardly seemed likely during early 1997 when, with Albania collapsing into civil turmoil and conflict sparked off by the pyramid investment scandal,[47] the United States not only refused to intervene but, with the support of the Federal Republic of Germany (FRG) and the UK, also prevented NATO from doing so.[48] It was left to Italy, with support and contributions from France and Greece, to put together an *ad hoc* multinational force for *Operation Alba*, a four-month humanitarian assistance and political stabilisation mission in the period leading up to Albanian parliamentary elections in the summer of 1997.

These events gave rise to some strong criticisms of NATO's apparent lack of collective interest; with arguments being made that this demonstrated the institution's unsuitability for dealing with post-Cold War security crises in the wider Europe. More specifically, the limitations of PfP as a promoter of stability amongst the partner states were criticised.[49] Although by no means all observers took this view,[50] NATO members evidently felt prompted into action.

Responding to a request from the Albanian government in August 1997, NATO staffers and planners set to work on devising a special PfP 'action plan' covering the reconstruction of the Albanian armed forces, which had virtually disintegrated earlier in the year. According to the director of the project in the NATO International Staff, no less than twelve teams of NATO advisers were dispatched to assess the situation on the ground and make recommendations to the Albanian Defence Ministry.[51] The challenge of Albania during the second half of 1997 became for NATO a matter of upholding its post-Cold War credibility and that of the PfP.

Although NATO's interest in Albania was not, therefore, initiated by events in neighbouring Kosovo, from early 1998 it did come increasingly to be driven by its members' wider concern with the developing crisis there. NATO foreign ministers, at their NAC meeting in May 1998, issued an important *Statement on Kosovo*, their first significant reference to the province. Amongst other things this document identified the 'security and stability' of both Albania and Macedonia as being a concern of NATO's.

Further to this, specific initiatives were announced which were designed to have a deterrent effect against any temptation, which might have existed on the part of the Milosevic government, to threaten either of these countries. The *Statement on Kosovo* announced that 'we are launching NATO-led assistance programmes to help

Albania and the former Yugoslav Republic of Macedonia to secure their borders, based on enhanced PfP activities and on bilateral assistance'. With regard to Albania, the statement announced the opening of a 'NATO/PfP Cell' – in effect a NATO office – in the capital, Tirana, as well as a major air-force exercise and a port visit by NATO's Standing Naval Force Mediterranean over the summer.[52] By publicly stating a NATO interest in the security and stability of these two countries, the *Statement on Kosovo* granted both Albania and Macedonia *de facto* NATO security assurances, if not formal legal guarantees. This was even before the build-up of NATO forces on their territories began as the Kosovo crisis escalated from the autumn of 1998.

The *Statement on Kosovo* also promised enhancements to Macedonia's PfP-based co-operation with NATO. In the Macedonian case, the statement announced the 'upgrading' of a PfP exercise – *Co-operative Best Effort* – scheduled to take place in the country in September 1998, and contained a promise to consider establishing a PfP training centre, which would be the first of its kind, in Krivolak. More immediately, in mid-June, the promised NATO air exercise – *Determined Falcon* – took place over Albania and Macedonia. This involved the participation of eighty-three aircraft from thirteen NATO member states and it was explicitly intended to send a deterrent signal to the Milosevic government.[53]

NATO forces on the ground in Albania and Macedonia

When *Operation Allied Force* was launched in March 1999, nearly 500,000 Kosovar refugees crossed into Albania. The Albanian government demanded NATO help to cope with the influx and this was forthcoming. In early April, it was announced that the Allied Command Europe Mobile Force (Land) – a multinational high-readiness brigade-strength force – would be deployed to Albania on *Operation Allied Harbour*. Its mission would be to construct accommodation and provide security and some semblance of order in the refugee camps.[54] For this mission it would be known as the 'Albania Force' (AFOR).

AFOR stayed on after the end of *Operation Allied Force* and the return of the refugees in June 1999. Initially its mission was to facilitate the safe and orderly return of the refugees (in so far as that was possible given the eagerness of many to return immediately, despite AFOR's advice to wait). Once the vast majority of the refugees had gone home, most of the troops assigned to AFOR remained. Its new role, having been renamed 'AFOR II', was to help safeguard the logistics tail and act as a reserve for the NATO-led forces in Kosovo itself. By the spring of 2000, during the course of its operations in Albania, AFOR had built or repaired over 200km of road, modernised Tirana Rinas airport and the airfields at Kukes and Korce, and greatly expanded the capacity of Durres as a port.[55] In October 2001 there were still 2,400 NATO troops in Albania.[56]

The Albanian government did not object to this continued presence, far from it. Albanian leaders could see that the physical deployment of a NATO force on their territory would help to ensure the continuation of the security assurances given in the *Statement on Kosovo*, and confirmed at the NATO summit in Washington in April 1999. In Washington the NATO assurances had been specifically linked to potential acts of aggression against countries in the region hosting NATO forces. It was hardly surprising, therefore, that in the autumn of 1999 the Speaker of the Albanian Parliament should refer to his country as a 'de facto ally' of NATO and state that a 'long term' NATO military presence was desirable. Nor was it surprising that the then Prime Minister should say that his country was 'open to the continuation of' the deployment of NATO forces.[57]

The NATO military presence on the ground in Macedonia had predated that in Albania. From the autumn of 1998, troops from European NATO states had begun to arrive in the country. Officially their task was to serve as the Extraction Force (XFOR), in case the OSCE's KVM got into trouble. There were doubts about the military utility of XFOR for the task at hand. It was pointed out that it was too small and poorly configured for the rescue of any but very small groups of OSCE personnel.[58] Given also that the force was being deployed in a somewhat haphazard fashion, a case can be made that the primary purpose behind the deployments was political signalling. This represented a continuation of the approach adopted earlier in the year by NATO with the air and naval exercises in Albania and Macedonia. The intention was to send a deterrent message to Milosevic.

Understandably the Macedonian government, like its counterpart in Albania, wanted something concrete in return for agreeing to host this force; i.e. a specific reiteration of the security assurances from NATO which it had originally obtained in May 1998. This was forthcoming when Solana and Clark visited Macedonia in November of that year in order to secure the in-principle agreement of the Macedonians to the deployment of XFOR. The Macedonian Foreign Minister subsequently told his colleagues at a meeting of NATO's Euro-Atlantic Partnership Council (EAPC) – the PfP's supervisory body – of 'the expected support, on a mutual basis, that has been reaffirmed during the recent visit of Secretary General Solana and General Clark to our country'.[59]

The NATO XFOR did not have to be used for the mission for which it was initially designated, as the KVM was withdrawn without hindrance from Kosovo in early March 1999. Nevertheless the force remained based on Macedonian territory for the duration of *Operation Allied Force* and indeed its numbers grew. During the NATO air operation it performed similar roles to the parallel AFOR in providing accommodation and order for the thousands of Kosovar refugees who arrived in Macedonia. It was also to form the basis for the first deployments of KFOR in June. In the autumn of 2001, around 5,000 troops were still being maintained under NATO command in Macedonia in order to contribute to KFOR's logistics tail and also to act as a reserve if required.[60] The Macedonian government had welcomed these continuing deployments.

Going further, Macedonian co-operation with NATO in this area has been seen, by its political leaders, as valuable preparation for eventual NATO membership. This rationale was summed up by the Macedonian Foreign Minister in front of his EAPC colleagues at the end of 1999, when he spoke of:

> the experience we are gaining through the co-operation with NATO and its member countries, as well as the Partners, particularly as a host country of the logistic base for the NATO peace forces in Kosovo, facilitating the largest part of the transit activities for the Kosovo peace operation and with the other activities and efforts ... contribute to the continuous and substantial progress in our relations with NATO, which have thus gained a new quality.[61]

By early 2001 NATO and its member states, for their part, seemed to be becoming ever more deeply committed to Macedonia's security. Following an outbreak of guerrilla activity by ethnic Albanians on the Kosovo-Macedonia border in March, NATO Secretary-General Lord Robertson stated that 'I want to emphasise that NATO is fully committed to supporting the security, stability and territorial integrity of the former Yugoslav Republic of Macedonia'.[62] These words were backed up by action. KFOR stepped up patrols on the Kosovo-Macedonia border with the aim of stopping Albanian guerrillas or their supplies from moving across it. By June 2001, 400 KFOR personnel were

reportedly part of 'Task Force Juno' patrolling the border region.[63] It
was *apropos* of this task that KFOR's US contingent had fired its first
shots since deploying to Kosovo nearly two years previously.[64]

More generally, NATO co-operation with the Macedonian
government was stepped up. Robertson announced that a 'Senior
Representative' from NATO would be seconded to the Macedonian
capital, where he subsequently established a 'NATO Cooperation and
Coordination Centre'. In May 2001, the NAC noted that 'improved
military coordination and the exchange of military information with
the Ministries of Defence and Interior' in Macedonia had also been
established.[65] Later, in the summer, a task force of several hundred
troops from European NATO member states was deployed, on
Operation Essential Harvest, to supervise the disarming of Albanian
rebels as part of a political agreement with the Macedonian government. A follow-on NATO force remained in the country on *Operation
Amber Fox*. In sum, by 2002 NATO had not only maintained but had
further developed its significant relationship with the Macedonian
government that had been begun during the Kosovo crisis. This relationship was, via the presence of the Senior Representative and other
NATO officials and teams not to mention the military task forces,
more overt and obvious than that which the institution maintained
with many of its own member states.

NATO's credibility

Probably the strongest overall reason why NATO has become so
deeply entangled in underwriting security and stability in South East
Europe is because the institution and its member states believe that
they have so much credibility tied up there. This sense pre-dates the
Kosovo crisis and has been apparent since at least the summer of 1995.
The stance of the United States has been crucial. Conventional
accounts of the reasons why the Clinton administration decided to
intervene actively in the Bosnian imbroglio in 1995, reversing previous
American reticence, stress the importance of domestic politicking.[66]
Such accounts underestimate or ignore the importance, for the then
President and his senior foreign policy advisers, of NATO's credibility.
That the very future of the institution was under threat if the Bosnian
civil war was not stopped was clear to numerous observers during 1994
and early 1995, as evidenced by the number of pessimistic articles and
commentaries which were being published at that time.[67]

The US-inspired NATO decision to launch *Operation Deliberate Force* in Bosnia from late August 1995 was mainly brought about by American concern to demonstrate, to both internal and external audiences, the cohesion, strength and effectiveness of NATO. This can be gleaned simply by looking at the relevant official statements of the time. On 30 August 1995, for example, a statement issued in the name of the Secretary-General declared that a key objective behind the decision to launch the strikes was to 'convince all parties of the determination of the Alliance to implement its decisions'. A similar statement issued a week later reiterated these words and added that 'no-one can now doubt our resolve to see this matter through'.[68]

Following the Bosnian Serbs' agreement to a ceasefire, and the opening of the negotiations for a peace deal in Dayton, Ohio in October 1995, NATO credibility remained a central part of the US agenda. Senior Clinton administration officials made public reference to it coupled, naturally, with references to how important the role of the US was in underpinning the credibility of NATO. The then Secretary of State, Warren Christopher, warned of 'the end of NATO' if the US was not prepared to help implement a Bosnian peace agreement by deploying troops on the ground. Then Defense Secretary William Perry, meanwhile, told a congressional committee that the successful implementation of an agreement would 'demonstrate the credibility of NATO'. Finally the President himself, in a television broadcast to the American people designed to put pressure on Congress to acquiesce in the sending of US troops to Bosnia, said that 'if we're not there, NATO will not be there; the peace will collapse ... and erode our partnership with our European allies'.[69]

Concerns about NATO's credibility have proved enduring. Following the initial deployment of some 20,000 US troops from late 1995 as part of the Bosnian Implementation Force (IFOR), the Clinton administration successively extended the deployment period and effectively forgot about periodic assertions that US troops were only in Bosnia for a finite period of time. It was clear to some as early as the spring of 1996 that the NATO-led forces in Bosnia could not simply be withdrawn according to some pre-determined timetable. Doing so would 'deal a blow to NATO's long-term credibility, given the prestige it [had] invested in IFOR'.[70]

Various deadlines for US withdrawal were, therefore, effectively fudged by the Clinton administration (and by Congress), and this practice continued into the Bush administration. In late 2001 there were still 3,500 US troops in Bosnia.[71] The Bush administration had gone quiet on previous 'promises' to seriously reduce or even eliminate the US military contribution to the NATO-led forces in both Bosnia and Kosovo.

The underlying robustness of commitments was demonstrated by the extent to which the NATO and US military presence remained essentially intact in the months following 11 September 2001. In the immediate aftermath, there was speculation that the Bush adminis-tration would denude its forces in South East Europe and give priority to the 'war on terror'. In fact, the US presence was only marginally adjusted. Six months after 11 September, the number of US troops in Kosovo was 5,300, which was just 100 below the level of the previous October.[72]

In July 2002, over 1,000 US troops were airlifted into Kosovo in a major exercise designed, according to KFOR commanders, to demonstrate the continuing strength of American commitment; not just in terms of forces on the ground, but also with so called 'over-the-horizon' troops (i.e. rapidly-deployable reinforcements). This exercise was quickly followed by a visit from the Chairman of the US Joint Chiefs of Staff, USAF General Richard Myers. He declared that whilst the US did face a challenge in 'trying to balance operations like here in the Balkans that is so vitally important in this region and the global war on terrorism', nevertheless, 'the Balkans is still a high priority with the US administration of President Bush'.[73]

Some have predicted that a NATO military presence in South East Europe will be required for '20 years or more'.[74] This bears out the validity of the argument made by Lawrence Freedman back in 1995:

> It is far easier to send troops in than to extricate them at a later date ...
> By then, the credibility of the intervener and probably the sponsoring institution – the Organisation for Security and Cooperation in Europe, European Union, United Nations or NATO – will have been invoked. Reputation, or saving face, becomes an extra interest ... the agonizing over a decision to admit failure and withdraw can be extremely intense.[75]

By the time the Kosovo crisis moved to the top of its agenda in 1998, NATO's credibility was already significantly invested in South East Europe; most especially in the maintenance of the Bosnian settlement which it was policing.

In this context it was certainly no coincidence that the first substantive NATO *Statement on Kosovo*, in May 1998, should open by stating that:

> We are deeply concerned by the situation in Kosovo. We deplore the continuing use of violence in suppressing political dissent or in pursuit of political change. The violence and the associated instability *risk jeopardising the Peace Agreement in Bosnia and Herzegovina* and endangering security and stability in Albania and the former Yugoslav Republic of Macedonia [emphasis added].[76]

Ultimately, self-interest prevails (own security)

Humanitarian concerns were mentioned in this statement, but the overall tone made clear that they were not of primary importance at the time. Rather, the worry was that unimpeded Serb activity in Kosovo might embolden both the Milosevic government in Belgrade and the Serbs in Bosnia to challenge the Dayton peace accords. Kosovo and Bosnia were linked together in the minds of many at NATO principally for this reason.

The preservation, or preferably enhancement, of NATO's credibility in South East Europe constituted a key stated objective – one might say an additional war aim – for western leaders during *Operation Allied Force*. In this context, 'credibility' came to depend increasingly on two factors. The first was the obvious one of 'winning', in the sense of compelling Milosevic to comply with the various demands which NATO had formulated. The second was the vital means to this end; maintaining the cohesion and basic political and diplomatic unity of all NATO members (whether they contributed aircraft to *Operation Allied Force* or not) behind the overall objectives of the campaign.

The extent to which the preservation of NATO's credibility became a distinct war aim in itself can be easily documented. For example, one week after the start of *Operation Allied Force*, Robin Cook was quoted as saying that 'the whole credibility of NATO is at stake – not just loss of face after earlier commitments, but confidence in our own security. It is in the national British interest to maintain NATO's credibility'. Shortly thereafter, Senator John McCain, an early challenger for the Republican presidential nomination in the United States, was quoted as saying that 'credibility is our most precious asset [in this campaign]. We have purchased our credibility with American blood'.[77] In the Pentagon's *After-Action Report* on Kosovo operations, 'ensuring NATO's credibility' was explicitly identified as being one of the 'primary interests' of the US and its allies in conducting operations.[78] In May 2000, the British House of Commons Select Committee on Foreign Affairs suggested that the humanitarian imperatives usually cited as the primary reason for the NATO intervention were at least partly a cover, to provide legitimacy for operations designed principally to underpin NATO's credibility.

NATO considered this cover necessary, in the Committee's view, because 'it is difficult to imagine a legal justification based upon the need to support any organisation's credibility'.[79]

Former SACEUR Clark, finally, has provided a good rationale for the prime role that the institution's credibility played in the calculations of NATO governments and leaders during the Kosovo crisis:

> Once the threat surfaces … nations or alliances are committed. Following through to preserve credibility becomes a matter of vital interest. Credibility is the ultimate measure of value for states and international institutions. Inevitably, sacrificing credibility carries long-term consequences far greater than the immediate issue, whatever it is.[80]

Conclusions

In terms, first, of its internal workings, it would be over-simplistic to suggest that NATO's performance during *Operation Allied Force* demonstrated that it 'doesn't work' in a real crisis. To be sure, many of its formal decision-making structures and procedures were quickly downgraded or sidelined and informal methods developed in their stead. This, however, suggests that the real value of 'NATO' lies not so much in its physical structures and processes as in the social networks and habits of working together that have built up around them. The conduct of *Operation Allied Force* suggested that the latter can be separated from the formal institutional structures and still function effectively.

Sir Michael Alexander sat as the UK's Permanent Representative on the NAC during the 1990–91 Gulf crisis. NATO was not formally involved in responding to this. Nevertheless, in Alexander's view a key role in facilitating the response of the US and its European allies was played by the informal habits of co-operation developed around NATO's structures. As he recalled:

> What really mattered was the existence of the enormous and very robust network of contacts and relationships between capitals, between military commanders, between logisticians and so on. This meant that it was very easy for people to pick up the telephone and speak to somebody else whom they have known and been exercising with and so on over the years. The whole habit of working together is so deeply engrained that problems always seemed soluble, they always looked manageable.[81]

The same core NATO strengths were present, and utilised to ultimately successful effect, during *Operation Allied Force* nine years after
the Gulf campaign.

Moving on to the external dimension, the term 'enlargement by
stealth' may not, in the final analysis, be the most appropriate one to
use to describe what has been happening because of its inherently
conspiratorial connotations. It implies that the institution and its
member states have had some kind of secret and sinister plan to extend
its boundaries and power as far as possible throughout Europe. In
reality, however, NATO has been sucked into a progressively wider and
deeper involvement in South East Europe on an incremental, *ad hoc*
and crisis-led basis.

Perhaps, therefore, the process could better be described as 'informal' or 'virtual' NATO enlargement. Albania and Macedonia have
been given security assurances in the context of a NATO presence in
the region that seems set to endure. The Kosovo crisis, whilst it did not
initiate the process of NATO engagement in South East Europe, was
nevertheless instrumental in spawning the security assurances that have
been given. The preceding crisis in Bosnia had produced no corre-
sponding assurances.

Overall, its response to the crisis in Kosovo revealed more about
NATO's underlying strengths as a highly interdependent and co-operative security community, than it did about its apparent structural limitations. This explains why the crisis has not led directly to much in the
way of structural reform or change at NATO. The crisis, which some
had suggested might lead to the debilitation, or even demise, of
NATO instead seems to have reinforced and further entrenched its
status as the core institution underpinning post-Cold War security in
the wider Europe.

Notes

1 M. Wörner, *Speech to the North Atlantic Assembly, London, 29 November
   1990* (Brussels, NATO Press Service, 1990), pp. 3–4.
2 Quoted in C. Bremner, 'Nato faults have prolonged war, says top
   general', *The Times* (5 May 1999).
3 G. Seigle, "Inflexible' NATO must improve its procedures', *Jane's
   Defence Weekly* (10 November 1999), 3.
4 Quoted in *Lessons of Kosovo: Volume I Report and Proceedings*, House of
   Commons Select Committee on Defence, Fourteenth Report, Session
   1999–2000, para. 94. Website reference www.parliament.the-stationery-
   office.co.uk/pa/cm199900/cmselect/cmdefence/347/34702.htm.

5 This was a two-week campaign of NATO airstrikes against Bosnian Serb military positions during late August and early September 1995. It contributed to the process that eventually resulted in the signing of the Dayton peace agreement for Bosnia.

6 *United States Policy Toward Federal Republic of Yugoslavia*, House of Representatives Committee on Armed Services, One Hundred Sixth Congress, First Session (Washington DC, US Government Printing Office, 1999), p. 13.

7 *Ibid.*, p. 42.

8 P. Webster, 'Alliance general cleared to bomb at will', *The Times* (3 April 1999). See also R. Jordan, 'NATO as a political organization', in V. Papacosma *et al.* (eds), *NATO After Fifty Years* (Wilmington, Scholarly Resources, 2001), p. 96.

9 See T. Judah, *Kosovo: War and Revenge* (New Haven, Yale University Press, 2000), p. 269. On the existence of this five-power group see also J. Hoekema, *NATO Policy and NATO Strategy in Light of the Kosovo Conflict* (North Atlantic Assembly, Defence and Security Committee, 1999), p. 8. Website reference www.naa.be/publications/comrep/1999/as252dsc-e.html.

10 P. Rudolf, 'Germany and the Kosovo conflict', in P. Martin and M. Brawley (eds), *Alliance Politics, Kosovo, and NATO's War: Allied Force or Forced Allies?* (Basingstoke, Palgrave, 2000), p. 138.

11 G. Kostakos, 'The Southern flank: Italy, Greece and Turkey' and P. Talas and L. Valki, 'The new entrants: Hungary, Poland and the Czech Republic', in A. Schnabel and R. Thakur (eds), *Kosovo and the Challenge of Humanitarian Intervention: Selective Indignation, Collective Action and International Citizenship* (Tokyo, United Nations University Press, 2000), pp. 166–80 and pp. 201–12.

12 The three main phases envisaged in *Operation Allied Force* were: 1) suppression of enemy air defences; 2) strikes against Serb forces in Kosovo; 3) strikes against military and other 'targets of value' in Serbia itself.

13 *Lessons of Kosovo: Volume I*, para. 98.

14 *Lessons of Kosovo: Volume II Minutes of Evidence*, House of Commons Select Committee on Defence, Fourteenth Report, Session 1999–2000, para. 871. Website reference www.parliament.the-stationery-office.co.uk/pa/cm199900/cmselect/cmdefence/347/0051701.htm.

15 *Lessons of Kosovo: Volume I*, para. 203.

16 *Lessons of Kosovo: Volume I*, fn. 461.

17 See, *inter alia*, B. Fenton, 'Kosovo air chief says French put pilots in danger', *Daily Telegraph* (22 October 1999) and G. Seigle, 'USA claims France hindered raids', *Jane's Defence Weekly* (27 October 1999), 3.

18 'US command structure in 'Allied Force' slammed', *Jane's Defence Weekly* (17 November 1999), 8.

19 *Lessons of Kosovo: Volume II*, para. 90.

20 'General who puts 'rapid' into Rapid Reaction Corps', *RUSI Journal*, 144:2 (1999), 27–8.

21 R. Fox, 'Gen. Strangelove and the wimps', *Spectator* (16 October 1999),

14–15. For further discussion on the dash and its consequences see Chapter 4, pp. 103–5.

22 P. Gallis (ed.), *Kosovo: Lessons Learned from Operation Allied Force* (Washington DC, Congressional Research Service, 1999), p. 11.

23 Gen. W. Clark, *Waging Modern War* (Oxford, PublicAffairs, 2001), ch. 15.

24 Fox, 'Gen. Strangelove and the wimps', p. 14.

25 Lt. Gen. Sir M. Jackson, 'KFOR: the inside story', *RUSI Journal*, 145:1 (2000), 16.

26 *Kosovo/Operation Allied Force After-Action Report* (Washington DC, Department of Defense, 2000), p. 16ff.

27 *Lessons of Kosovo: Volume II*, para. 92.

28 I. Daalder and M. O'Hanlon, *Winning Ugly: NATO's War to Save Kosovo* (Washington DC, Brookings, 2000), p. 106.

29 *United States Policy Toward Federal Republic of Yugoslavia*, p. 13.

30 R. Connaughton, *Military Intervention and Peacekeeping: The Reality* (Aldershot, Ashgate, 2001), p. 203.

31 J. Thomas, *The Military Challenges of Transatlantic Coalitions* (Adelphi Paper 333) (London, International Institute for Strategic Studies, 2000), pp. 47–8.

32 *United States Policy Toward Federal Republic of Yugoslavia*, p. 40.

33 *United States and NATO Military Operations Against the Federal Republic of Yugoslavia*, House of Representatives Committee on Armed Services, One Hundred Sixth Congress, First Session (Washington DC, US Government Printing Office, 1999), p. 31.

34 Quoted in M. Evans, 'General wanted US to call the shots in Kosovo', *The Times* (27 January 2000).

35 *Winning Ugly: NATO's War to Save Kosovo*, Brookings Press Briefing, June 2000. Website reference www.brook.edu/pa/transcripts/20000 608/keynote.htm.

36 *After-Action Report*, pp. 20–1.

37 *United States and NATO Military Operations*, p. 19.

38 Judah, *Kosovo: War and Revenge*, p. 269.

39 *Lessons of Kosovo: Volume I*, para. 281.

40 For such suggestions see, *inter alia*, J. Simon, 'Does Eastern Europe belong in NATO?', *Orbis*, 37:1 (1993), 32–4 and D. Stuart, 'NATO's future as a pan-European security institution', *NATO Review*, 41:4 (1993), 18–19.

41 *Study on NATO Enlargement* (Brussels, NATO, 1995), p. 23.

42 P. Cornish, *Partnership in Crisis: The US, Europe and the Fall and Rise of NATO* (London, Pinter, 1997), p. 78.

43 *Press Communiqué M-1(94)2* (Brussels, NATO,1994).

44 I. Szonyi, 'The Partnership for Peace as a process of adaptation', *Journal of Slavic Military Studies*, 11:1 (1998), 22.

45 *Ibid.*, pp. 22–6.

46 *Ibid.*, pp. 26–9.

47 For background on this crisis and its consequences see M. A. Smith, *Albania 1997–1998* (Camberley, Conflict Studies Research Centre, 1999).

48 R. Hendrickson, 'Albania and NATO', *Security Dialogue*, 30:1 (1999), 111–12. See also G. Dinmore, R. Graham and K. Done, 'Albania pleads with NATO to halt slide into anarchy', *Financial Times* (14 March 1997).

49 See *Anarchy in Albania: Collapse of European Collective Security?*, British American Security Information Council. Website reference www.basicint. org/bpaper21.htm.

50 Fatmir Mema, for example, argued that Operation Alba helped to strengthen co-operation between participating NATO and PfP countries. See 'Did Albania really need Operation 'Alba'?', *Security Dialogue*, 29:1 (1998), 61.

51 *Securing Peace in South-Eastern Europe*, North Atlantic Assembly. Website reference www.naa.be/publications/special/rr-tirana99.html; G. Katsirdakis, 'Albania: A case study in the practical implementation of Partnership for Peace', *NATO Review*, 46:2 (1998), 22–6.

52 *Statement on Kosovo*. Website reference www.nato.int/docu/pr/1998/p98-061e.htm.

53 *Atlantic News*, 3020 (16 June 1998).

54 Press Conference by NATO Spokesman Jamie Shea, Air Commodore, David Wilby and Commander Fabrizio Maltinti, SHAPE. Website reference www.nato.int/kosovo/press/p990408a.htm.

55 Private briefing on AFOR operations, London, April 2000.

56 *The Military Balance 2001–2002* (London, International Institute for Strategic Studies, 2001), p. 80.

57 *Securing Peace in South-Eastern Europe*.

58 The force's commander himself admitted this. See T. Ripley, 'NATO Extraction Force has limited capabilities', *Jane's Defence Weekly* (13 January 1999), 4.

59 Presentation by Macedonian Minister of Foreign Affairs Aleksandar Dimitrov, 8 December 1998. Website reference www.nato.int/docu/speech/1998/s981208r.htm.

60 *The Military Balance 2001–2002*, p. 94.

61 Address by Mr Aleksandar Dimitrov, Minister of Foreign Affairs of the Republic of Macedonia, 16 December 1999. Website reference www.nato.int/docu/speech/1999/s991216.htm.

62 Statement by the Secretary General on the Situation in the former Yugoslav Republic of Macedonia (Press Release (2001)032). Website reference www.nato.int/docu/pr/2001/p01-032e.htm.

63 M. Evans, 'Skopje asks for Nato troops', *The Times* (15 June 2001).

64 M. Evans, 'US force opens fire in Kosovo', *The Times* (8 March 2001). See also 'Oh no, not war in Macedonia as well', *The Economist* (10 March 2001), 45–6.

65 Statement by the Secretary General on the situation in the former Yugoslav Republic of Macedonia (Press Release (2001)041). Website reference www.nato.int/docu/pr/2001/p01-041e.htm. Final Communiqué: Ministerial Meeting of the North Atlantic Council Held in Budapest. Website reference www.nato.int/docu/pr/2001/p01-077e.htm.

66 See, *inter alia*, F. Ajami, 'Under Western eyes: the fate of Bosnia', *Survival*, 41:2 (1999), 43ff.

67 For a sampling see J. Chace, 'Present at the destruction', *World Policy Journal*, X:2 (1993), 89–90; 'Patching up NATO', *The Economist* (19 November 1994), 18–20; B. Clark and B. Gray, 'United front splinters', *Financial Times* (30 May 1995); L. Silber and A. Robinson, 'NATO rift widens as Clinton urges action on Bosnia', *Financial Times* (28 July 1995).

68 *Press Release (95)73* and *Press Release(95)79* (Brussels, NATO, 1995).

69 Christopher: A. Marshall, 'Bosnia: now for the hard part', *Independent on Sunday* (8 October 1995). Perry: J. Martin and L. Silber, 'Clinton team starts Congress troops plea', *Financial Times* (18 October 1995). Clinton: *Weekly Compilation of Presidential Documents*, 31:48 (1995), 2062.

70 L. Silber and B. Clark, 'West fearful for post-IFOR Bosnia', *Financial Times* (1 April 1996).

71 *The Military Balance 2001–2002*, p. 28.

72 October 2001 figure: *Ibid*. March 2002 figure: *KFOR Contingent: United States of America*. Website reference www.nato.int/kfor/kfor/nations/usa.htm.

73 See *Rapid Guardian 02-3* and *Top US Officer visits MNB(E) Soldiers*. Website reference www.nato.int/kfor/welcome.html.

74 'NATO takes root in Bosnia', *Defense News* (2 March 1998).

75 L. Freedman, 'Bosnia: does peace support make any sense?', *NATO Review*, 43:6 (1995), 20.

76 *Statement on Kosovo*.

77 Cook: P. Riddell, 'Former peacenik Cook warms to heat of battle', *The Times* (30 March 1999). McCain: A. Sullivan, 'America's hawks go into hiding', *Sunday Times* (4 April 1999).

78 *After-Action Report*, p. 1.

79 *Kosovo Volume I: Report and Proceedings of the Committee*, House of Commons Select Committee on Foreign Affairs, Fourth Report, Session 1999–2000 (London, The Stationery Office, 2000), p. xxviii.

80 Clark, *Waging Modern War*, pp. 460–1.

81 Authors' interview with Sir Michael Alexander, UK Permanent Representative on the North Atlantic Council 1986–92, March 1993.

Chapter 3

South East European settlements? Democratisation, nationalism and security in former Yugoslavia

The end of the conflicts in Bosnia (1995) and Kosovo (1999) created for NATO an important place in the post-conflict 'peace-building' that represents a sustained effort to create a new international order in South East Europe. The idea that such peace-building efforts involve attempts to inculcate norms and values is a key feature of the process and a significant source of controversy. Just as NATO's 'humanitarian intervention' over Kosovo highlighted the normative tension between the doctrine of non-intervention in sovereign states versus efforts to promote respect for human rights that transcend state boundaries, the subsequent efforts at peace-building have revealed other normative conundrums. For NATO and other international institutions, this has made South East Europe a normative labyrinth where democracy, 'stateness', identity and security are difficult to bring together. Oliver Richmond argues that the resulting tension creates 'a normative discourse ... focusing on humanitarianism, culture and identity, and motivated by a need to regain "order" and protect the *status quo* on the part of the dominant actors of the international system'.[1]

NATO has taken a prominent security role in the international attempts to make work the political settlements in Bosnia, Kosovo and, to a lesser extent, Macedonia. It is worth considering the prospects for the long-term success of the Alliance's objectives of underwriting military security in the region while at the same time upholding the norms aimed at developing democratic states with multicultural identities that lay at the heart of these settlements. This chapter will examine the international attempts at peace-building in the former Yugoslavia[2] by focusing on the challenges to efforts to bring lasting stability posed by democratisation, ethnic nationalism and the promotion of security.

NATO's peace-building roles in Bosnia, Kosovo and Macedonia

The deployment of the NATO IFOR to Bosnia in 1995 in the wake of the Dayton agreement and associated UNSC Resolutions marked the beginning of the Alliance's role in peace-building in the region. Reaching peak strength of 60,000, IFOR existed for a one-year mission before transforming itself into the smaller Stabilisation Force (SFOR) in December 1996. SFOR was initially given a mandate for eighteen months but this has been extended repeatedly, giving the operation a virtually open-ended timeframe. The improving security situation has allowed significant reductions in SFOR. Between 1996 and 1999 it stood at 32,000 personnel, with its deployed level in early 2002 standing at about 20,000. This represented about one-third of the original IFOR strength.[3]

The second major, and now concurrent, peace-building operation for NATO began in June 1999 with the deployment of KFOR, at an initial strength of nearly 50,000 and an open-ended time commitment in its peace-building role.[4] Three years after its initial deployment, KFOR strength had dropped to approximately 35,000 with further reductions to around 30,000 being mooted.[5] In addition to SFOR and KFOR, NATO deployed troops to Macedonia from the summer of 2001 to assist in ending the insurgency in that country and to support the implementation of the internal political settlement.[6] Although small in overall numbers, the Macedonian deployments form part of a much larger pattern of NATO troop commitments in the region.

NATO's considerable investment in manpower, resources and time in the former Yugoslavia is directed, as noted, toward the overall objective of peace-building. This concept originated in former UN Secretary-General Boutros Boutros-Ghali's report called *An Agenda for Peace*, first published in 1992. In *An Agenda for Peace*, Boutros-Ghali defined peace-building as 'action to identify and support structures which will tend to strengthen and solidify peace in order to avoid a relapse into conflict'.[7] It is clear that the essence of this definition has shaped that employed by NATO, which states that:

> Peace building covers actions that support political, economic, social, and military measures and structures, aiming to strengthen and solidify political settlements in order to redress the causes of conflict. This includes mechanisms to identify and support structures that tend to consolidate peace, advance a sense of confidence and well being, and support economic reconstruction.[8]

A more succinct definition describes peace-building as having the overall aim 'to transform conflicts constructively and to create a sustainable peace environment'.[9]

It is clear from these definitions that peace-building embraces a broad spectrum of activity in the military, political, social and economic spheres. Charles-Philippe David has argued that the full gamut of peace-building activity falls into three key areas: 'security transition', 'democratic transition' and 'socio-economic transition'.[10]

The broad agenda of peace-building is well illustrated by the declaratory aims of NATO's engagement in Bosnia and Kosovo. For example, the published statement of the SFOR mission in Bosnia takes the NATO forces into areas of peace-building not strictly militarily orientated:

> The Stabilisation Force (SFOR) will deter hostilities and stabilise the peace, contribute to a secure environment by providing a continued military presence in the Area of Responsibility (AOR), target and coordinate SFOR support to key areas including primary civil implementation organisations, and progress towards a lasting consolidation of peace, without further need for NATO-led forces in Bosnia and Herzegovina.[11]

A similar pattern of broad involvement in peace-building can also be seen in the mission of KFOR. Key elements include to:

- establish and maintain a secure environment in Kosovo, including public safety and order
- monitor, verify and when necessary, enforce compliance with the conditions of the Military Technical Agreement and the UCK [KLA] Undertaking [to disarm]
- provide assistance to the UN Mission in Kosovo (UNMIK), including core civil functions until they are transferred to UNMIK.[12]

From the missions of both SFOR and KFOR several important features can be observed. Although the missions are broadly couched to support an array of peace-building activity, the role of SFOR and KFOR in the 'security transition' constitutes the core activity. Deterring a resumption of hostilities and the demilitarisation and demobilisation of warring parties are security functions which both SFOR and KFOR have played major and positive roles in carrying through, particularly in the early phases of their deployment. SFOR and KFOR have also played a part in ensuring public safety and order, although this is only an explicit part of the mission in the case of

KFOR.[13] What is especially striking about these forces' place in the security transition in Bosnia and Kosovo is the range of levels at which NATO forces contribute to the maintenance of security. The impact of the Alliance's part in peace-building touches the regional, state, sub-state and individual levels of security.[14]

Although NATO is contributing to the 'socio-economic transition' dimension of peace-building in both Bosnia and Kosovo, it is the political settlement or 'democratic transition' that is central to the success or failure of peace-building efforts. The political dimension is shaped above all by a set of norms that provide the essential framework of the peace-building process and give the most important criteria for measuring success. The security and socio-economic aspects of peace-building support this normative component of the political settlement. Therefore, NATO's contributions to peace-building in the region have to be measured against the prospects of success or failure in the establishment of the norms inherent in the political transition. For the success of the overall efforts at peace-building, establishing and entrenching the norms is the crucial variable. As David has stressed, 'the merit of peace building thus hinges on its capacity to change a potential or actual strife-ridden situation to a state of durable peace'.[15]

Normative underpinnings: from Dayton to the Stability Pact

Dayton agreement: democracy, human rights and multiculturalism for Bosnia?

The General Framework Agreement for Peace in Bosnia and Herzegovina, initialled in Dayton, Ohio in November 1995 and formally signed in Paris one month later, brought to an end the armed conflict and initiated a process of peace-building in Bosnia. The Dayton agreement as it has since been known, provided for a comprehensive political settlement to the bloodiest European conflict since the end of the Second World War. The conflict had resulted in thousands of deaths, hundreds of thousands displaced from their homes by ethnic cleansing and physical destruction of property and infrastructure on a scale not seen in Europe for forty years. In addition to ending the violence, the Dayton agreement sought the promotion of long-term stability by attempting to reverse the bitter legacy of the Bosnian conflict. It was this *raison d'être* that led to the norms of democracy, human rights and multiculturalism being woven into the fabric of its text.

Annex 4 of the agreement, detailing the 'Constitution of Bosnia and Herzegovina', clearly envisaged the creation of a post-conflict democracy. It stated that 'Bosnia and Herzegovina shall be a democratic state, which shall operate under the rule of law and with free and democratic elections'. The human rights regime in Bosnia was to be uncompromising in its rigour of application. 'Bosnia and Herzegovina and both Entities', stated Annex 4, 'shall ensure the highest level of internationally recognised human rights and fundamental freedoms'. All of these aims were consistent with trends in the international settlement of post-Cold War conflicts that made democratisation and enhancement of human rights important elements of the post-conflict peace-building process. Given the Bosnian conflict's large-scale ethnic cleansing, another key normative feature embedded in the Dayton agreement was the re-building of a multicultural society. To this end, Annex 4 made constitutional provision that 'all refugees and displaced persons have the right freely to return to their homes of origin'.[16]

Another annex created a number of mechanisms to foster the return of refugees and displaced persons. The mechanisms contained in Annex 7 included measures against discrimination and harassment with international monitoring by the United Nations High Commissioner for Refugees (UNHCR).[17] This strong commitment to rebuild a multicultural Bosnia, however, suffered from an inherent contradiction within the *General Framework Agreement* insofar as it made legitimate two separate 'entities' with their own political institutions within the Bosnian state.[18] In a *de facto* way, the entities reflected the outcome of the conflict in terms of ethnic cleansing and population displacement.[19] It was difficult to disguise the fact that the federal structure of Bosnia contained in reality two separate states with two separate armies. Richard Holbrooke, who played a key role in the reaching of the Bosnia settlement, considered this aspect of the Dayton agreement a 'flaw'.[20] The confederal structure of the Bosnian state has worked against the unitary norms at the heart of the Dayton political settlement.

Democratisation and a multicultural society in Kosovo?

In June 1999, UNSC Resolution 1244 initiated the peace-building process for Kosovo. The end of the conflict there yielded not so much a final settlement as a skeleton process that was supposed to lead, eventually, to a political settlement. Despite a paucity of detail, Resolution 1244 nevertheless planted much the same normative seeds as the Dayton agreement. The main text of the Resolution stressed that the 'international civil presence' had the role of 'protecting and promoting human rights' and 'assuring the safe and unimpeded return of all refugees and displaced persons to their homes in Kosovo'. The implications of this requirement were to restore the pre-conflict multi-cultural society in Kosovo such as it had existed (with around 90 per cent of the population being ethnic Albanians).

Annex 2 of Resolution 1244 contained the most substance as regards an ultimate political settlement. Here it was made clear that establishing democracy was part of the international community's intention for Kosovo's future. This annex provided for the:

> establishment of an interim administration for Kosovo as a part of the international civil presence under which the people of Kosovo can enjoy substantial autonomy within the Federal Republic of Yugoslavia, to be decided by the Security Council of the United Nations. The interim administration to provide transitional administration while establishing and overseeing the development of provisional democratic self-governing institutions to ensure conditions for a peaceful and normal life for all inhabitants in Kosovo.

It would seem, therefore, that 'democratic self-governing institutions' were to be established within a Kosovo forming part of the FRY. The context was, in fact, not so clear cut. Elsewhere in the text of Annex 2, the eventual context for the development of democracy in Kosovo was more ambiguous. It foresaw:

> a political process towards the establishment of an interim political framework agreement providing for substantial self-government for Kosovo, taking full account of the Rambouillet accords and the principles of sovereignty and territorial integrity of the Federal Republic of Yugoslavia and the other countries of the region, and the demilitarization of UCK. Negotiations between the parties for a settlement should not delay or disrupt the establishment of democratic self-governing institutions.[21]

It is important to remember that the Rambouillet accords held out the possibility of eventual independence for Kosovo. The reference in Resolution 1244 to the 'principles of sovereignty and territorial integrity of the Federal Republic of Yugoslavia and the other countries of the region', however, suggested otherwise with its implicit tilt toward the maintenance of the territorial *status quo* and hence Kosovo in the FRY. This contradictory element regarding the political and territorial future of Kosovo injects a major degree of uncertainty. The Dayton settlement arguably created too many entities or states in the context of Bosnia, but in the case of Resolution 1244 there is no clear determination on the future status of Kosovo in terms of potential statehood.

The question of the future of Kosovo is tied to wider problems in the region. Resolution 1244 linked the resolution of the issue of Kosovo to the need for a region-wide approach. This found expression in the creation of the so-called 'Stability Pact for South Eastern Europe'.

The Stability Pact: aims, process and democratic agenda

During the 1990s, the various conflicts in the former Yugoslavia sent tremors of potential instability throughout the wider South East European region. The consequences for neighbouring states of the Yugoslav conflicts could be seen in such things as the economic costs associated with loss of trade and the social pressures of having to host, in some cases, sizeable refugee populations. It was this wider perspective of regional problems that prompted the international community to launch the Stability Pact process in 1999. It was designed to do two things. First, to address the issues facing the South East European region as a whole and not simply particular areas such as Bosnia and Kosovo. Second, to initiate a process that would effectively integrate the peace-building and stability-enhancement efforts of interested governments and international and non-governmental organisations.

The normative dimension of the Stability Pact signifies an extension of those norms embedded in Dayton and the Kosovo agreements. At the heart of the Stability Pact, launched on 10 June 1999 in Cologne, are norms of democracy, multiculturalism and human rights. The major difference from earlier peace-building initiatives is the broader political agenda to impart them in the region. In the eyes of the pact's promoters, the norms are viewed as essential building blocks to a more stable and secure order both within and between states in this part of Europe.

The European Union was the initiator of the Stability Pact process on the eve of the end of *Operation Allied Force*. Its Cologne summit sought to bring into existence an integrated and comprehensive approach to political, social and economic reconstruction.[22] In the summit's final communiqué, the central and certainly ambitious stated aim of the Stability Pact was to achieve 'lasting peace, prosperity and stability for South Eastern Europe'. The Stability Pact process is meant to operate as a 'framework for co-ordination' for the multifarious participants engaged in the project. Organisationally, the Stability Pact created four 'Working Tables'. They are: the South Eastern Europe Regional Table; the Working Table on Democratisation and Human Rights; the Working Table on Economic Reconstruction, Development and Co-operation and, finally, the Working Table on Security Issues. The Regional Table is the co-ordinating body for the other three tables.[23] The Stability Pact process received the endorsement of its regional participants a month later in a follow-up summit in Sarajevo, which formally launched its organisational machinery. Tasked with the role of providing over-arching direction for the process was a Special Co-ordinator appointed by the Council of the European Union but coming under the auspices of the OSCE on a day-to-day basis. Bodo Hombach, a German diplomat, was appointed as the first Special Co-ordinator at the Sarajevo summit.[24]

The introduction of democracy, economic prosperity and security into the South East European region thus form the core objectives of the Stability Pact. Moreover, the Stability Pact's 'headline goals' embrace a number of other norms related to democracy; including human rights, multiculturalism and the fair treatment of national minorities. The Cologne summit communiqué illustrated the centrality of these norms in the Stability Pact's goals. It spoke of the aims of the pact being to:

- bring about mature democratic political processes, based on free and fair elections, grounded in rule of law and full respect for human rights and fundamental freedoms, including the rights of persons belonging to national minorities, the right to free and independent media, legislative branches accountable to their constituents, independent judiciaries [and the] deepening and strengthening of civil society
- preserve the multinational and multiethnic diversity of countries in the region, and protecting minorities
- ensure the safe and free return of all refugees and displaced persons to their homes.

In a sweeping vision of the democratic ambitions of the Stability Pact process, the summit document also unabashedly concluded that 'lasting peace in South Eastern Europe will only become possible when democratic principles and values, which are already actively promoted by many countries in the region, have taken root throughout, including the Federal Republic of Yugoslavia'.[25]

The most important vehicle for the accomplishment of these normative aims is Working Table I, on Democratisation and Human Rights. Working Table I sets out the following as its primary task in its work plan:

> The main strategic aim of the Working Table on Democratisation and Human Rights is to anchor democracy and respect for human rights throughout the region, including by institutionalising OSCE commitments and principles in the countries in the region, also through membership of the Council of Europe, including accession to its Convention on Human Rights and implementation in practice of its political and human rights codes, where appropriate.[26]

In order to deliver on these aims, the Working Table has created a number of 'task forces and initiatives' covering areas such as human rights and national minorities; good governance; gender issues; media; education and youth; refugee returns and parliamentary exchange.[27] This ambitious agenda requires resources and, as a consequence, Working Table I obtained initially 165 million Euros (£100 million) to finance its projects.[28] As indicated above, Stability Pact norms, rather unsurprisingly, reflect the democratic and human rights norms embedded in the major international treaties and agreements of the OSCE and the Council of Europe. The significance of this link is to ground them in the wider norms of the international system.

The Stability Pact's democratic and multicultural norms, like those enshrined in the Dayton and Kosovo settlements, are being promoted in a region that has recently experienced the brutal consequences of ethnic nationalism. This ethnic nationalism in South East Europe must be reckoned with in attempts to impart democratic norms to build stability. The introduction of these norms brings into sharp focus an important challenge. The success or failure of attempts to impart democratic norms depends on how nationalism is understood by both the norm givers and their recipients. Therefore it is necessary to examine the meaning of ideas of nationalism and ethnicity and how they impact on the democratic and multicultural norms which are the foundation of international peace-building efforts in the former Yugoslavia.

Friend or foe?
Nationalism's relationship to democratic norms

Nationalism remains a field of study that is 'vast and ramified'.[29] Yet, despite the varieties of meanings and academic approaches involved in the study of nationalism and ethnicity, there is a dominant orthodoxy. It sees national or ethnic identities as being 'situational' and the 'property of individuals rather than of collectivities'.[30] According to this view, national identity and ethnicity are secondary issues, able to be swept aside by more potent universal forces such as social class, economic development, global interdependence or secularisation.[31] Anthony Smith, in his examination of the major strands of this dominant 'modernist' and 'instrumentalist' school has summarised them in the following manner:

> First, nations and nationalism are regarded as inherently modern – in the sense of recent – phenomena; that is, they emerged in the last two hundred years, in the wake of the French Revolution. Second, nations and nationalisms are treated as the products of the specifically modern conditions of capitalism, industrialism, bureaucracy, mass communications and secularism. Third, nations are essentially recent constructs, and nationalisms are their modern cement, designed to meet the requirements of modernity. Finally, ethnic communities, or ethnies, to use a convenient French word, though much older and more widespread, are neither natural nor given in human history, but are mainly resources and instruments of elites and leaders in their struggles for power.[32]

For the instrumentalists, the nation is seen as the 'imagined community' of Benedict Anderson's highly influential study of nationalism. This seductive phrase encapsulates the artificiality of nations and nationalism in the eyes of this school of thought. Anderson has argued that 'the convergence of capitalism and print technology on the fatal diversity of human language created the possibility of a new form of imagined community, which in its basic morphology set the stage for the modern nation'.[33]

'Primordialism' stands in complete contrast to the instrumentalist school of thought. The primordial school, although of many hues, generally maintains that nations and consequently nationalism, are more deeply rooted in history and can be seen as organic; part of the naturally occurring order and representing unbreakable social bonds. Proponents of primordialism consider that 'ethnic identities have biological and even genetic foundations, and that the motivation for ethnic and kinship affiliation comes from these socio-psychological forces internal to the individual and related to primordial human needs for security and, more importantly, survival'.[34]

The primordialist position has gained some fresh credibility as a consequence of the conflicts in the former Yugoslavia but it has also been heavily criticised for its determinism.[35] The primordialist camp certainly embraces a broad spectrum of views. Primordialist thought can encompass both ethnic nationalist extremists and more gentle academic observers. The common ground of this range of views is that nations and nationalism are seen to have qualities that are deeply rooted and unchanging.

Some work falls between the instrumentalist and primordialist schools. The work of Anthony Smith defines nationalism 'as an ideological movement, for the attainment and maintenance of self-government and independence on behalf of a group'.[36] Seen from the perspective of instrumentalism, his definition is entirely consistent with similar instrumentalist views. He sees the nation, nationalism and ethnicity as changeable and changing phenomena. Smith departs from the instrumentalist approach with his views concerning the deep-rooted and durable cultural qualities of national identity. He believes that these are firmly rooted in early modern ethnic communities, which he calls 'ethnies'. He considers many cultural attributes, but for him language is clearly one of the most important elements of national identity:

> Authenticity and dignity are the hallmarks of every aspect of ethnic culture, not just its ethno-history. Of these the best known and most important is language, since it so clearly marks off those who speak it from those who cannot and because it evokes a sense of immediate expressive intimacy among its speakers. The outstanding role played by philologists grammarians and lexicographers in so many nationalisms indicates the importance so often attached to language as an authentic symbolic code embodying the unique inner experiences of the ethnie. Though language is not the only significant aspect of the nation … it remains a vital symbolic realm of authentication and vernacular mobilisation.[37]

Smith's thinking has some important implications. He underscores the diversity and staying power of nations and nationalism. While the instrumentalists see nationalism as a transitory phenomenon, over-taken by new forces such as globalisation, and the primordialists see nationalism as part of an enduring natural order, Smith argues that it is something that continues to have necessity and function within a 'modern plural world order'.[38] Moreover, Smith views nationalism as a phenomenon that is too complex to fit neatly into one distinct category or another. The broadness of Smith's thinking was well reflected when he wrote that 'no nation, no nationalism, can be seen as purely the one or the other, even if at certain moments one or the other of these elements predominates in the ensemble of components of national identity'.[39]

Applying a specific understanding of nationalism to problems in the international arena can have enormous implications. Yet, one of the reoccurring and trenchant criticisms of the international relations field concerns the relatively little attention that has been given to the problem of nationalism.[40] Although the volume of literature on ethnic conflict has undoubtedly increased,[41] it nevertheless is deficient in considering the basic assumptions about how nationalism is understood in the context of these conflicts. It is clear, however, that instrumentalist thinking dominates analysis of the international challenges posed by nationalism. This has important implications, not least for those attempting to measure the prospects of success or failure in introducing democratic norms in an area stricken with ethnic conflict. Importing norms based on an understanding of nationalism alien to the region might lead to some significant difficulties for the norm givers.

Nationalism, democracy and the state

The state stands at a significant crossroads in the debates on the issues related to democratic norms and nationalism. As Linz and Stepan have argued, 'modern democratic governance is inevitably linked to stateness, without a state, there can be no citizenship; without citizenship, there can be no democracy'.[42] The notion of citizenship is also central to the idea of 'civic nationalism'; in a civic national identity it is one's citizenship that determines national identity. Where civic nationalism prevails, the focus is on the individual rather than any collective ethnic identity:

> In a liberal democracy the individual is taken as the cornerstone of the deeply divided society while ethnic affiliations are ignored by the state. All individuals are accorded equal civil and political rights and judged by merit. They compete and are free to mix, integrate, assimilate, or alternatively form separate communities as long as they do not discriminate against others. The privatization of ethnicity in liberal democracy maximizes individual rights but minimizes collective rights.[43]

Examples of countries that embrace civic nationalism are the United
Kingdom and the United States. These states possess a civic national
identity where democracy, citizenship and national identity are closely
intertwined with the state. With the individual's rights at the centre,
the combination of democracy and civic nationalism is meant to
minimise the potential conflict within the ethnic, cultural and linguis-
tic diversity contained within the state's borders. This model, however,
has broader implications beyond the borders of particular states where
civic nationalism prevails.

Civic nationalism is also reflected in the international norms
relevant to democracy and national identity. In terms of the 'interna-
tionalisation' of minority rights, the emphasis on the individual rather
than collective rights has prevailed in the post-Second World War
period.[44] Previously, in the broad sweep of history, the evolution of
international minority rights law was grounded in the treatment of
religious minorities; suggesting more of a collective thrust to minority
rights than one centred on the individual.[45] Nevertheless, present-day
norms largely reflect the experience of states possessing a civic form of
nationalism. This reality raises some important questions about civic
nationalism. How effective is it in preserving ethnic identity while
preventing inter-communal conflict among disparate groups within the
state? Can democracy only exist alongside civic nationalism?

In addressing the first question, the record of democratic states
possessing a civic nationalism is seen as being generally good. They are
seen as being inclusive of minority groups while integrating them into
an overarching civic nationalist identity. Not all analysis, however, sees
civic nationalism as being completely benign in its treatment and
respect for the identities of ethnic minorities. Indeed, some critics have
identified serious shortcomings in the democratic-civic nationalism
model. Hans Köchler has argued that:

> The traditional nation-state is based on an authoritarian ideology in terms
> of the ethnic, religious and regional status of the individual (the citizen).
> This ideology corresponds to a centrist power structure and to the regret-
> table fact that population groups which differ from majority populations
> (in terms of their ethnic, religious, cultural orientation and so forth) do
> not enjoy equal rights.[46]

What is clear is that under the civic nationalism model, the majority
group has the ability to *impose* a collective identity at the expense of
other ethnic groups in the state.

Anthony Smith has gone further, in arguing that civic nationalism offers no better alternative than its ethnic counterpart on the crucial matter of its treatment of minorities:

> The common view fails to grasp the nature of civic nationalism. From the standpoint of affected minorities, this kind of nationalism is neither as tolerant nor as unbiased as its self-image suggests. In fact, it can be every bit as severe and uncompromising as ethnic nationalisms. For civic nationalisms often demand, as the price for receiving citizenship and its benefits, the surrender of ethnic community and individuality, the privatization of ethnic religion and the marginalization of the ethnic culture and heritage of minorities within the borders of the national state.[47]

The 'price for receiving citizenship' is expensive in terms of group identity according to Smith. He argues that it 'delegitimizes and devalues the ethnic cultures of resident minorities ... and does so consciously and deliberately'.[48]

The conventional wisdom regarding the second question suggests that democracy and civic nationalism have a symbiotic relationship. The existence of democracy in conditions of ethnic nationalism is seen as problematic, if not contradictory. In his *Politics in Eastern Europe*, George Schöpflin observed that:

> The nation in its ethnic dimension functions in politics as a category that is connected primarily to the state and to definitions of identity. It is not the medium through which the multiplicity of cross-cutting and contradictory interests find articulation and, it is hoped, aggregation. Rather, the nation is a relatively static entity, as it must be if it is to act as the foundation of the community, and one that transcends everyday politics. The nation is sacralised and cannot be the subject of the bargains and compromises needed for the smooth functioning of democracy.[49]

Schöpflin, however, does not dismiss nationhood, or more specifically 'ethnicity', as unimportant to democracy. Indeed he argues that 'democratic nationhood is composed of three key, interdependent elements: civil society, the state and ethnicity'. The central thrust of his argument is that 'ethnicity, far from being an exaggerated or pathological condition is essential to certain aspects of nationhood and thus to democracy'.[50]

Jeff Richards has similarly argued against the view that only civic nationalism is compatible with liberal democratic norms. Not viewing this as credible, Richards has stressed that:

> The attempt to make a rigid distinction between 'good' civic nationalism which is liberal democratic and 'bad' ethnic nationalism, which is organic,

democratic is neither accurate nor helpful. One must synthesise rather than dichotomise between civic and ethnic/organic democracy. Ultimately the test of democracy is respect and toleration for individual choice and rights. In considering the relationship between citizenship and national identity the cognate concepts of ethnicity, nationality and citizenship must not be fused together. The tendency to do so, given the underlying assumptions of nationalism and the rationale of the nation-state, is very strong.[51]

Richards' and Schöpflin's departure from the conventional wisdom is supported by the fact that states exist that are practising 'ethnic democracy', a model that combines 'a real political democracy with explicit ethnic dominance'.[52] Many examples can be identified of democracy and ethnic nationalism existing together successfully. The post-Second World War FRG, Israel and the post-Communist Czech Republic, Hungary, Poland and Slovenia all bring together strong ethnic national identities and 'real political democracy'. In these examples democratic aggregation of interests takes place in a largely monocultural ethnic state.

Despite what these examples suggest about the possibility of democracy operating successfully other than alongside a civic national identity, the most commonly held assumptions see civic nationalism as benign and argue that modern democracy cannot exist alongside anything but this type of nationalism in the international system. These assumptions form the foundation of the international norms concerning democracy and ethnicity as applied to peace-building in South East Europe. This is well illustrated by the example of a report spawned by the Stability Pact process. Working Table I produced a draft report on *The Promotion of Multi-Ethnic Society and Democratic Citizenship in South Eastern Europe* in February 2000. A team of advisors from the Council of Europe drafted this report, which was to form the basis of an 'action plan'. During its preparation the team enjoyed the co-operation of the OSCE High Commissioner on National Minorities and included a consultation process that saw a delegation travel to four states in South East Europe; Albania, Bosnia, Croatia and Macedonia.

The report's section headed 'basic concepts and general objectives' clearly contained certain assumptions regarding the type of nationalism best associated with democratisation:

The concept of 'multi-ethnic and multi-cultural society' is put forward as an important avenue for overcoming the problems which have resulted from an – often ethnocentric – thinking in rigid categories: a heritage of exclusivity, exclusion and compartmentalisation which did not allow for a genuine dialogue between all people, [or] a common forum (both in a political and in a social sense) for the articulation of the different wishes and needs and a common ground for living together.

The paper emphasised the need for the normative element outlined above to be moved into the realm of policy; 'it is now urgent to move forward and re-create the pillars of multi-ethnic and multi-cultural society'. This, it was argued, 'should be done not in an ad hoc manner but through a principled approach on the basis of existing common European standards that are directly relevant and should be applied in each country'. As a consequence of these basic principles, two objectives were set out to guide Working Table I; 'the promotion and, where necessary, rehabilitation of multi-ethnic and multi-cultural society, and the development of democratic citizenship'.

The report envisaged that these things be developed hand in hand; 'these two objectives have to be seen in conjunction: multi-ethnic and multi-cultural society must be firmly rooted in a common effort to promote democratic values, especially equal citizenship rights and the equal empowerment of all citizens for sharing responsibility for the life of the country as a whole'. Multiethnic society and democratic citizenship, in the view of the report's authors, have to be seen as 'mainstreaming concepts' and an 'integral part of decision-making in all policy areas'.[53] What this Stability Pact report demonstrates, when stated in the simplest terms, is that civic nationalism is regarded as good and ethnic nationalism as bad when juxtaposed against the entrenching of democracy.

The model suggested in the Stability Pact report concentrates only on the first of the three pillars (civil society) postulated in Schöpflin's model of democracy and nationhood. Although the desirability of constructing a healthy civil society is much in evidence in the report, the inter-relationship with the state and ethnicity is conceived as a problem. The fact that states in South East Europe are weak – or have failed in some cases in former Yugoslavia – is attributed to a lack of legitimacy linked to the deleterious effects of ethnic nationalism.

The lack of legitimacy that underpins the weak or failed states in the region may not be a product of ethnic nationalism *per se* but, rather, the weakness of states and civil society in accommodating it. Hence ethnicity only becomes a 'disease' when other components of the body of the state are weak.[54] The fixation on the civic model, moreover, may make it more difficult to establish democracies in conditions where ethnic nationalism prevails. While no one can deny the savagery that has attended ethnic nationalism in parts of the former Yugoslavia, to see ethnic nationalism as illegitimate and, in normative terms, as needing to be transmogrified into a civic identity assumed compatible with democracy in practice has produced its own difficulties. Indeed, the risk of imposing particular approaches or models in promoting democracy in post-conflict situations is increasingly recognised.[55] How likely is it that these 'mainstreaming concepts' will succeed in building democracy and pushing into the background ethnic identity in the cases of Bosnia and Kosovo?

Democracy, nationalism and security in Bosnia and Kosovo

Bosnia

In the case of Bosnia, the construction of a multicultural democratic state, where ethnic nationalism has been supplanted by the supposedly more benign civic national identity has made very limited progress. Evidence of this can be seen in the poor rates of repatriation of refugees and internally displaced persons to areas across the inter-entity lines (dividing the Serb Republic from the Muslim-Croat Federation). According to official statistics this has been very limited.

Statistics collected by the UNHCR or the Office of the High Representative (in effect the internationally appointed governor of Bosnia) do not always make clear how many people are refugees returning to Bosnia and how many are moving back to areas from which their group had been ethnically cleansed during the conflict. Despite this caveat, the reports of the High Representative to the UN Secretary-General from 1996 to 2002 do not give the impression that much progress has been achieved. Efforts to restore something akin to the pre-conflict multiethnic settlement pattern have not made significant progress toward meeting the normative goals.[56]

Although a report by the International Crisis Group (ICG) argues that there has been some positive movement, most press reports argue that change has been more modest in scope.[57] Indeed, pessimism seems to prevail as indicated by a *Washington Post* report that quotes an ICG official as saying that 'the ethnic cleansers are winning the battle to shape postwar Bosnia'.[58] Between 1995 and 1999, only 80,000 people out of the 600,000 that had returned to Bosnia had 'gone to areas where their ethnic groups are in the minority'.[59] Statistics published in a March 2002 report by the High Representative show 'minority' returns increasing, but it is too early to assess the significance of any apparent trend.[60]

NATO's role in the military implementation of the Dayton agreement undoubtedly has registered important gains. The disarming of the warring parties, cantonment of weapons and the continued presence of SFOR have insured against any regression into conflict.[61] In terms of establishing a longer-term basis for peace and stability in Bosnia, based on democratic norms and the promotion of a civic national identity, the progress has been far less encouraging, however. And, as David Bosco has perceptively commented, 'for Bosnia, demographics is destiny'.[62]

The difficulties in establishing a multicultural civic national identity in Bosnia clearly impact on NATO's efforts at peace-building, particularly if they are based on unaccepted norms. This has led to a major debate over whether the normative underpinnings of Dayton should be altered. In the case of Bosnia, it is an 'integration or partition' debate. Some commentators have argued that partition, or accepting ethnic separation, is the only viable solution after a terrible 'ethnic war'.[63] Others see such an approach as abhorrent, arguing that it legitimates ethnic cleansing and does not bring lasting stability.[64] Pragmatic policy-makers, who have experience with Bosnian problems, see no option but to persist; with the present arrangements being the least bad option in terms of the risk of rekindling the conflict.[65] In academic circles there has been a similar debate on the merits of integration versus partition. This has highlighted both the difficulties with the existing Dayton settlement and the risks of embarking on a new course.[66]

Kosovo

NATO's and others' efforts to restore and promote a multicultural Kosovo have met with even less success so far. With the entry of KFOR into Kosovo there followed a Serb exodus spurred on by fear and violent attacks on Serbian cultural and religious sites. This replaced the earlier flight of Albanians from Kosovo, before and during *Operation Allied Force*.[67] It is estimated that around three-quarters of the pre-conflict Serb population has left the province, with approximately 100,000 Serbs remaining and living in a few enclaves.[68] The tensions between the two communities inside Kosovo are violently symbolised by the sporadic conflict in the divided city of Mitrovica.[69]

In the face of the *de facto* separation or departure of the Serb population, some members of the international community continue to make vigorous efforts to keep remaining Serbs *in situ* or entice back those who have departed.[70] Significantly, the United Nations Interim Administration Mission in Kosovo has been cautious about promoting the too-rapid return of Serb refugees in the absence of a secure environment.[71] The demographic reality in Kosovo today makes the Albanians an absolute majority; making up approximately 95 per cent of the population. Kosovo thus possesses an ethnic uniformity that few states in Europe can claim.

As in the case of the integration versus partition debate concerning Bosnia, Kosovo has generated a similar discussion, more along the lines of 'autonomy versus independence'.[72] Separation from the FRY is a possibility included in UNSC Resolution 1244 as discussed earlier. The issue of statehood for Kosovar Albanians has huge implications not only for Kosovo, but also for the whole South East European region.[73] Addressing this issue requires facing the possibility of redrawing the boundaries of at least one state in South East Europe. It is a prospect the international community traditionally has been reluctant to contemplate in addressing minority (or even majority) rights.[74]

Overall, the international projects to create or restore multicultural societies in Bosnia and Kosovo have seen little measurable progress to date. Similarly, the efforts to cultivate democratic citizenship have registered only modest gains in the face of collectivist ethnic identities and questions of self-determination. In Bosnia, the Dayton settlement at least provided for a state that could bestow citizenship on its peoples. Despite the retention of a common state structure with a common citizenship, however, individual identification remains strongly tied to ethnic groups and/or neighbouring states or nations such as Croatia and Serbia. Only the Muslim community has any clear affinity with the Bosnian state.[75] In the case of Kosovo, the central obstacle to cultivating democratic citizenship is structural; if citizenship requires a state, then it is a basic condition currently lacking for the inhabitants of Kosovo. Kosovo is in a *de jure* sense still part of a Yugoslav state. This is a circumstance that has little or no legitimacy in the eyes of Kosovar Albanians. According to the conventional wisdom discussed earlier, democratic citizenship and the state are inextricably linked. Yet this is precisely what the Kosovar Albanians currently lack and the international community is not showing much desire to bestow statehood in the foreseeable future.

Conclusions

The sustained efforts of NATO and the international community to build a new and more peaceful international order in South East Europe raise some serious questions regarding the relationship between democracy, nationalism and ultimately security. The apparent difficulties in introducing democratic reforms and cultivating the civic national identity called for in the Dayton and Kosovo settlements and the Stability Pact can be attributed to the obduracy of ethnic nationalism.

General Jackson, the first commander of KFOR during 1999, offered some sobering thoughts on the difficulties of introducing democratic norms tied to a civic understanding of nationalism in the Kosovo context:

> We have soldiers living in Serb apartments where they are isolated. We have permanent guards on all Orthodox churches and monasteries without which they would be burnt and bombed. We even escort little old ladies to the bread shop to buy their bread, but on the way a Kosovar Albanian teenager will give the sign of throat-slitting to her face. In terms of what outside intervention in the sense of soldiers, and policemen and civil administrators can achieve, what this tells me is that there is a limit: we're talking about people's attitudes, people's perceptions – and that's what needs to be changed if we are to achieve the concept which underpins 1244 of a new Kosovo: democratic, liberal, reconciled, multi-ethnic. I'm afraid that my deduction is that there's a very long way to go indeed.[76]

Despite the stubborn persistence of ethnic nationalism in the face of international efforts to introduce a new normative base, analysts are sometimes dismissive of its importance and power. Susan Woodward, a well regarded observer of the Yugoslav conflicts, wrote that 'the label of nationalism is not sufficient to describe a situation or predict behaviour ... because of its empty-vessel character – its absence of programme outside the insistence on political power for some imagined community'.[77] The difficulty in making inroads with international norms in places like Bosnia and Kosovo suggests that ethnic nationalism is far from being an 'empty-vessel' and it is an identity that will not easily be replaced. If this is the case, then it is likely to give international peace-building efforts in South East Europe a decidedly long-term character.

For NATO and other agencies engaged in peace-building, finding a means of making democratic norms accessible to those possessing an ethnic identity is the key to effectively tackling the security problems of the region. In this regard, a more differentiated approach to norm transmission may yield better long-term prospects for security and stability. It may also entail moving away from conventional western notions of multicultural society. Where ethnic groups have become separated by violence, it may be more desirable and practical to attempt to build democracy in a monoethnic context. The application of a solution based on such an approach could apply to the two entities of Bosnia and to Kosovo. Such solutions have been adopted in the past and they may be the only viable option.[78]

NATO's efforts to try to prevent ethnic conflict from leading to civil war in Macedonia suggest that separation is not the first option to pursue if ethnically mixed communities remain mostly intact and not traumatised by brutal violence. Accepting ethnic separation as the starting point for introducing democratic norms in failed states and societies, however, is driven by the need to bring security not only to regions and states but also to individuals. If the need for individual human security and the promotion of democratic norms are best advanced together in a monoethnic setting, then the prize of long-term stability may prove less elusive. By matching norms to realities, the structural problems that have hitherto impeded international peace-building efforts in South East Europe could yet be swept away, to the benefit of security and stability in this troubled part of the world.

Notes

1 O. Richmond, 'States of sovereignty, sovereign states and ethnic claims for international status', *Review of International Studies*, 28:2 (2002), 383.
2 The former Yugoslavia is a kind of sub-region within South East Europe comprising states and territories that were part of Communist Yugoslavia until the early 1990s. Today, the former Yugoslavia thus embraces Bosnia, Croatia, the FRY (officially still including Kosovo), Macedonia and Slovenia.
3 See *NATO's Role in Bosnia and Herzegovina*. Website reference www.nato.int/docu/facts/2000/role-bih.htm, and P. Valpolini, 'Changing the Guard in Bosnia', *International Defence Review* (April 1997).
4 R. Connaughton, 'Can KFOR win the peace?', *Jane's Defence Weekly* (14 July 1999).
5 'Thankless tasks', *The Economist* (31 August 2002), 30.
6 T. Ripley, 'NATO's hardest mission … in only 30 days?', *Jane's Defence Weekly* (22 August 2001) and T. Ripley, 'NATO assigns follow-on force for Macedonia', *Jane's Defence Weekly* (3 October 2001).

7 As quoted in *Peace Support Operations (Joint Warfare Publication 3-50)* (London, Ministry of Defence, nd), Glossary-2.

8 *Ibid.*, pp. 1–2.

9 L. Reychler, 'Conceptual framework', in L. Reychler and T. Paffenholz (eds), *Peacebuilding: A Field Guide* (Boulder, Lynne Rienner, 2001), p. 12.

10 C-P. David, 'Does peacebuilding build peace? Liberal (mis)steps in the peace process', *Security Dialogue*, 30:1 (1999), 28–9.

11 *SFOR Mission*. Website reference www.nato.int/sfor/organisation/mission.htm.

12 *KFOR Mission*. Website reference www.nato.int/kfor/kfor/objectives.htm.

13 *Ibid*. Given the functional differences between military and police forces, it is not always ideal to employ the former in a public safety and order role. See A. Hills, 'The inherent limits of military forces in policing peace operations', *International Peacekeeping*, 8:3 (2001), 79–98.

14 For more on the different levels of security, see B. Buzan, *People, States and Fear: An Agenda for International Security Studies in the Post-Cold War Era* (New York, Harvester Wheatsheaf, 1991) and B. Buzan *et al.*, *Security: A New Framework for Analysis* (Boulder, Lynne Rienner, 1998).

15 David, 'Does peacebuilding build peace?', p. 28.

16 'Annex 4: Constitution of Bosnia and Herzegovina', *The General Framework Agreement*. Website reference www.nato.int/ifor/gfa/gfa-an4.htm.

17 'Annex 7: Agreement on refugees and displaced persons', *The General Framework Agreement*. Website reference www.nato.int/ifor/gfa/gfa-an7.htm.

18 'Annex 4: Constitution of Bosnia and Herzegovina'. The entities are a Muslim-Croat Federation and a Serb Republic.

19 P. Williams, 'The international community's response to the crisis in former Yugoslavia', in B. Magas and N. Malcolm (eds), *The War in Croatia and Bosnia-Herzegovina 1991–1995* (London, Frank Cass, 2001), pp. 279–80.

20 R. Holbrooke, *To End a War* (New York, The Modern Library, 1999), p. 363.

21 *Resolution 1244 (1999)*. Website reference www.un.org/Docs/scres/1999/99sc1244.htm.

22 The Stability Pact has twenty-nine participants including states in Europe, North America and Asia (Japan) and a host of organisations and institutions including the EU, NATO, OSCE, Council of Europe, UN, International Monetary Fund and World Bank. See *Stability Pact Information Note*. Website reference www.seerecon.org/News/ETSP/SPC.htm.

23 *Stability Pact for South Eastern Europe*. Website reference www.seerecon.org/KeyDocuments/KD1999062401.htm.

24 *Sarajevo Summit Declaration*. Website reference www.stabilitypact.org/SUMMIT.htm.

25 *Stability Pact for South Eastern Europe*.

26 *Workplan: Stability Pact for South Eastern Europe.* Website reference www.ceps.be/Research/SEE/workplan.htm.

27 *Working Table I: Democratisation and Human Rights, Task Forces/Initiatives.* Website reference www.stabilitypact.org/WT-1/TOC-WT1.htm.

28 'Address by Stability Pact Special Co-ordinator Bodo Hombach, Tokyo 15 May 2000'. Website reference www.stabilitypact.org/Speeches/Speech%20Tokio%20May%2015%20Hombach.htm.

29 J. Hutchinson and A. D. Smith (eds), *Nationalism* (Oxford, Oxford University Press, 1994), p. 3. For an excellent summary of the various strands of the debates on nationalism see A. D. Smith, *The Nation in History: Historiographical Debates about Ethnicity and Nationalism* (London, Polity Press, 2000).

30 A. D. Smith, *Nations and Nationalism in a Global Era* (London, Polity Press, 1995), p. 30.

31 M. Weiner, 'People and states in a new ethnic order?', *Third World Quarterly*, 13:2 (1992), 317–18.

32 Smith, *Nations and Nationalism in a Global Era*, p. 29.

33 Quoted in Hutchinson and Smith, *Nationalism*, p. 95.

34 F. Harvey, 'Primordialism, evolutionary theory and ethnic violence in the Balkans: opportunities and constraints for theory and policy', *Canadian Journal of Political Science*, 33:1 (2000), 3.

35 *Ibid.*, pp. 1–24. See also Smith, *Nations and Nationalism in a Global Era*, pp. 31–5.

36 A. D. Smith, *Theories of Nationalism* (London, Duckworth, 1971), p. 171.

37 Smith, *Nations and Nationalism in a Global Era*, p. 66.

38 *Ibid.*, p. 153.

39 Smith, *The Nation in History*, p. 25.

40 See, *inter alia*, F. Hinsley, *Nationalism and the International System* (London, Hodder and Stoughton, 1973); J. Pettman, 'Nationalism and after', in T. Dunne *et al.* (eds), *The Eighty Years' Crisis: International Relations 1919–1999* (Cambridge, Cambridge University Press, 1998), pp. 149–64. See also S. Ryan, 'Explaining ethnic conflict: the neglected international dimension', *Review of International Studies*, 24:3 (1998), 161–77.

41 For a small sampling see, *inter alia*, M. Brown (ed.), *Ethnic Conflict and International Security* (Princeton, Princeton University Press, 1993); W. Duncan and G. Holman, *Ethnic Nationalism and Regional Conflict: The Former Soviet Union and Yugoslavia* (Boulder, Westview Press, 1994); S. I. Griffiths, *Nationalism and Ethnic Conflict: Threats to European Security (SIPRI Research Report 5)* (Oxford, Oxford University Press, 1993); and T. R. Gurr and B. Harff, *Ethnic Conflict in World Politics* (Boulder, Westview Press, 1994).

42 J. Linz and A. Stepan, *Problems of Democratic Transition and Consolidation* (Baltimore, The Johns Hopkins University Press, 1996), p. 28.

43 S. Smooha and T. Hanf, 'The diverse modes of conflict regulation in deeply divided societies', in J. Hutchinson and A. D. Smith (eds), *Ethnicity* (Oxford, Oxford University Press, 1996), p. 332.

44 J. Jackson Preece, 'Minority rights in Europe: from Westphalia to Helsinki', *Review of International Studies*, 23:1 (1997), 84–7.

45 G. Gilbert, 'Religio-nationalist minorities and the development of minority rights law', *Review of International Studies*, 25:3 (1999), 389–410.

46 H. Köchler, 'The concept of the nation and the question of nationalism: the traditional "nation state" versus a multi-cultural "community state"', in M. Dunne and T. Bonazzi (eds), *Citizenship and Rights in Multicultural Societies* (Keele, Keele University Press, 1995), p. 43.

47 Smith, *Nations and Nationalism in a Global Era*, p. 101. See also E. Mortimer, 'A mild patriotism', *Financial Times* (7 August 1996).

48 Smith, *Nations and Nationalism in a Global Era*, p. 102.

49 G. Schöpflin, *Politics in Eastern Europe* (Oxford, Blackwell, 1993), p. 278. This view is echoed in B. Denitch, *Ethnic Nationalism: The Tragic Death of Yugoslavia* (Minneapolis, University of Minnesota Press, 1994), p. 143.

50 G. Schöpflin, *Nations, Identity, Power: The New Politics of Europe* (London, Hurst and Co., 2000), p. 35.

51 J. Richards, 'Ethnicity and democracy: complementary or incompatible concepts?', in K. Cordell (ed.), *Ethnicity and Democratisation in the New Europe* (London, Routledge, 1999), p. 23.

52 Smooha and Hanf, 'The diverse modes of conflict regulation in deeply divided societies', p. 330.

53 *The Promotion of Multi-Ethnic Society and Democratic Citizenship in South Eastern Europe*. Website reference http://greekhelsinki.gr/english/reports/stability-pact-1-2-2000.html.

54 Schöpflin, *Nations, Identity, Power*, pp. 41–2.

55 B. Pouligny, 'Promoting democratic institutions in post-conflict societies: giving diversity a chance', *International Peacekeeping*, 7:3 (2000), 31–2.

56 *Reports by the High Representative for Implementation of the Peace Agreement to the Secretary-General of the United Nations, March 1996-May 2000*. Website reference www.ohr.int/reports/.

57 *Bosnia's Refugee Logjam Breaks: Is the International Community Ready? (ICG Balkans Report 95)*. Website reference www.crisisweb.org/projects/bosnia/reports/30may00.pdf. See also I. Guzelova, 'Bosnia refugees trickle back home', *Financial Times* (3 July 2000).

58 R. J. Smith, 'Outside efforts do little to mend fractured Bosnia', *Washington Post* (23 January 2000).

59 Statement by Principal Deputy Special Advisor to the President and Secretary of State for Kosovo and Dayton Implementation Ambassador James Pardew, to the House International Relations Committee, 4 August 1999. (Washington DC, United States Information Agency, 1999).

60 21st Report by the High Representative for Implementation of the Peace Agreement to the Secretary-General of the United Nations, 5 March 2002. Website reference http://www.ohr.int/other-doc/hr-reports/default.asp?content_id=7025.

61 P. Neville-Jones, 'Dayton, IFOR and alliance relations in Bosnia', *Survival*, 38:4 (1996–97), 53.

62 D. Bosco, 'Reintegrating Bosnia: a progress report', *Washington Quarterly*, 21:2 (1998), 66.

63 R. Pape, 'Partition: an exit strategy for Bosnia', *Survival*, 39:4 (1997–98), 26. Ivo Daalder suggests a half way house: splitting off the Serb portion of Bosnia and fully integrating its Croat-Muslim Federation. See his 'Bosnia after SFOR: options for continued US engagement', *Survival*, 39:4 (1997–98), 13.

64 The arguments for this view are fully explored in M. Kramer and A. Siljak, 'Separate doesn't equal ethnic peace', *Washington Post* (21 February 1999) and R. Kumar, *Divide and Fall? Bosnia in the Annals of Partition* (London, Verso, 1997).

65 Holbrooke, *To End a War*, p. 365.

66 One of the most comprehensive critiques of the partition option can be found in S. Bose, *Bosnia after Dayton: Nationalist Partition and International Intervention* (London, Hurst and Co., 2002), pp. 149–203.

67 See K. Done, 'Bombing of Serb cathedral condemned', *Financial Times* (2 August 1999); P. Smucker, 'NATO and UN clash as KLA terror campaign goes on', *Daily Telegraph* (24 June 1999) and R. Wright, 'Fear sparks move toward ghettos', *Financial Times* (24 June 1999).

68 E. Cody, 'Out of work and hope, Serbs evacuate Kosovo', *Washington Post* (17 February 2000) and R. J. Smith, 'A year after the war, Kosovo killing goes on', *Washington Post* (12 June 2000).

69 R. J. Smith, 'Diversity divides a town in Kosovo', *Washington Post* (16 February 2000) and S. Wagstyl, 'Razor wire to stay in city filled with hate', *Financial Times* (24 March 2000).

70 Report of the Secretary-General on the United Nations Interim Administration Mission in Kosovo, 6 June 2000 (S/2000/538) (New York, United Nations, 2000). See also P. Finn, 'U.S. plans to return 700 Serbs to Kosovo', *Washington Post* (16 April 2000).

71 *Kosovo Volume I: Report and Proceedings of the Committee*, House of Commons Select Committee on Foreign Affairs, Fourth Report, Session 1999–2000 (London, The Stationery Office, 2000), p. lxvii.

72 See, *inter alia*, D. Allin *et al.*, *What Status for Kosovo? (Chaillot Paper 50)* (Paris, Western European Union Institute for Security Studies, 2001).

73 For a range of views on the vexing issues of self-determination and secession see A. Buchanan, 'Self-determination and the right to secede', *Journal of International Affairs*, 45:2 (1992), 347–65; A. Etzioni, 'The evils of self-determination', *Foreign Policy*, 89 (1992–93), 21–35; J. Mayall, 'Sovereignty, nationalism and self-determination', *Political Studies*, 47:3 (1999), 474–502 and K. Shedadi, *Ethnic Self-Determination and the Break-up of States (Adelphi Paper 283)* (London, International Institute for Strategic Studies, 1993).

74 See J. Jackson Preece, 'Self-determination, minority rights and failed states'. Website reference www.ippu.purdue.edu/failed_states/1999/papers/Jackson-Preece.html and Richmond, 'States of sovereignty, sovereign states and ethnic claims for international status', pp. 381–402.

75 Smith, 'Outside efforts do little to mend fractured Bosnia'.

76 Lt. Gen. Sir M. Jackson, 'KFOR: the inside story', *RUSI Journal*, 145:1 (2000), 17–18.

77 S. Woodward, 'War: building states from nations', in T. Ali (ed.), *Masters of the Universe? NATO's Balkan Crusade* (London, Verso, 2000), p. 204.
78 See two articles by Chaim Kaufman: 'Possible and impossible solutions to ethnic civil wars', *International Security*, 20:4 (1996), 136–75 and 'When all else fails', *International Security*, 23:2 (1998), 120–56. See also J. McGarry and B. O'Leary (eds), *The Politics of Ethnic Conflict Regulation* (London, Routledge, 1993), pp. 1–40.

Chapter 4

Kosovo, NATO and Russia

In the eyes of some observers, the Kosovo crisis posed the greatest threat to relations between Russia and NATO since the end of the Cold War. It also, according to some, seemingly demonstrated the impotence and marginalisation of Russia as an actor in European security affairs. In order to test and explore the validity of these propositions the discussions in this chapter first chart the course of Russian policy towards, and involvement in dealing with, the Kosovo crisis. Following this, attention will turn to an examination of the longer term impact of the crisis on relations between Russia and NATO.

Russia and the Kosovo crisis

Drifting apart from NATO, September 1997–March 1999

Russia and the leading NATO members were extensively engaged in discussing what to do about the developing crisis in Kosovo during 1997 and 1998. Two main forums were utilised for the conduct of these conversations, which produced a greater degree of agreement than is sometimes supposed. They were the Contact Group and the UNSC.

Kosovo was first discussed at a specially convened meeting of Contact Group foreign ministers on the sidelines of the annual session of the UN General Assembly in New York in September 1997. In a brief statement, they voiced 'deep concern over tensions in Kosovo' and warned both Serbs and Albanians 'against any resort to violence to press political demands'. No sanctions were threatened in the statement, should either side – or both – fail to heed this warning. Nevertheless the western participants and Russia managed to reach agreement on their preferences for the future status of Kosovo. They stated that 'we do not support independence and we do not support maintenance of the status quo. We support an enhanced status for Kosovo within the FRY'.[1] In effect this would have restored the *status quo ante* of the period up to 1989, before President Milosevic removed much of the autonomy formerly enjoyed by Kosovo within Communist Yugoslavia.

When Russia and the NATO members began to disagree, it was over the possible use of coercion in order to impose a settlement on Milosevic. The Contact Group considered the imposition of sanctions at a meeting in London in March 1998, in the face of worsening violence in Kosovo. The proposed sanctions were:

a. A 'comprehensive arms embargo against the FRY, including Kosovo'.
b. A ban on supplying 'equipment to the FRY which might be used for internal repression, or for terrorism'.
c. 'Denial of visas for senior FRY and Serbian representatives responsible for repressive action by FRY security forces in Kosovo.'
d. A ban on 'government-financed export credit support for trade and investment ... in Serbia'.

The London statement noted that 'the Russian Federation cannot support measures 'c' and 'd' above for immediate imposition. But if there is no progress towards the steps called for by the Contact Group, the Russian Federation will then be willing to discuss all the above measures'.[2]

Russia had thus not simply opted out of imposing sanctions as some observers subsequently claimed.[3] Its opposition was focused on those elements of the proposed sanctions package that were directed specifically against the Serbs. Elements 'a' and 'b' were not opposed. This was because they would impact upon the KLA as well as Serb forces, if weapons and repressive equipment were prevented from entering the FRY 'including Kosovo'. Even with regard to the sanctions directed specifically against the Serbs, the statement carefully noted that Russia might be willing to impose these too if the Milosevic government proved intransigent.

UNSC Resolution 1160, passed in March 1998, imposed a comprehensive arms embargo on the FRY 'including Kosovo', as called for by the Contact Group. It also threatened 'the consideration of additional measures' should the FRY authorities not prove willing to enter into a serious political dialogue over the future of Kosovo.[4] This resolution invoked Chapter 7 of the UN Charter, which provides for 'action with respect to threats to the peace, breaches of the peace, and acts of aggression'. The invocation of Chapter 7 was regarded in some important quarters at NATO as opening the door to potential military enforcement action if the arms embargo did not prove sufficient.

The Russian government supported Resolution 1160. According to Russian press commentary, it did so for two reasons. First, in order to send what it hoped would be a final warning to Milosevic and, second, because its government did not want Russia to be isolated within the Security Council.[5] None of this meant, however, that the Russian government was happy to countenance the use of force. Indeed, the differences on this crucial issue, which began to loom large during the second half of 1998, became the major source of division and discord between Russia and NATO over the subsequent handling of the Kosovo crisis.

In September 1998, the Security Council passed Resolution 1199. This made a series of specific demands of the FRY government and the leaders of the Albanian community in Kosovo. For the first time it called for 'international monitoring' on the ground in the province in order to verify compliance with these demands. As with the predecessor Resolution 1160, it threatened 'to consider further action and additional measures to maintain or restore peace and stability in the region'.[6]

The fact that its government also supported Resolution 1199 provoked some dissent inside Russia, chiefly on the grounds that the resolution's terms might be used by NATO countries as cover for military action, without further recourse to the UN.[7] But, as Catherine Guicherd has pointed out, UNSC Resolutions providing for consideration of 'additional measures' did not give *carte blanche* to member states. Rather, they 'have usually been interpreted as requiring further action by the Security Council to allow military action'. This understanding was given added clarity and weight in the cases of Resolutions 1160 and 1199 by the fact that 'Russia and China both had accompanied their votes by legally valid declaratory statements spelling out that the resolutions should not be interpreted as authorising the use of force'.[8]

An assumption that NATO members would return to the Security Council to request authorisation to use force seems naive in retrospect given Russian opposition. Yet, it should be recalled that, up to this point, NATO had treated Russia as a full and equal partner in its efforts to tackle the Kosovo crisis. Indeed, Russia's role and input had been *greater* than that of most NATO members, due to its status on the Security Council and membership of the Contact Group. Subsequently, however, the Russians scarcely helped their own cause – or the UN's – by making clear that they would, under no circumstances, entertain *any* possibility of approving NATO military strikes in the Security Council.

Tim Judah has recounted a story from Richard Holbrooke which, even if apocryphal in some details, nevertheless does fairly illustrate the essential rigidity of the underlying Russian position. Holbrooke described an informal Contact Group discussion in October 1998 between the then German Foreign Minister, Klaus Kinkel, and his Russian counterpart, Igor Ivanov:

> Ivanov said: 'If you take it [the issue of using force] to the UN, we'll veto it. If you don't we'll just denounce you.' Kinkel says he wants to take it to the Security Council, as do the British and French ... So, Kinkel says: 'Let's have another stab at it.' But Ivanov says: 'Fine, we'll veto it.' And Kinkel asks again and Ivanov says: 'I just told you Klaus, we'll veto it.'[9]

This confirmed the public line from Ivanov that, if NATO sought a UN mandate for military action, Russia would 'undoubtedly exercise its veto'.[10]

In a 2000 report, the Independent International Commission on Kosovo concluded that Russia's 'rigid commitment to veto any enforcement action' constituted 'the major factor forcing NATO into an unmandated action' in its subsequent bombing campaign.[11] The inflexibility of the Russians (and Chinese) on the Security Council was even criticised – albeit indirectly – by the UN Secretary-General. In his annual report to the General Assembly in September 1999, Kofi Annan stated that 'the choice, as I said during the Kosovo conflict, must not be between ... Council division, and regional action'. He added that 'the Member States of the United Nations should have been able to find common ground in upholding the principles of the Charter, and acting in defence of our common humanity'.[12] Oleg Levitin, a former Russian Foreign Ministry official who worked on its Balkan Desk and in the Contact Group, subsequently argued that Russian policy on Kosovo generally had been inflexible and unimaginative during this period.[13]

The Russian government may also have believed at this time that

Problems of agreement / relative-gains

it had an additional veto over what NATO might do. On 29 January 1999, the Contact Group issued its summons to the Serbs and Albanians to attend negotiations at Rambouillet. This was followed by a session of the NATO NAC on 30 January, which agreed that:

> NATO is ready to take whatever measures are necessary in the light of both parties' compliance with international commitments and requirements, *including in particular assessment by the Contact Group of the response to its demands,* to avert a humanitarian catastrophe, by compelling compliance with the demands of the international community and the achievement of a political settlement. The Council has therefore agreed today that the NATO Secretary General may authorise air strikes against targets on FRY territory [emphasis added].[14]

This ratcheting-up of the NATO airstrike threat provoked little protest in Moscow at the time. The Russians may have thought that the 30 January statement, suggesting that NATO members would act *only* if the Contact Group determined that the FRY government was being obstructive, gave Russia, as a Contact Group member, a *de facto* veto over any use of force.

Significant deterioration in relations between Russia and NATO did not become apparent until after the Rambouillet meeting got underway. Over the course of the negotiations, which broke up and then reconvened the following month in Paris, the souring of relations was pronounced, however. Marc Weller, who was present at Rambouillet as an adviser to the Albanian delegation, has provided a succinct summary:

> Throughout the talks, significant rifts in the Contact Group were visible, relating to the political settlement, to the implementation force and to the threat or use of force as a tool of achieving a settlement. These divisions became more pronounced towards the conclusion of the conference, when a collapse of the talks appeared likely. In fact, one might say that towards the end, the talks were less about Kosovo and more about relations within the Contact Group.[15]

Perhaps the key bone of contention between the Russian representatives and their western counterparts was over the Russian perception that, not only was NATO biased against the Serbs, it was actively seeking to engineer a situation whereby the talks would fail, with the Serbs being blamed. NATO would then have a pretext to begin bombing.[16] Some western observers, for their part, suspected the Russians of not only being partisan in favour of the Serbs, but of acting as the latter's *de facto* representatives at Rambouillet.[17]

As it became increasingly clear that an agreement would not be reached in France, the prospect of NATO military action began to loom large. It was made clear by the United States that NATO reserved the right to launch airstrikes without consulting Russia, the UN or anybody else.[18] In February and March 1999, the prospect of airstrikes was moving up the agenda and Russian opposition to them was simultaneously becoming sharper and more vocal.

Operation Allied Force, *March–June 1999*

The launch of *Operation Allied Force* on 24 March 1999 followed the final breakdown of negotiations. In New York, Sergei Lavrov, Russia's Permanent Representative on the UNSC, told a specially convened meeting of the council that his country was 'profoundly outraged' by the launch of airstrikes. In the view of the Russian government, he said:

> Those who are involved in this unilateral use of force against the sovereign Federal Republic of Yugoslavia – carried out in violation of the Charter of the United Nations and without the authorization of the Security Council – must realize the heavy responsibility they bear for subverting the Charter and other norms of international law and for attempting to establish in the world, de facto, the primacy of force and unilateral diktat.[19]

It was arguable, as noted above, that Russia itself bore part of the blame for 'subverting the Charter' in this instance. Because it had been making clear for months that any attempt by NATO to use the UN would be doomed to failure, the Russian government, in effect, colluded with those NATO countries that were hardly predisposed to involving the UN in the first place.

The Russian government, under Boris Yeltsin, severed most of its institutional links with NATO on the day the bombing began. Much was made of this in both the Russian and western media, where it was frequently suggested that Russia had 'broken off links with the West'. In reality the Russian action was carefully calibrated and targeted and it did not amount to anything so drastic. The Yeltsin administration resisted calls from the Russian Communist Party amongst others to terminate its military presence in Bosnia as part of the NATO-led SFOR.[20] The government opted instead to make limited and symbolic 'adjustments' to its SFOR contingent. These included withdrawing its deputy commander[21] and two signals officers responsible for communications with NATO.[22] In this way Russia could indicate its displeasure whilst maintaining the substance of its military co-operation with NATO forces on the ground in Bosnia. On the wider diplomatic front, the Russian government maintained normal diplomatic relations with all NATO governments, including the United States.

Although its immediate *rhetorical* response was subsequently described as being 'of a pitch unheard in the entire post-Cold War period',[23] the Yeltsin government was clear from the start and explicitly that its *practical* response to the NATO 'aggression' would be circumscribed. Following the initial bombing raids on the FRY, Ivanov stated that 'Russia does not intend to take any [military] countermeasures with respect to NATO'.[24] It was clear that Russia lacked the means to take such measures even if it had wanted to. The only military response was to deploy an intelligence collection ship, the *Liman*. A rumoured deployment of warships from the Black Sea Fleet never materialised.[25]

There were, in addition, three reasons behind this policy of *limited* disruption of relations. First, the Yeltsin government felt that it could not afford – literally – to take any action which might jeopardise the financial and economic support that it received from western countries and institutions such as the International Monetary Fund (IMF).[26] In spring 1999 the Russian economy had barely begun to recover from the effects of a currency crisis the previous summer. Second, there was an underlying fear of being isolated, or rather in this case of Russia isolating itself. President Yeltsin expressed this clearly one month into the bombing. 'In spite of NATO's aggressive actions, we cannot break with the Western countries' he said, 'we cannot lead ourselves into isolation because we are in Europe and no one will kick us out of Europe'.[27] In some quarters, finally, there was a sense of impotence; that there was nothing Russia could do to stop the bombing anyway.[28]

In his initial response to the bombing, on 24 March, Yeltsin, whilst announcing the suspension of institutional links with NATO, was careful to keep the door open in one particularly important area. He stated that 'the sooner negotiations are resumed, the greater the chance the international community will have of finding a political settlement. *Russia is prepared to continue working closely with the other members of the Contact Group for the sake of achieving this goal*' [emphasis added].[29] From the very beginning of *Operation Allied Force*, the best opportunity for Russia to avoid becoming isolated or marginalised and to demonstrate that it was not completely impotent, lay in the diplomatic sphere. Thus it was scarcely surprising that, from day one, Russian leaders concentrated their energies on efforts to broker a diplomatic settlement and to make their country an indispensable partner in doing so.

First off the mark was the then Prime Minister, Yevgeny Primakov. Primakov put special effort into cultivating the French and, especially, the German governments. This was shrewd diplomacy. Primakov was almost certainly calculating that the chances of an acceptable settlement package being constructed would be enhanced if he could build a sympathetic coalition inside NATO generally, rather than dealing exclusively with the United States. In addition, he probably calculated that these two continental European countries would be more amenable to according Russia a key role in the diplomacy than the US. By cultivating them, therefore, Russia might thus better establish itself as a vital factor in the diplomatic equation.

The latter element of Primakov's strategy soon began to yield results. At the end of March, *Rossiiskaya Gazeta* quoted 'French diplomatic sources' as saying that 'the small door leading to peace in the Balkans has one key, it is in Russia's hands'.[30] One week later, the German Foreign Ministry stated that 'the German government believes that a solution to the conflict in Kosovo can be found only through close cooperation with Russia'.[31]

Following these initial 'successes', President Yeltsin decided to become more directly involved. He did so on 14 April 1999 by appointing former Prime Minister Viktor Chernomyrdin to be his 'special representative for the conflict in Yugoslavia'. In effect this meant that Primakov was being sidelined. The latter, indeed, was to be sacked by Yeltsin as Prime Minister the following month. Yeltsin's decision to shuffle his pack was prompted by several concerns. One was domestic politicking.[32] As Russian commentator Vladimir Baranovsky noted, 'the coming parliamentary and presidential elections are always present in a very conspicuous way in nearly all the steps taken by the leading Russian politicians in connection with the Yugoslav developments'.[33] By the spring of 1999, Yeltsin had evidently decided that he did not want Primakov to succeed him as President. Thus, the latter's power base was progressively undermined.

Nezavisimaya Gazeta identified other reasons for Yeltsin choosing Chernomyrdin. It opined that 'the President had to put all national efforts to resolve the Yugoslav crisis into the hands of a man who would be completely under Boris Yeltsin's control'. Chernomyrdin was, in addition, 'so well known in the world that he can negotiate as an equal with Western and Yugoslav leaders'.[34]

By the middle of April, three weeks after the start of *Operation Allied Force*, Russian leaders had succeeded in securing a role in the diplomatic negotiations that would eventually contribute to a settlement of the Kosovo crisis. In assessing the nature and extent of the influence that Russia had on the terms of the final settlement, it is necessary first of all to consider NATO's own starting point, which was agreed just before Chernomyrdin's appointment. In a statement released after a NAC meeting on 12 April, the member states set out five demands which President Milosevic was expected to meet before the bombing could be called off. They were:

- a verifiable end to Serb military action and repression in Kosovo
- the withdrawal from Kosovo of Serb military, police and paramilitary forces
- the stationing in the province of an 'international military presence'
- the unconditional and safe return of refugees and displaced persons and 'unhindered access to them by humanitarian aid organisations'
- willingness to work, on the basis of the draft Rambouillet agreement, on a settlement of the political status of Kosovo.[35]

Two days after these five points were agreed, ironically on the day that Chernomyrdin was appointed to his special envoy's job, Primakov's efforts with the German government yielded their most tangible fruit. A German 'peace plan' was unveiled. Actually this description, although widely used in the media, was inaccurate on two counts. First, the proposals did not amount to a 'plan' as such. Rather, they were presented as a series of suggested steps by which a settlement might be reached. Second, the proposals were not exclusively German. They had been agreed jointly by German and Russian diplomats. The vital importance of Russian involvement was repeatedly stressed on the German side, although it suited the Russians to have the proposals presented formally by the FRG in order to increase the chances of a positive reception within NATO.[36]

The *de facto* Russo-German proposals incorporated NATO's five demands, but there were also four significant additions. First, it was proposed that the Group of Eight (G8) provide the framework within which the eventual proposals to be put to Milosevic be agreed. This reflected the obvious Russian interest in institutionalising Russia's involvement as a full and equal participant in the international diplomatic efforts. The Contact Group was evidently seen as a busted flush, having more or less fallen apart in France. The membership of the G8 was virtually identical however; with Canada and Japan sitting alongside Russia and the five leading NATO members. Thus it seemed to offer a comparable forum.

The second key element in the Russo-German proposals was United Nations involvement. The UN had not been mentioned in NATO's 12 April statement, other than in a passing reference to any final settlement of the status of Kosovo being 'in conformity [with] ... the Charter of the United Nations'. In the Russo-German proposals, however, the UN was assigned major roles. In the first place, any agreement should, it was proposed, be implemented via a UNSC Resolution. It was further suggested that the UN should be in charge of the 'transitional administration' of Kosovo pending a final settlement of its status.

The third new element was the proposal that any settlement must include agreement on demilitarising the KLA, which had not figured at all in NATO's 12 April demands. Ensuring that this was part of any eventual settlement was motivated by the long-standing Russian view that NATO was biased against the Serbs. Finally, a bombing pause was proposed once the withdrawal of Serb military and other forces had begun; this to be made permanent once the withdrawal was completed.[37]

The initial response from NATO collectively to these initiatives seemed frosty. At the Washington summit in late April, NATO's five demands were simply repeated verbatim and, for good measure, it was stated that 'there can be no compromise on these conditions'.[38] Behind the scenes, however, things were more fluid. According to then US Deputy Secretary of State, Strobe Talbott, Yeltsin put through a telephone call to President Clinton towards the end of the summit (the five demands had been reaffirmed on the first day). During this conversation, it was agreed that Chernomyrdin should negotiate directly with the US on forming an agreed position, which could then be presented to Milosevic.

Talbott, who was designated by Clinton as Chernomyrdin's chief interlocutor on the American side, subsequently stated that:

> I think [this] can be seen as a bit of a turning point, because until Viktor Chernomyrdin engaged on behalf of President Yeltsin and the Russian government, the Russian position was basically kind of just say no ... But when President Yeltsin decided to dispatch Mr Chernomyrdin, who was a close ally and associate of his, and had been his prime minister for a long time ... it represented an attempt to use the prestige of Russia and the

diplomatic energy of Russia and the skills of Mr Chernomyrdin to see if despite our disagreement over the need for the bombing campaign, we could agree on the terms by which the bombing campaign could come to an end.

Talbott acknowledged that there had been pressure on the western side, at the summit, to accommodate the Russians. He recalled 'a real sense of tension building' and a 'widespread feeling that [Kosovo] was going to spoil much else of what was going on between the US and Russia, between the West and Russia, between NATO and Russia'.[39]

Following the NATO summit, things began to move quickly. From late April, Chernomyrdin and Talbott began a series of meetings designed to flesh out a common negotiating position. In early May, Finnish President Martti Ahtisaari joined them, as the representative of the European Union. It was widely recognised that the initial Chernomyrdin-Talbott talks represented the opening of a new phase in diplomatic efforts to end the crisis.[40] It was accepted on all sides that the Russians were not there purely for form's sake or to make up the numbers.

Chernomyrdin's presence in the newly formed diplomatic troika fulfilled two key functions. First, by late April and after a month's worth of bombing, the Clinton administration had come round to the view, as Erik Yesson has put it, that 'NATO could not bring to bear sufficient leverage on Serbia by itself; other actors had to participate'.[41] The best-placed 'other actor' seemed to be Russia, with its historic engagement in South East Europe and sympathy for the Serbs. Chernomyrdin played on this, telling his western interlocutors that 'if you want to persuade Milosevic you have to convince me first'.[42]

Second, Chernomyrdin was able to develop a 'good cop/bad cop' approach with Ahtisaari in what Talbott called the 'hammer and anvil' strategy. As the Deputy Secretary of State explained, 'the notion was that Chernomyrdin would be the hammer and would pound away on Milosevic, and President Ahtisaari would be the anvil against who the pounding would take place, so that Milosevic would know what he had to do in order to get the bombing stopped'.[43]

It is noteworthy that Talbott himself did not travel to Belgrade during the diplomatic endgame in late May and early June. Rather, he left it to Chernomyrdin and Ahtisaari to execute their hammer and anvil strategy. For this to work it was essential that all three negotiators had reached solid agreement on a common negotiating position in advance. The Americans had to be sure that the Russians were firmly on board. Otherwise there was a chance that Chernomyrdin might depart from the agreed script in Belgrade. As Talbott later put it, 'the logic of … the tri-lateral diplomacy among President Ahtisaari, Mr Chernomyrdin and ourselves was to basically close down the gaps that existed among the various parts of the international community', which otherwise President Milosevic might have been able to exploit.[44]

It is an inaccurate caricature to – as some have done[45] – portray Russia as having been little more than the 'messenger boy' or 'post office' transmitting NATO's demands to Milosevic. The demands that were transmitted differed in significant respects, and not just 'in nuance',[46] from those that NATO had originally laid down on 12 April 1999. None of NATO's original demands were deleted. The differences lay in what was subsequently added in. These additions were the best measurement of Russia's diplomatic influence and success.

The principles upon which the eventual settlement was based were agreed at a meeting of G8 foreign ministers on 6 May 1999. Use of the G8 forum in itself reflected a concession to Russian (and German) requests as put forward in their joint proposals of 14 April. The G8 principles incorporated the 12 April NATO demands but amplified them in significant ways. In so doing they also reflected key elements of the 14 April Russo-German proposals. The main additions were:

- The 'international presences' to be deployed in Kosovo following a Serb withdrawal should be both 'civil and security'.
- These presences should be 'endorsed and adopted by the United Nations'.
- The G8 statement agreed on the 'establishment of an interim administration for Kosovo to be decided by the Security Council of the United Nations'.
- The 'demilitarization of the UCK' (KLA) was identified as an integral part of an overall political settlement.[47]

Overall, as Dov Lynch has noted, the G8 settlement 'contained important elements of success for Russia'.[48] Of course the Russians had to agree some compromises in return, as is normal practice in diplomatic intercourse.[49]

Jockeying for position, June–July 1999

One key issue had not been resolved before Milosevic accepted the NATO/G8 demands. This was the nature and extent of a Russian military presence, working with NATO, in post-settlement Kosovo.

Chernomyrdin had accepted that the international security presence should be NATO-led. This was incorporated into UNSC Resolution 1244, which put into place the agreed settlement.[50] The specific question of Russian participation was effectively set aside for subsequent consideration, in order to prevent it from holding up the overall deal.[51] What happened next demonstrated that, for all their diplomatic co-operation since the end of April, substantial underlying distrust remained between Russia and NATO.

On the day after Resolution 1244 was passed, some 200 Russian troops detached themselves from the Russian SFOR contingent in Bosnia. They undertook a pre-emptive march to the airport in Pristina, arriving before the first NATO troops from the newly formed KFOR. Various explanations for the 'dash to Pristina' have been put forward. In the West, conspiracy theorists suggested that Serb forces, on their way out of Kosovo, had arranged to give back to the Russians military equipment that the latter had covertly supplied during the conflict. A variation on this theme had the Serbs handing over the wreckage of the highly sensitive US F-117 'stealth' fighter, which had been shot down early on in the NATO bombing campaign.[52] In Russia, meanwhile, some explanations focused on the perceived need for Yeltsin (assuming that the dash was, indeed, ordered by him) to pull off a dramatic gesture to distract attention from political travails at home.[53] Others argued that it was designed to reinforce the point that Russia remained an important player in South East European affairs.[54]

Still others have argued that the dash represented only the initial deployment of an intended substantial force. Its purpose was allegedly to occupy the northern part of Kosovo, where the majority of its Serbian population lived, and assist the Milosevic government in effectively partitioning the province. This particular conspiracy theory has enjoyed high-level support. Former National Security Adviser Zbigniew Brzezinski advanced it, in hearings before the US Senate Committee on Foreign Relations in October 1999.[55] In his memoir of the Kosovo crisis, General Clark makes clear that he also believed that partition was the Russian objective.[56] Yet, as Clark also noted in his memoirs; 'if the Russians really wanted to enter and establish a sector in the north of Kosovo, they could simply drive across the border [i.e. from Bosnia through Serbia], even if we blocked the airfield, and plant their flag. Reinforcements could be flown in to airfields in Serbia and driven in'.[57] Why, therefore, dispatch a symbolic force to a high-profile site in the provincial capital when a more substantial force could have been dispatched directly to northern Kosovo?

The most likely explanation is that the Russian bottom line was about ensuring that they had *some* actual military presence, however small, in the heart of Kosovo at the start of the post-conflict phase and were not, therefore, frozen out completely by NATO. The nature of the Russian involvement in KFOR had not yet been agreed, as noted. Many in Russia evidently felt that, when the crunch came, they could not trust NATO to ensure that Russia's views would be adequately respected in Kosovo unless Russia itself moved to establish facts on the ground before NATO arrived. Thereafter, and like it or not, NATO members would be compelled to negotiate a mutually acceptable Russian role in KFOR. This, in essence, is what subsequently happened.

By July 1999, it was clear that relations between Russia and the West had survived the Kosovo crisis essentially intact, if far from in rude health. The discussions above have demonstrated that at no time during the crisis had there been a *complete* breakdown in relations. There certainly did exist a substantial mistrust of NATO amongst Russian political and military leaders, as evidenced by the pre-emptive dash to Pristina. But the prevailing Russian view was summed up in *Vremya MN*:

> During the Balkan war, Russia made the most important choice in our country's recent history. We didn't ally ourselves with NATO, but, thank God, we didn't become its enemy either. Now, Russia and the West can become partners who may not have any reason to love each other, but have to work together if only because there's no getting away from each other.[58]

Russia and NATO since the Kosovo crisis

The period between June 1999 and September 2001 was characterised by a deliberate Russian policy of gradually and incrementally restoring those links and co-operation with NATO that had been broken off at the start of *Operation Allied Force*. This process was begun during the last months of the Yeltsin administration. Co-operation in KFOR[59] necessitated re-establishing some kind of institutional channel of communication between Russia and NATO at the political level, to allow for the discussion of Kosovo-related issues.

On 23 July 1999, the NATO-Russia Permanent Joint Council

(PJC) met for the first time since before the start of *Operation Allied Force*. The PJC had been established in the summer of 1997 to provide a forum for consultation between Russia and the NATO members. It had, however, failed to live up to expectations with Russia and NATO both investing relatively little political capital in the forum. On the other hand, for all its limitations the PJC was the only extant politico-diplomatic structure for the carrying on of Russia–NATO discussions. Therefore, the use of it was more by default than Russian desire.

The Russian side was at pains to make clear that PJC meetings would not wipe the slate clean and did not signal a return to business as before. Rather, the Russian government emphasised that the PJC was being reactivated solely for the purpose of discussing issues 'in a clearly defined sphere: interaction within the framework of KFOR'.[60] A moderate upgrading was announced two months later when the Russian government decided to send back its chief military representative to NATO. However, it declared that this signalled no change in its basic approach of restricting contacts to those deemed necessary in order to maintain Russia's voice in KFOR.[61]

No further progress was possible during the remainder of the Yeltsin Presidency, seemingly bearing out the predictions of pessimists who had argued that Russia–NATO relations were unlikely to ever be restored to their pre-crisis levels.[62] At the least, it was widely assumed inside Russia during the second half of 1999 that no further progress on restoring relations with NATO was possible until after the forthcoming parliamentary and presidential elections.[63]

Balancing this, however, was the view, widely expressed by Russian political leaders, that Russia would have to learn (again) to live with NATO on the European stage. As Igor Ivanov expressed it in October 1999: 'like it or not, NATO is a reality in today's international arena, primarily in Europe but also in the world in general'. Four months later, Primakov expressed a similar view when he said that 'we have to talk, as NATO is a real force and this should be taken into account'.[64] Once the elections were out of the way, therefore, and a new President installed in office, it seemed likely that, notwithstanding the bitterness left by the Kosovo crisis, Russia's political leaders would continue – and perhaps accelerate – the process of gradually re-establishing ties with NATO.

President Yeltsin announced his resignation at the end of 1999 having, it was widely assumed, manoeuvred his preferred successor, Vladimir Putin, into pole position for the forthcoming presidential election. Putin wasted little time, early in 2000, in making clear his interest in not only continuing with the incremental restoration of links with NATO, but in moving them forward in qualitative terms. In February, Lord Robertson visited Moscow on the first high-level NATO official trip to Russia since *Operation Allied Force*. He met with Putin and Ivanov. The two sides agreed on a statement pledging to 'intensify their dialogue in the Permanent Joint Council … on a wide range of security issues that will enable NATO and Russia to address the challenges that lie ahead and to make their mutual cooperation a cornerstone of European security'.[65] In other words, consultations within the PJC would, from henceforth, take place on other issues in addition to those relating to KFOR.

Robertson was, sensibly, careful to avoid the appearance of triumphalism over this agreement. He restricted his public assessment to the understated comment that 'we've moved from permafrost into slightly softer ground'.[66] Nevertheless, there was little doubt that this was the most significant step forward since the end of *Operation Allied Force*. In Russia, *Segodnya* asserted that 'it's safe to say that the crisis in Russia–NATO relations has been overcome, or almost overcome'.[67] It is important to note, however, that the moves made between June 1999 and February 2000 resulted in the restoration of the *status quo ante*; i.e. the Permanent Joint Council. No thought appeared to have been given by NATO members to developing new and better consultative machinery with Russia. To be fair, prior to the severe jolt induced by the events of 11 September 2001, it was not easy to see what a better alternative to the existing PJC-based framework might look like.[68]

In March 2000, Putin made headlines both at home and abroad following a British television interview. Most of the attention focused on his response to a question about possible Russian membership in NATO. 'Why not?' was Putin's reply. This was widely interpreted as a strong political signal to the NATO members that Putin wanted to see relations further improved and developed, in a qualitatively significant way.[69]

In Brussels, Robertson, in a statement, said that although 'at present Russian membership of NATO is not on the agenda', nevertheless, NATO recognised 'the need for partnership between the Alliance and Russia, and will work hard to build on our existing links'.[70] The indications by Putin that the 'existing links' were not sufficient and should be superseded by something more did not elicit a NATO response at this time.

The impact of 11 September 2001

Initially, in the days and weeks following the terrorist strikes on New York and Washington DC on 11 September 2001, it seemed as if their effect would be felt more in confirming the objectives that Putin had already signalled rather than in ushering in anything dramatically new. In late September, the Russian President was quoted as calling on NATO to admit Russia to membership; a clear echo of his television interview eighteen months previously.[71] Putin seemingly wanted to take advantage of western – especially US – interest in constructing the broadest possible international coalition for the impending 'war on terror' in order to persuade NATO members to respond more dynamically than hitherto to his signals in favour of enhanced relations and more co-operation. Following a meeting with Robertson in early October, Putin was quoted as saying that 'we have got the impression that our signals in favour of closer co-operation have been heard'.[72] Positive mood music had also been picked up at a PJC meeting at the end of September.[73] Thus far, however, there had been little more than words.

The prospects of this situation changing seemed especially promising in November. Amongst NATO members there was talk that Russian representatives might be given co-decision-making rights – in effect a veto – in a new 'council of twenty' at NATO headquarters. Tony Blair was publicly credited with the initiative behind this idea, perhaps because he was reckoned to have a particularly good personal relationship with the Russian President.[74] In fact, on a visit to Moscow that month, Lord Robertson attributed similar ideas to the US, FRG, Italy and Canada.[75]

Robertson's public remarks on his visit to Russia were most noteworthy for his candid admission of the lack of substance in Russia–NATO relations to date. In a speech to the Diplomatic Academy in Moscow, Robertson said that 'the current state of NATO–Russia relations is not sufficient to deal seriously with the new security challenges that confront us today and tomorrow'. He added that:

> Our Partnership has remained a nervous one ... Fundamental differences in perception persist, above all regarding the future of the European security architecture, and the respective roles NATO and Russia should play within this architecture. The 1999 Kosovo crisis exposed these fundamental differences in perception.[76]

In effect, Robertson used his November 2001 visit to formally propose the 'council of twenty' to the Russian government. He gave it a provisional name – the 'Russia-North Atlantic Council' (RNAC). This new body, he explained:

> would involve Russia having an equality with the NATO countries in terms of the subject matter and would be part of the same compromising trade-offs, give and take, that is involved in day-to-day NATO business. That is how we do business at 19. The great United States of America, the mighty France and Germany, the United Kingdom have an equal voice to tiny Luxembourg and even tinier Iceland. But we get compromises. We build consensus. So the idea would be that Russia would enter that. That would give Russia a right of equality but also a responsibility and an obligation that would come from being part of the consensus-building organization. That is why I say a new attitude is going to be required on both sides if this is going to work. But if it works, it obviously is a huge change, a sea change in the way in which we do business.[77]

From these remarks, it was clear that Robertson envisaged the RNAC serving, in significant part, to 'discipline' the Russians. This might prevent them from repeating what some westerners regarded as a dilettante approach under the 'Founding Act' (the name given to the 1997 agreement on Russia–NATO relations, which had established the PJC). By 2001, NATO officials could point to a number of instances where Russia had obstructed the implementation of the Founding Act's provisions; by, for example, repeatedly holding up the opening of a NATO military liaison mission in Moscow.

Consensus-building has achieved an almost mystical status amongst NATO member states. This was evident during the course of *Operation Allied Force*. As noted in Chapter 2, constant reference was made throughout the campaign to the primary importance of maintaining allied solidarity and cohesion. That this *was* maintained was regarded within NATO, and elsewhere, as a major – if not the prime – reason why Milosevic eventually conceded. According to NATO officials subsequently, there was never any significant prospect of consensus-breaking. This, they explained, was because of the strenuous efforts made in developing basic consensus on NATO's objectives *before* military operations were launched. Once achieved, the consensus was something that no member – large or small – would lightly break.[78] Thus, one can understand the idea that bringing Russian representatives into the consensus-building process would have positive effects in encouraging them to engage more seriously and constructively with NATO than hitherto.

NATO foreign ministers formally endorsed the RNAC proposal at their meeting in December 2001. They stated that the aim of establishing a new council would be to 'identify and pursue opportunities for joint action at 20', by creating 'new, effective mechanisms for consultation, cooperation, joint decision, and coordinated/joint action'. Significantly, by promising to create 'new, effective mechanisms', NATO members were tacitly admitting that their existing co-operative arrangements with Russia had been ultimately *ineffective*. The ministers were careful to reaffirm that Russia was being offered a more substantial voice but ultimately no veto over core areas. 'NATO', they stated, 'will maintain its prerogative of independent decision and action at 19 on all issues consistent with its obligations and responsibilities'.[79]

As the year 2002 began, representatives from NATO and Russia set to work on trying to turn the RNAC idea into reality. The talks got underway against the general background – certainly in Russia – of a sense that whatever 'bounce' had been given to the country's relations with the West in general, and the United States in particular, by 11 September had substantially dissipated. In January 2002, an editorial in *Izvestia* argued that 'everything [is] just like it was before ... Sept. 11 changed nothing. The Americans are the same as they were before. Russia and its president need not expect a special approach, leniency or solidarity on the part of the sole superpower'.[80] *Vremya MN*, meanwhile, noted that 'the latest illusory honeymoon in relations with the US lasted less than five months'.[81]

At first, the course of negotiations in the spring of 2002 appeared to confirm the suspicions of the Russian pessimists. For their part, Russian negotiators seemed to some in the West to be unable or unwilling to break away from an approach which alternated between making over-ambitious demands and putting forward ideas seemingly designed to weaken and undermine NATO.[82]

The NATO position reportedly hardened at this time, under pressure from a divided Bush administration.[83] In February 2002, a widely cited report in the *Financial Times* claimed that NATO members had reached agreement on restricting the scope of Russian input. Reportedly, Russia would not be offered decision-making rights on matters pertaining to 'the vital interests of any one Nato country' or 'issues that involve military decisions'. It was also reported that NATO members had agreed on a 'retrieval' mechanism, allowing them to withdraw an issue from the new council 'if consensus proves impossible'.[84]

A sense of approaching *impasse* was apparent at this time. In early March, the Russians were reported to have 'submitted a proposal which focused very heavily on substance', whereas NATO members 'had agreed a position that focused on … structure, modalities and principles'. As a result, ideas for the new council were 'still at a relatively early stage of exploration'.[85] In an interview published in *The Times*, Igor Ivanov revealed that negotiations 'were not going well', a situation that he attributed to 'the refusal by some to overcome Cold War stereotypes'.[86]

Yet, the December 2001 NATO meeting had pledged that the new council would be ready at, or even before, the next foreign ministers' gathering which was scheduled for May 2002 in Reykjavik. This imposed a deadline that would have been highly politically and diplomatically embarrassing – for both sides – to have missed. Thus, in Reykjavik the NATO ministers announced the creation of what was now to be officially known as the 'NATO-Russia Council' (NRC) to replace the existing PJC.

According to press reports, the NRC would give Russia co-decision-making rights in nine issue areas, including significant ones such as military crisis management, counter-terrorism, non-proliferation of weapons of mass destruction and theatre missile defence. This appeared to confound pessimists who had speculated that nothing of substance would emerge from the Russia–NATO negotiations. As such, it provoked enthusiastic media commentary. *The Times*, for example, called the NRC 'the most far-reaching change in the North Atlantic alliance since Nato was founded in 1949'.[87] The *Guardian* was only slightly less enthusiastic in describing the new arrangement as 'one of the most fundamental shifts in European security since the collapse of communism'.[88]

Important provisos were, however, reportedly included in the new arrangement. One was the retrieval mechanism, allowing NATO members to withdraw an issue from discussion in the NRC if the prospects for consensus being reached with the Russians looked poor. This opened the door to potential disagreements over who should decide when such an *impasse* had been reached. There was also reported ambiguity over whether or not NATO members would reserve the right to formulate common positions in advance of meetings with the Russians.[89] This was an important issue. It had been one of the main complaints from the Russian side in the PJC since 1997.

Two weeks after the Reykjavik meeting, leaders from the nineteen NATO member states met in Rome with President Putin to formally set the seal on their new council. Their agreed communiqué was upbeat and effusive. The nine areas for co-operative endeavour, which had been flagged up in Reykjavik, were confirmed. It was stated that the NRC would 'provide a mechanism for consultation, consensus-building, cooperation, joint decision, and joint action for the member states of NATO and Russia'.[90] NATO officials stressed the importance of the consensus-building element, confirming that a significant part of the institution's intention with the new council was to educate their Russian interlocutors in the ways of responsible multilateral decision-making.[91]

If this sounded somewhat patronising, it also represented perhaps the best hope of NATO members taking the new council seriously in the sense of really intending to develop joint decision-making and implementation procedures with the Russians. The Rome communiqué appeared quite clear on this score, stating that 'the members of the NATO-Russia Council ... will take joint decisions and will bear equal responsibility, individually and jointly, for their implementation'. Taken at face value this seemed unequivocal. The recent history of Russia–NATO relations cautioned against taking such statements at face value however. The 1997 Founding Act – the first attempt to create a lasting Russia-NATO institutional relationship – was also supposed to provide the means 'for joint decisions and joint action ... to the maximum extent possible'.[92] But this had never been developed.

In substantial part, the failure of the Founding Act had been due to the approach of the Russians, as noted earlier. However, NATO members must also bear part of the blame. They had never been willing to engage in genuinely thorough-going multilateral consultations, preferring instead to formulate common positions amongst themselves in advance of PJC meetings and then engage in rather desultory and non-binding conversations with the Russians. As a result of the failure by all parties to invest more political capital and effort in it, the PJC was effectively moribund even before its failure to perform any useful role during the Kosovo crisis.[93]

What were the prospects of the new NRC turning out differently? There could be no guarantees. However, optimists could point to two differences with 1997. First, there was some evidence that both sides had learnt from the failure of the PJC. NATO leaders in 2001–02 explicitly stated their willingness, from the start of negotiations, to bring Russian representatives into their hallowed consensus-building practices. The Russians, for their part, accepted the implied obligation that this placed on them to participate constructively and positively in the often frustrating and laborious task of building consensus amongst different countries.

There was also the prospect of the new arrangements being institutionalised to a greater degree. Russia was to maintain a permanent mission at the NATO headquarters, as opposed to just sending representatives to meetings, as had been the case with the PJC. The 2002 agreement also pledged that a 'Preparatory Committee' would be established to undertake the necessary staff-work in advance of NRC meetings. This apparently innocuous administrative announcement belied a more profound potential change. The Preparatory Committee would include 'Russian representation at the appropriate level'. This would, if implemented in good faith, allow the Russians to be involved at the crucial agenda-setting and preparation stages of the consultative process. It would make it more difficult for NATO members to present them with pre-cooked 'alliance positions'.

Underlying this, second, was an emerging perception that western – and especially United States – policy towards Russia was now in the process of undergoing a sea-change as a result of the events of 11 September 2001. In Rome, Lord Robertson spoke of the:

> expectations that this will not be just another glizty protocol event, but a real breakthrough. Expectations that the new NATO-Russia Council will not just talk but will act, not just analyse but prescribe, not just deliberate but take decisive action ... and if we need a reminder of why, then there is a simple answer. There is a common enemy out there. The man and woman in the street, be it Petrovka Street or 66th Street, knows it, feels it and they expect us to address it. 11 September 2001 brought death to thousands of people in one act of terrible, criminal violence. But it also brought a message to the leaders of the democratic world. Find solutions and find them together.[94]

In the wider domain, opinion was more mixed. Some observers and commentators continued to argue that Russia–NATO relations were as they had always been – hollow and lacking substance – and that the new NRC was unlikely to change that. In the UK, the *Guardian*, adopting in its editorial a markedly cooler tone than had its reporter at Reykjavik, wrote of the 'phoney piazza of platitudes' in Rome.[95]

For a growing number of commentators, however, a more positive and important change was underway. In an insightful commentary, *The Economist* argued that 'America's relations with Russia are better than at any time since the end of the second world war and are improving'.

Three reasons were cited in support of this contention. The first was renewed concern in the US that terrorists or 'rogue' states might gain access to ex-Soviet nuclear materials, either through theft or covert Russian sales, unless the Russians were persuaded and/or helped to secure their stockpiles. Second, the Bush administration was reported to be taking a renewed interest in Russia's role as a major producer of oil and gas. As such, a closer US partnership with Russia might help reduce the former's level of dependence on energy supplies from the Middle East. Third, and most direct, the administration wanted to maintain, for the long haul, the practical co-operation and assistance which Putin had been giving to the war on terror since the autumn of 2001.[96]

Conclusions

The story of Russia's involvement in the Kosovo crisis tells us important things about its status and role in post-Cold War European security affairs. Most important, from the evidence of the crisis Russia has not been as weak, in terms of diplomacy, and its relations with NATO not as unbalanced as is sometimes supposed. In the period April–June 1999, it played a key diplomatic role in bringing about the Kosovo settlement.

Nevertheless, it can be argued that during the crisis Russia had effectively used its diplomacy to make up for a measurable decline in influence and power overall. The diplomatic success cannot easily disguise Russia's general decline as a power. In this context, Lawrence Freedman has written that 'if [Russia] continues to be treated as a great power, that is because others choose to do so, not because they must'.[97]

In 2000, Ivo Daalder and Michael O'Hanlon argued that the long-term impact of the Kosovo crisis on Russia–NATO relations was likely to be 'modest'.[98] Events since then have confirmed the validity of their conclusion. Relations between Russia and the West, and in particular between Russia and the United States, have been much more profoundly affected by the events of 11 September 2001.

Notwithstanding this, relations have, so far, remained ultimately unfulfilled. Neither side has clearly identified to the other – nor, in all probability, worked out for itself – what it wants from the relationship. The Russian government has, at various times, been vocal and clear in asserting what it did *not* want; chiefly the eastward enlargement of NATO's membership and unilateral military action over

Kosovo. But it has proved vaguer and more reticent when it has come to identifying and fleshing out the nature and parameters of its relationship with the institution.

Notes

1 'Statement of the Contact Group Foreign Ministers, New York, 24 September 1997', in M. Weller, *The Crisis in Kosovo 1989–1999. International Documents and Analysis, Volume 1* (Cambridge, Documents and Analysis Publishing, 1999), p. 234.

2 'Statement by the Contact Group, London, 9 March 1998', *ibid.*, pp. 235–6.

3 See, *inter alia*, T. Judah, *Kosovo: War and Revenge* (London, Yale University Press, 2000), p. 144 and I. Daalder and M. O'Hanlon, *Winning Ugly: NATO's War to Save Kosovo* (Washington DC, Brookings, 2000), p. 220.

4 *Resolution 1160 (1998)*. Website reference www.un.org/Docs/scres/1998/sres1160.htm.

5 *Kommersant-Daily* (3 April 1998). Translated in *The Current Digest of the Post-Soviet Press* [hereafter *CDPSP*], 50:14 (1998), 23.

6 *Resolution 1199 (1998)*. Website reference www.un.org/Docs/scres/1998/sres1199.htm.

7 *Izvestia* (25 September 1998). *CDPSP*, 50:39 (1998), 19–20.

8 C. Guicherd, 'International law and the war in Kosovo', *Survival*, 41:2 (1999), 26–7.

9 Judah, *Kosovo: War and Revenge*, p. 183.

10 *Izvestia* (7 October 1998). *CDPSP*, 50:40 (1998), 14.

11 Independent International Commission on Kosovo, *Kosovo Report* (Oxford, Oxford University Press, 2000), p. 161.

12 Secretary-General Presents his Annual Report to General Assembly (Press Release SG/SM/7136GA/9596). Website reference www.un.org/News/Press/docs/1999/19990920.sgsm7136.html.

13 O. Levitin, 'Inside Moscow's Kosovo muddle', *Survival*, 42:1 (2000), 130–40.

14 'Statement by the North Atlantic Council on Kosovo, 30 January 1999', in Weller, *The Crisis in Kosovo*, p. 416.

15 M. Weller, 'The Rambouillet conference on Kosovo', *International Affairs*, 75:2 (1999), 251. See also *Nezavisimaya Gazeta* (23 February 1999). *CDPSP*, 51:8 (1998) [sic], 18.

16 For a development of the argument that Rambouillet 'was set up to fail' see M. MccGwire, 'Why did we bomb Belgrade?', *International Affairs*, 76:1 (2000), 12ff.

17 Judah, *Kosovo: War and Revenge*, p. 198; Weller, 'The Rambouillet conference on Kosovo', p. 251.

18 In a press briefing on 21 February, State Department spokesperson James Rubin said that 'the fact that Russia doesn't support military action is not a surprise, but NATO's authority has been given to Secretary General

Solana. He has that authority and he doesn't need to seek political authority from any other body'. See 'James Rubin, Press Briefing on the Kosovo
peace talks, Rambouillet, France, 21 February 1999', in Weller, *The Crisis
in Kosovo*, p. 451.

19 'Security Council Provisional Record, 3988th Meeting, 24 March 1999,
5.35 p.m. (NY time), Extract', in Weller, *The Crisis in Kosovo*, pp.
499–500.

20 The Communist leader, Gennady Zyuganov, had called for this on the day
after air operations were launched. *Sovetskaya Rossia* (27 March 1999).
CDPSP, 51:12 (1999), 5.

21 D. Lynch, '"Walking the Tightrope": The Kosovo conflict and Russia
in European security, 1998–August 1999', *European Security*, 8:4
(1999), 68.

22 E. Yesson, 'NATO and Russia in Kosovo', *RUSI Journal*, 144:4
(1999), 21.

23 M. Andersen, 'Russia and the former Yugoslavia', in M. Webber (ed.),
Russia and Europe: Conflict or Cooperation? (Basingstoke, Macmillan,
2000), p. 197.

24 *Vremya MN* (26 March 1999). *CDPSP*, 51:12 (1999), 3–4.

25 D. Hoffman, 'Attacks stir Cold War feelings in Russia', *Washington Post*
(4 April 1999).

26 M. Smith, *Russian Thinking on European Security after Kosovo*
(Camberley, Conflict Studies Research Centre, 1999), p. 6.

27 Lynch, '"Walking the Tightrope"', p. 70.

28 *Izvestia* (25 March 1999). *CDPSP*, 51:12 (1999), 9.

29 *Rossiiskaya Gazeta* (26 March 1999). *CDPSP*, 51:12 (1999), 3.

30 *Rossiiskaya Gazeta* (31 March 1999). *CDPSP*, 51:13 (1999), 2.

31 *Trud* (8 April 1999). *CDPSP*, 51:14 (1999), 5. See also B. Posen, 'The
war for Kosovo', *International Security*, 24:4 (2000), 67.

32 See C. Wallander, *Russian Views on Kosovo: Synopsis of May 6 Panel
Discussion* (PONARS Policy Memo 62). Website reference www.csis.org/
ruseura/ponars/policymemos/pm_0062.pdf.

33 V. Baranovsky, 'Russia's interests are too important', *International
Affairs* (Moscow), 45:3 (1999), 11.

34 *Nezavisimaya Gazeta* (15 April 1999). *CDPSP*, 51:15 (1999), 12.

35 *The Situation in and Around Kosovo* (*Press Release M-NAC-1(99)51*).
Website reference www.nato.int/docu/pr/1999/p99-051e.htm.

36 Daalder and O'Hanlon, *Winning Ugly*, pp. 165–6; Posen, 'The war for
Kosovo', p. 67.

37 *Kosovo Peace Plan*. Website reference www.basicint.org/peaceplan.htm.

38 *Statement on Kosovo (Press Release S-1(99)62)*. Website reference
www.nato.int/docu/pr/1999/p99-062e.htm.

39 Transcript of interview with Talbott in *Frontline: War in Europe*. Website
reference www.pbs.org/wgbh/pages/frontline/shows/kosovo/inter-
views/talbott.html.

40 See, *inter alia*, *Kommersant* (28 April 1999). *CDPSP*, 51:17 (1999), 7;
Segodnya (29 April 1999). *CDPSP*, 51:17 (1999), 9.

41 Yesson, 'NATO and Russia in Kosovo', p. 24.

42 Transcript of interview with Chernomyrdin in *Frontline: War in Europe*. Website reference www.pbs.org/wgbh/pages/frontline/shows/kosovo/interviews/chernomyrdin.html.
43 Talbott interview, *Frontline: War in Europe*. See also Daalder and O'Hanlon, *Winning Ugly*, p. 169.
44 Talbott interview, *Frontline: War in Europe*.
45 See, *inter alia*, Smith, *Russian Thinking on European Security after Kosovo*, pp. 7–9; *Izvestia* (7 May 1999). *CDPSP*, 51:18 (1999), 4.
46 As Dana Allin has suggested. See D. Allin, *NATO's Balkan Interventions (Adelphi Paper 347)* (London, International Institute for Strategic Studies, 2002), p. 64.
47 Statement by the Chairman on the Conclusion of the Meeting of the G8 Foreign Ministers on the Petersberg. Website reference www.g7.utoronto.ca/g7/foreign/fm990506.htm.
48 Lynch, '"Walking the Tightrope"', pp. 75–6.
49 For an assessment of the overall 'balance sheet' see Andersen, 'Russia and the former Yugoslavia', pp. 201–2.
50 *Resolution 1244 (1999)*. Website reference www.un.org/Docs/scres/1999/99sc1244.htm.
51 Daalder and O'Hanlon, *Winning Ugly*, pp. 172–3.
52 *Ibid.*, p. 118.
53 *Segodnya* (14 June 1999). *CDPSP*, 51:24 (1999), 1.
54 *Izvestia* (15 June 1999). *CDPSP*, 51:24 (1999), 3; *Slovo* (16–17 June 1999). *CDPSP*, 51:24 (1999), 5.
55 *The War in Kosovo and a Postwar Analysis* (Washington DC, Committee on Foreign Relations, United States Senate, September/October 1999), pp. 79–87.
56 Gen. W. Clark, *Waging Modern War* (Oxford, PublicAffairs, 2001), ch. 15.
57 *Ibid.*, p. 387.
58 *Vremya MN* (5 July 1999). *CDPSP*, 51:27 (1999), 8.
59 For the text of the agreement on Russian participation in KFOR see *Agreed Points on Russian Participation in KFOR*. Website reference www.nato.int/kfor/resources/documents/helsinki.htm.
60 *Russia and European security (Document A/1722)* (Paris, Assembly of the Western European Union, 2000). Website reference www.assembly-weu.org/en/documents/sessions_ordinaires/rpt/2000/1722.html. See also *Kommersant* (24 July 1999). *CDPSP*, 51:30 (1999), 19.
61 *Trud* (8 September 1999). *CDPSP*, 51:36 (1999), 20.
62 See, *inter alia*, Wallander, *Russian Views on Kosovo*.
63 *Kommersant* (24 July 1999). *CDPSP*, 51:30 (1999), 19.
64 Ivanov: *Nezavisimaya Gazeta* (12 October 1999). *CDPSP*, 51:41 (1999), 3; Primakov: E. MacAskill, 'NATO and Russia re-establish ties as tensions ease', *Guardian* (17 February 2000).
65 Joint Statement on the Occasion of the Visit of the Secretary General of NATO, Lord Robertson, in Moscow on 16 February 2000. Website reference www.nato.int/docu/pr/2000/p000216e.htm.
66 Quoted in 'NATO and Russia re-establish ties as tensions ease'.
67 *Segodnya* (17 February 2000). *CDPSP*, 52:7 (2000), 19.

68 See S. Croft *et al.*, 'NATO's triple challenge', *International Affairs*, 76:3 (2000), 499.

69 See, *inter alia*, *Izvestia* (7 March 2000). *CDPSP*, 52:10 (2000), 5; *Kommersant* (7 March 2000). *CDPSP*, 52:10 (2000), 5; 'The fist unclenched', *The Times* (6 March 2000).

70 Statement by Lord Robertson, NATO Secretary General, on Acting President Putin's Interview with the BBC (Press Release (2000)023). Website reference www.nato.int/docu/pr/2000/p00-023e.htm.

71 R. Boyes, 'Putin is impatient for Nato welcome', *The Times* (27 September 2001).

72 Quoted in C. Bremner, 'Russia and West to work more closely on security', *The Times* (4 October 2001).

73 *Kommersant* (28 September 2001). *CDPSP*, 53:39 (2001), 6–7.

74 See, *inter alia*, *Noviye Izvestia* (20 November 2001). *CDPSP*, 53:47 (2001), 20–1; M. Evans, 'Blair plans wider role for Russia with Nato', *The Times* (17 November 2001).

75 Press Conference with NATO Secretary General, Lord Robertson, 22 November 2001. Website reference www.nato.int/docu/speech/2001/s011122b.htm.

76 A New Quality in the NATO–Russia Relationship. Speech by NATO Secretary General, Lord Robertson at the Diplomatic Academy, 22 November 2001. Website reference www.nato.int/docu/speech/2001/s011122a.htm.

77 Press Conference with NATO Secretary General, Lord Robertson, 22 November 2001.

78 Authors' interviews with officials at NATO headquarters, November 2001.

79 *Press Communiqué M-NAC-2(2001)158*. Website reference www.nato.int/docu/pr/2001/p01-158e.htm.

80 *Izvestia* (12 January 2002). *CDPSP*, 54:2 (2002), 18.

81 *Vremya MN* (19 January 2002). *CDPSP*, 54:3 (2002), 3.

82 See M. Evans, 'Russian bid to "weaken" Nato alienates West', *The Times* (16 March 2002).

83 See K. Bosworth, 'The effect of 11th September on Russia–NATO relations'. Paper presented to the annual conference of the British Association for Slavonic and East European Studies, Cambridge, April 2002, pp. 12-13.

84 J. Dempsey, 'Nato woos Russia with offer of closer relations', *Financial Times* (25 February 2002). This article was subsequently criticised within NATO circles as being 'highly inaccurate'. See *A Summary of the Meetings at NATO and SHAPE of the Joint Monitoring Group on the NATO-Russia Founding Act*. NATO Parliamentary Assembly. Website reference www.nato-pa.int/publications/special/av076-jmg-rus.html.

85 *A Summary of the Meetings at NATO and SHAPE of the Joint Monitoring Group*.

86 M. Binyon, 'Russia "will stand by coalition even if Iraq is attacked"', *The Times* (15 March 2002).

87 'The new alliance', *The Times* (15 May 2002).

88 I. Traynor, 'Russia and Nato reach historic deal', *Guardian* (15 May 2002).

89 For differing views about what NATO members had agreed on this score see M. Evans, 'Russia to move into Nato HQ', *The Times* (15 May 2002) and J. Dempsey and R. Wolffe, 'In from the cold', *Financial Times* (15 May 2002).

90 NATO–Russia Relations: A New Quality. Declaration by Heads of State and Government of NATO Member States and the Russian Federation. Website reference www.nato.int/docu/basictxt/b020528e.htm.

91 R. Owen and M. Evans, 'Nato and Russia sign deal to end 50 years of fear', *The Times* (29 May 2002).

92 *Founding Act on Mutual Relations, Cooperation and Security between NATO and the Russian Federation*. Website reference www.nato.int/docu/basictxt/fndact-a.htm.

93 See M. A. Smith and G. Timmins, *The EU, NATO and Russia since 1991* (London, Routledge, forthcoming), ch. 2.

94 Remarks by NATO Secretary General, Lord Robertson at the NATO-Russia Summit. Website reference www.nato.int/docu/speech/2002/s020528b.htm

95 'Follies in the forum', *Guardian* (29 May 2002).

96 'Reaching out to Vladimir', *The Economist* (25 May 2002), 54. See also 'Meeting as friends', *The Times* (24 May 2002) and T. Hames, 'Bush can take comfort from friends in unlikely places', *The Times* (30 May 2002).

97 L. Freedman, 'The new great power politics', in A. Arbatov *et al.* (eds), *Russia and the West: The 21st Century Security Environment* (London, M. E. Sharpe, 1999), p. 34.

98 Daalder and O'Hanlon, *Winning Ugly*, p. 198.

Chapter 5

The EU's military dimension: a child of the Kosovo crisis?

One of the most frequently cited 'lessons' of the Kosovo crisis has been the alleged extent to which it spurred West European leaders to address a perceived need for Europe to do more for its own military security. Member states of the European Union decided to establish a 'European Security and Defence Policy' (ESDP) in the months following *Operation Allied Force*. Daalder and O'Hanlon have written that 'the growing consensus on the need for a European defense capability is a direct consequence of the Kosovo crisis'.[1] Others have argued in similar vein.[2]

The discussions in this chapter will critically examine this view. They will consider the long- and short-term origins of the ESDP and assess the extent to which the Kosovo crisis was the key driver leading to the decisions by EU members formally to create it in 1999.

The long-term evolution of the ESDP

The Cold War years

The most basic of what may be called the 'permissive facilitators' for the development of the ESDP can be found in the nature of the European Union itself. The idea encapsulated in the concept of 'functional integration' (sometimes called the 'Monnet method') has exercised significant influence on political leaders in continental EU countries. The impact has been most especially important in France and the FRG because these two countries have traditionally acted as the main 'motor' driving forward the process of European integration.

Functional integration thinking suggests that the process of 'construct-ing Europe' is one of continuing forward movement based on the so-called 'spillover effect'. The completion of a major integrative endeavour in one sector opens the way to the launch of new efforts in others. The original Treaty of Rome in 1957 famously did not define an ultimate end-point for what was then called the European Economic Community (EEC). Rather, the stated overall objective was the construction of an open-ended 'ever closer union among the peoples of Europe'.[3]

The potential for developing a military dimension to the European integration process has been present since the formative decade of the 1950s. Indeed, in the early part of that decade, there was a serious plan to create an integrated military capability by the six states that were later to become founder members of the EEC.[4] This was the proposed 'European Defence Community' (EDC), first advanced by the French government in 1950. It collapsed in 1954 when the French National Assembly refused to ratify the treaty setting it up. The EDC proposal failed for a variety of reasons including political instability in France, fears about the consequences of German rearmament and American and British ambivalence.[5] Thereafter, attention amongst 'the Six' shifted to an alternative next step,[6] the development of a 'Common Market'. The Treaty of Rome initiated this in 1957. For the remainder of the Cold War era, European military integration, other than in NATO, remained off the agenda. The EEC developed a kind of insti-tutional aversion to military issues. As Walter Hallstein, the first President of the European Commission, noted, '[we] don't waste time talking about defence. In the first place we don't understand it. In the second place we'll all disagree'.[7] Yet the logic of functional integration ensured that the prospect of eventual military integration was never totally lost.

During the early 1980s an attempt was made to 'reactivate' the Western European Union (WEU). At that time the WEU was a group-ing of seven EEC members that had originally been established, as the Western Union, back in 1948 as a forum for co-operation in various areas, including military security. Although they had made a start on developing some collective military infrastructure during the early Cold War years, it is doubtful that any of its founding members[8] really believed that they could mount a credible joint defence effort against the Soviet Union by themselves. Rather, they wished to demonstrate a willingness to make an effort in order to lever the United States into a transatlantic military alliance. This effort proved successful with the

signing of the Washington Treaty in April 1949. Thereafter, the puta-
tive Western Union military infrastructure programmes were simply
taken over by NATO.

The revived WEU achieved little of consequence in an operational
capacity during the 1980s but it did perform one important political
role. It became a repository for keeping alive the dream of ultimately
adding a military dimension to the process of European integration. In
1987, WEU members issued a *Platform on European Security Interests*,
which opened with the statement that 'we are convinced that the
construction of an integrated Europe will remain incomplete as long as
it does not include security and defence'.[9] For as long as the Cold War
order remained in place, these words were not likely to produce any
kind of action. But change was coming.

After the Cold War: marking time with the WEU

From the early autumn of 1990, following the collapse of Communist
rule in Central Europe, the WEU began to assume a more significant
status in the plans of some important West European governments.
They saw in the strategic upheavals the opportunity to move ahead
with the development of a military dimension to the European
integration process. In September 1990, the first public proposal
was made. Italy's then foreign minister came forward with a suggestion
to prepare the WEU for rapid absorption by the then European
Community (EC).[10] This, if effected, would give EC members
a mutual security guarantee under Article V of the WEU's Brussels
Treaty. The EC would also acquire a ready-made collective defence
infrastructure – albeit an underdeveloped one – based upon the
WEU's political and military consultative committees.[11] The Italian
proposal was, subsequently, supported by France and the FRG in
December 1990.

As for the UK, then Foreign Secretary Douglas Hurd gave the first
public expression of the view of John Major's government in Berlin in
the same month. Hurd said that his government supported the case for
'a revitalised WEU', one which could 'bring a clear European view ...
to discussion within the [NATO] alliance'. He also held out the possibility of European military operations being conducted under the
auspices of the WEU; but only in situations when NATO did not or
could not act itself.[12] This was a significant qualification on the extent
to which the UK was prepared to see things develop, and there was

nothing in Hurd's remarks to suggest that the UK favoured trans-
planting the WEU into the EC. Yet the British had crossed a Rubicon
of sorts. As Ken Booth and Nicholas Wheeler have noted, all WEU
member governments by the end of 1990[13] 'accepted that NATO
[would] have to be 'Europeanised' to some degree'.[14]

In the autumn of 1991 the Italians and British agreed upon a
compromise proposal. This envisaged that the WEU would be established as a kind of 'bridge' between a new European Union and
NATO, whilst retaining its own institutional identity. In this way,
according to the Anglo-Italian *Declaration on European Security and
Defence* issued in October, the WEU could act as 'the defence component of the [European] Union and as the means to strengthen the
European pillar of the [NATO] Alliance'.[15]

The compromise that was most evident in this joint statement was
the Italian one. The Italians had abandoned their previous position
supporting the direct development of an EU military component.
Instead, under the bridge formula, the EU would need to request
an autonomous institution to undertake military operations on its
behalf. But the UK had also made important concessions. As suggested
by Booth and Wheeler, the Major government had, in effect, conceded
that an effective NATO monopoly of European military affairs was
no longer tenable now that the Cold War was over. The British
accepted in principle that the EU could develop a defence component,
albeit indirectly.

Despite the rhetorical posturing of the time, no other member
government was *really* prepared to develop a direct EU military
component. The Anglo-Italian bridge formula was accepted virtually
word-for-word as the basis of the agreements on defence matters
reached at the Maastricht summit in December 1991. Overall, the
contents of the *Treaty on European Union* (TEU) were a severe
disappointment to those who did favour quick or decisive progress
on the military front. A declaratory breakthrough was contained in
Title V Article J.4, where it was stated that, for the first time, the
new Union's 'common foreign and security policy shall include all
questions relating to the security of the Union'. Previously, under the
terms of the Single European Act of 1987, only the political and
economic dimensions of security had been included, with the military
element deliberately left out. Yet Article J.4 was vague in the extreme,
noting only an aspiration towards 'the *eventual* framing of a common
defence policy, which *might in time* lead to a common defence'
[emphases added].[16]

Nevertheless, after the TEU was signed, moves were quickly set in hand to develop the operational capacity of the Western European Union. It was decided to establish a military planning cell at its head-quarters, which was to move from London to Brussels at the beginning of 1993. WEU member states also decided at their meeting in the FRG in June 1992 on potential operational tasks for the organisation. These were in the areas of humanitarian assistance, peacekeeping and 'tasks of combat forces in crisis management'.[17] Furthermore, the WEU was quickly tasked with taking on a real operation, in South East Europe.

In retrospect, the July 1992 decisions to dispatch separate NATO and WEU naval flotillas to the Adriatic, to monitor compliance with UN sanctions against the combatants in the Bosnian civil war, represented the beginning of an ultimately terminal decline in the WEU's reputation. The WEU deployment was a premature attempt, apparently instigated by the Italian government, to demonstrate that there was substance behind the 'Petersberg Tasks' which had been agreed the previous month. Whereas the NATO operation could rely on its established multinational command structures and standing naval forces, the WEU one was an improvised affair which, although under the 'political direction' of the WEU's Ministerial Council, in practice relied on Italian command and control structures. Far from confirming its utility, this only served to demonstrate the WEU's relative *lack* of operational capacity. Moreover, the deployment of two flotillas to do the same job attracted unfavourable media attention suggesting that western governments were more interested in arcane institutional competition rather than in making a serious effort to deal with the developing Bosnian crisis.[18]

In 1993 it was decided to fuse the two operations under NATO command. Although in theory they would now come under the political direction of both the NAC and the WEU Ministerial Council, in practice it would be NATO that from now on would call the tune. The 1993 decision was prompted by considerations of operational efficiency and, specifically, by the changing nature of relations between France and NATO. This mattered because hitherto the French govern-ment under President François Mitterrand had been widely regarded as the most determined to see the WEU develop real operational capa-bilities and roles; to the detriment, some suspected, of NATO itself. A developing France-NATO *rapprochement*, begun under Mitterrand but especially evident from 1995 under his successor Jacques Chirac, thus had the consequence of helping to ensure that momentum was lost in the operational development of the WEU.[19]

This is not to say that the WEU was simply left to wither and die. However, it was striking that the success or otherwise of efforts to empower it would rest substantially in the gift of NATO, and especially the United States. The first attempt was announced at the NATO summit in Brussels in January 1994. Here member states agreed to create 'Combined Joint Task Forces' (CJTF) with the stated purpose, amongst others, of providing for 'separable but not separate military capabilities that could be employed by NATO or the WEU'.[20] The CJTF agreement represented in effect a tacit acceptance by WEU member states (who were also all members of NATO) that further attempts to conduct operations separately from, or even in competition with, NATO were ruled out. If the Brussels agreement were implemented, future WEU operations would take place on the basis of resources and assets provided by NATO.

The adoption of the CJTF concept thus represented a trimming of sails on the part of WEU member states. Reduced ambitions were also evident in their refusal seriously to consider further significant operational commitments. In December 1992, the WEU's then Secretary-General, Willem van Eekelen, suggested possible ground-force deployments in Bosnia.[21] His suggestion was ignored. Two years later it was the turn of the French to be rebuffed when they reportedly urged their WEU partners to intervene militarily in Rwanda.[22] WEU member states were also castigated by the institution's own Parliamentary Assembly, which published a report stating that:

> The theoretical framework exists, but apparently the political will among the changing coalitions of member states to implement a policy to which everybody has agreed is still lacking. The reluctance to act, which is particularly manifest in the time-consuming beating around the bush and procedural battles in the Council, is tarnishing the image of the organisation. This is especially exasperating when it concerns limited operations such as [in the Bosnian town of] Mostar where swift action would be possible with a coalition of the willing.

Member state behaviour was, in short, according to this report, characterised by 'shuffling, reluctance, and hesitant, slow actions'.[23]

Another attempt was made to sort things out at a NAC meeting in Berlin in June 1996. The Berlin meeting implicitly acknowledged that the CJTF concept had failed to get off the ground. The Berlin statements were thus effectively a reaffirmation, in beefed-up language, of what had already supposedly been agreed. NATO ministers pledged concrete support for the 'development of the European Security and

Defence Identity within the Alliance'. They also stated that 'this identity will be grounded on sound military principles and supported by
appropriate military planning' which would 'permit the creation of
militarily coherent and effective forces capable of operating under the
political control and strategic direction of the WEU'. Furthermore, the
ministers promised that they would 'prepare, with the involvement of
NATO and the WEU, for WEU-led operations'. There could be a
double-hatting of officers within NATO command structures in order
that they could quickly take command of WEU-led operations if
required. Finally, NATO members pledged to undertake 'at the
request of and in coordination with the WEU, military planning and
exercises for illustrative WEU missions identified by the WEU'.[24]

These agreements seemed to hold out the prospect of a solid institutional relationship being developed between the WEU and NATO;
one in which the two institutions could function in future division-of-
labour operations as two distinct and equal partners. Press coverage of
the Berlin meeting was mostly positive. Many reports used phrases
such as 'a turning point for NATO' in suggesting that the decisions in
some way significantly reduced the role and power of the United States
within the institution and concurrently increased the scope and potential for Europe-only military operations.[25]

Once the dust had settled, however, an equally striking consensus
formed amongst academic analysts and observers that Berlin did *not*
represent the great 'rebalancing' of US–West European relations that
many had at first assumed. Paul Cornish, Philip Gordon and John
Ruggie all examined the Berlin decisions and their likely impact on
both NATO and the WEU; and all came to the same basic conclusion.
By providing for the evolution of a European Security and Defence
Identity *within* NATO, dependent upon NATO member states agreeing to 'loan' operational assets to the WEU and release double-hatted
personnel, the Berlin decisions guaranteed a *de facto* US veto over
future WEU-led military operations. More generally, they made it
'most unlikely that a serious rival to NATO could now develop' as
Cornish put it.[26]

A number of French leaders, including Laurent Fabius, Paul
Quiles and Gabriel Robin, were (or claim to have been) aware all along
that the Berlin decisions were less radical than they at first appeared.[27]
However, the Chirac government was prepared to give the US a
chance to prove its good faith, although it was disappointed when it
became clear that the Berlin decisions might not be all that they had
seemed. Although the sense of let-down did not lead the French to

terminate any of the various elements of their 1995–96 *rapprochement* with NATO, it certainly helped to slow down development of the CJTF concept.[28]

The new push forward, 1998–99

The discussions in the first section here have shown that the idea of a military dimension to the overall process of European integration had never completely died since the failure of the EDC project in 1954. On the other hand, nor had a *decisive* push towards creating one yet been successfully made. Developments in the years 1998 and 1999 were to take matters further than they had ever been taken before in this respect. This time-period, of course, coincided with the Kosovo crisis coming to the boil and the US-led NATO response.

This proximity of timing has, in itself, been sufficient to convince some observers that the crisis must, therefore, have been solely, or at least largely, responsible for the new push towards the ESDP. In order to test and explore this assessment, the discussions in this section focus upon the two EU member states that have been the main movers behind the process. They are the United Kingdom and France. In each case the relative importance of the Kosovo crisis in shaping their attitudes and policy will be determined, *vis-à-vis* other potential causal factors.

The United Kingdom

The most significant catalyst for the new push forward was the change in British policy. This was not immediately apparent after the Blair government took office in May 1997. Initial statements suggested continuity from the previous Conservative administration. One of Tony Blair's first tasks following his election was to attend the EU's Amsterdam summit in June 1997. The resulting Treaty of Amsterdam effectively reaffirmed, using slightly different language, the existing understandings on military issues dating back to the 1991 TEU, including the British-inspired bridge role for the WEU.[29] British leaders made it quite clear at that time that they were strongly opposed to any change in the *status quo*. On his return from Amsterdam, Blair told the House of Commons that 'getting Europe's voice heard more clearly in the world will not be achieved through merging the

European Union and the Western European Union or developing an unrealistic common defence policy. We therefore resisted unacceptable proposals from others'. Then Defence Secretary George Robertson was subsequently quoted as saying that it would be a 'Trojan horse in NATO to give the EU a role'. As late as May 1998, Robin Cook stated that 'we do not see the European Union becoming a defence organisation ... we will be working for better co-operation between the EU and the WEU but not for merger between them'.[30]

The Prime Minister first revealed a willingness to change this line at an 'informal' EU summit meeting in Pörtschach, Austria in October 1998. Blair did not unveil a fully formed proposal here. Rather, he signalled a willingness to drop the inflexible opposition to reconsidering the role of the WEU and its relationship with the EU that had characterised British policy since Maastricht. 'I simply want to start the debate,' he said in a press conference after the meeting.[31]

Perhaps the most popular interpretation of Blair's motives for signalling a change in British policy has been that he was seeking to *assert British leadership with regard to EU military affairs in order to compensate for non-participation in the single currency project*. Support for this view can be adduced from the timing. The Pörtschach meeting took place just over two months before the EU's single currency was due to be officially launched on 1 January 1999. Minds in London were bound to be concentrated on the potential fall-out from the UK's non-participation in the project of the moment. Taking a lead in revisiting military questions would, on this argument, make sense for the UK, as military matters were things which it was widely regarded as being 'good at' by its European partners. Blair hinted that a compensation strategy was in his mind. At his Pörtschach press conference he stated that 'we need to allow fresh thinking in this *and it is important for Britain to be part of that thinking and not for us simply to stand there and say we are not*' [emphasis added].[32]

Such a compensation strategy had not seemed necessary before about the middle of 1998. The British had assumed that, despite their refusal to join the single currency at the beginning, they would not lose influence within the EU. This was reflected in the Blair government's expectation that the UK would be a full participant in the institutional structures overseeing the new currency. In the spring of 1998, however, after a sometimes acrimonious debate, the UK had to agree that the key forum for managing the currency on a day-to-day basis – the so-called 'Euro-11' group – would only permit non-participants to attend as observers.

Having been rebuffed in this area, the British government set about, as a matter of some urgency, trying to find a means to shore up its position within the EU and, indeed, provide a foundation for Blair's stated desire to 'lead in Europe'. The timeframe was tight, with 1 January 1999 as an immutable deadline. This may help to explain the impression that the UK was making policy 'on the hoof' for a time during the second half of 1998.[33] There had simply not been time, prior to Pörtschach, to work up a more concrete or detailed policy in an area that would require significant change in the traditional British position.

More flesh was put on the bones six weeks later at an Anglo-French summit in St Malo. Blair and Chirac agreed that:

> The European Union needs to be in a position to play its full role on the international stage ... To this end, the Union must have the capacity for autonomous action, backed up by credible military forces, the means to decide to use them, and a readiness to do so, in order to respond to international crises ... In order for the European Union to take decisions and approve military action where the [NATO] Alliance as a whole is not engaged, the Union must be given appropriate structures and a capacity for analysis of situations, sources of intelligence, and a capability for relevant strategic planning, without unnecessary duplication, taking account of the existing assets of the WEU and the evolution of its relations with the EU. In this regard, the European Union will also need to have recourse to suitable military means (European capabilities pre-designated within NATO's European pillar or national or multinational European means outside the NATO framework).[34]

This agreement codified and confirmed the nature and extent of the shift in the British position. For the first time, the UK was agreeing to the EU developing its own military dimension, based on concrete planning structures, and to member states assigning armed forces for potential EU military operations. The fact that Blair had chosen to advance matters in partnership with the French was significant and points to a second element in his overall European leadership agenda; *a desire to establish the UK as co-equal with the traditional Franco-German motor within the EU*. Blair had identified a window of opportunity. Not only did the UK have the opportunity to initiate a new proposal, but to do so in collaboration with one of the parties in the traditional EU motor.

President Chirac had provided a *de facto* opening in August 1998. In an address to French ambassadors in Paris, Chirac reiterated that:

> For France, [the WEU] is destined to become the European Union's defence agency, progressively integrated into its institutions, while, of course, retaining its links with NATO. In this context, we shall have to see whether we need to establish, when the time comes, a Council of EU Defence Ministers to affirm our solidarity in this sphere.[35]

In 1998 the WEU's Brussels Treaty in effect reached its expiry date (Article XII stipulated that it was to remain in force for fifty years).[36] That year was, therefore, an opportune time to consider once again the future of the WEU and, indeed, whether it should have one as a distinct institution. Chirac's response was to try to revive interest in the incorporation of the WEU into the European Union. In 1990–91, this idea had been set aside chiefly because of British opposition. In 1998, on the other hand, the French revived the notion at precisely the time that the Blair government was looking for a 'big idea' for a potential compensation strategy.

The fact that its treaty ran out in 1998 also drew attention to the extent to which the *WEU had seemingly outlived its usefulness*. It had not developed any significant operational capabilities during the 1990s, following the adoption of the 'bridge' formula in Maastricht. Undoubtedly, the major portion of blame for this failure belongs to the member states. They had not displayed the necessary collective political will to, for example, deploy ground forces in Bosnia, intervene to halt the genocide in Rwanda or deal with the collapse of order in Albania during the spring of 1997. The reluctance to seriously consider a WEU intervention in this last instance was seen as being a particular blow to the institution's credibility.[37]

The complicated triangular relationship into which the WEU had been bound with the EU and NATO at Maastricht was largely a consequence of British initiative, as noted. Thus, the WEU's perceived lack of utility in places like Bosnia and Albania was an especial embarrassment to the British government and further evidence that the UK was a reluctant, indeed obstructive, European. It could be argued that the UK had deliberately engineered, at Maastricht, the creation of arrangements that it knew all along would prove to be unworkable in practice.

British disenchantment with, and sense of embarrassment about, the WEU was a supporting consideration in inducing the Blair government to become more flexible about its future. At an informal meeting of EU defence ministers in November 1998, Robertson publicly referred to the existing NATO-WEU-EU triangle as 'cumbersome'[38] Later, Richard Hatfield, Policy Director at the Ministry of Defence, told the House of Commons Select Committee on Defence that:

> A major part-impetus for [the] developing [British] policy came from the Ministry of Defence because the purely practical arrangements that had been developed did not give us a great deal of confidence. You had a system where the EU, as one political organisation, although a very important one, was going to, if it got into crisis management ... avail itself of another organisation, the WEU, which had a very limited military infrastructure and capability, which, in turn, would turn to a third organisation, which we all think is a very good organisation – NATO. Essentially, the Ministry of Defence started to think about this, and our view was we ought to try and simplify this into a pragmatic arrangement and get a proper relationship between the two big players. That played into a wider debate that was going on inside government and that, in brief, led to the start of the process we have got now.[39]

In alluding to the 'wider debate that was going on inside government', Hatfield's testimony suggested that the Ministry of Defence had acted opportunistically in seizing a political moment (created by Blair's search for a compensation strategy) to simplify a cumbersome and impractical institutional arrangement. The Defence Committee was somewhat sceptical of this assertion however. It noted that 'Mr Hatfield's attempt to pass off the latest European defence initiative as a purely practical response to some institutional problems seems a (perhaps deliberate) understatement of its significance. No choices about the future of the [NATO] Alliance are made on pragmatic grounds alone'.[40] The scepticism seems justified. There can be little doubt that the principal underlying reasons for the British policy shift were political rather than pragmatic.

The role of the Kosovo crisis

A number of academic analysts have argued that a further significant source of pressure for change in British policy came from the Prime Minister's alleged dismay at the European Union's impotence in the face of the emerging crisis in Kosovo. This, they note, had begun to move up the agenda during the British Presidency of the EU between January and June 1998.[41]

During the UK Presidency, EU members, acting through their Common Foreign and Security Policy (CFSP) mechanism, issued three statements and agreed on two 'Common Positions' with regard to

Kosovo. The purpose of this activity was clear: 'to put pressure on Belgrade to find a peaceful settlement to the Kosovo problem'. This objective was declared in March 1998, when the EU adopted a Common Position imposing a range of military and economic sanctions on the Milosevic government.[42] Yet this activity did little other than point up the EU's impotence in situations where economic and political pressure was insufficient to change the behaviour of recalcitrant leaders.

Three months later, another CFSP statement conceded that, far from diminishing following the imposition of EU sanctions, Serb activities in Kosovo had reached 'a new level of aggression'. To all intents and purposes EU member states conceded their own inability to do anything further to stop this aggression. They stated that 'the EU encourages international security organisations to pursue their efforts ... and to consider all options, including those which would require an authorization by the UNSC under Chapter VII'. In effect, the EU was inviting NATO to sort things out, by force if necessary.[43]

One should not underestimate the motivational effects that a blow to the pride, prestige and credibility of leaders on the international stage can have. Alexander Vershbow, the US Ambassador to NATO, subsequently attributed Blair's policy shift mainly to what he called the 'Holbrooke effect':

> The Kosovo experience, and the Bosnia experience before that, drove home the harsh reality that, at the present time, only the United States has the ability to marry military power to diplomacy as a means of managing – and resolving – crises. Diplomacy backed by force was the secret to Dick Holbrooke's success.

Vershbow added that 'the lesson for the EU was clear: without more military muscle to back it up, the EU's Common Foreign and Security Policy could never duplicate the Holbrooke effect'.[44]

Without using the term itself, senior government ministers in the UK articulated a desire to see the EU develop the means to bring its own version of the Holbrooke effect into play; with the UK naturally playing a leading role. This was clearly expressed by Blair in what was probably the most significant European speech of his first premiership; delivered in Warsaw in October 2000. Having asserted that 'for Britain ... being at the centre of influencing Europe is an indispensable part of influence, strength and power in the world', Blair described the kind of Europe that he had in mind:

In a world with the power of the USA; with new alliances to be made with the neighbours of Europe like Russia; developing nations with vast populations like India and China; Japan, not just an economic power but a country that will rightly increase its political might too; with the world increasingly forming powerful regional blocks ... Europe's citizens need Europe to be strong and united. They need it to be a power in the world. Whatever its origin, *Europe today is no longer just about peace. It is about projecting collective power* [emphasis added].

The Prime Minister went on to offer a sound-bite summary of his core message; 'such a Europe can, in its economic and political strength, be a superpower; a superpower, but not a superstate'.[45]

In summarising the motivations of the British government – the key player in making possible the decisions to finally develop an ESDP during 1998–99[46] – it can be stated that *influence* and *leadership* were the predominant considerations. This applied in the sense of both British leadership within the European Union, and EU influence in the international arena. Most immediately and particularly, however, the Blair government was concerned to ensure that self-exclusion from the Euro did not lead to a diminution in the UK's status and influence within the EU.

The emerging Kosovo crisis provided the backdrop, during 1998, for the reformulation of British policy. It undoubtedly helped to focus attention and concentrate minds in London. It is unlikely, however, that it was the *decisive* factor for the UK. Given the other, political, pressures on the Blair government it is highly likely that the Pörtschach/St Malo initiatives would have been developed anyway.

France

Earlier discussions in this chapter have noted the development of a *rapprochement* between France and NATO under the Chirac Presidency from 1995. This was premised on substantial reforms of NATO's structures and procedures – most especially on the military side. These were not, in French eyes, sufficiently realised in the period following the NATO Berlin meeting in 1996. As a result, the *rapprochement* petered out short of full French reintegration into the NATO military structures from which President Charles de Gaulle had withdrawn in the 1960s.

The issue of 'Europeanisation' in military affairs was very much in play for the French before the Kosovo crisis. Attention during the period 1995–97 was focused on developing a significant European Security and Defence Identity *within NATO* rather than a military arm for the EU. What changed the focus for France were not any perceived lessons of the Kosovo crisis. Rather, there existed a sense of disappointment, and indeed betrayal, caused by the failure of NATO and the United States, as French leaders saw it, to proceed in the spirit of the Berlin decisions.

Supplementing this, the year 1998 was significant in that, as noted above, the WEU's Brussels Treaty expired. This provided a natural opportunity for reflections on its future and President Chirac had attempted to reopen an old debate in his remarks to the French ambassadors in the summer, where he proposed that the WEU be absorbed into the European Union. Thus, as Chirac stated in June 1999, 'as far as the discussion on the need for a European defence dimension is concerned, it had begun well before the Kosovo crisis'.[47]

This had also been partly due to the influence of the functional integration view on official French thinking. It has long been reflected in official thinking in France to a significantly greater extent than in the UK, with the result that French statements can sound somewhat discordant, or dreamy, to Anglo-Saxon ears. President Chirac provided a good example when addressing the NAC in June 2001. He stated that 'the progress of European defence is irreversible since it is part and parcel of the general and far-reaching process of building Europe. The advent of a European Union, occupying its full place on the international scene, is ordained by history'.[48]

The impending launch of the Euro at the beginning of 1999 produced a key convergence of views between France and the UK. Their two governments were, to be sure, approaching this event from different angles. For the French the Euro's launch created opportunities to consider what the next steps in the 'process of building Europe' should be. For the British, as discussed above, the emphasis was much more on developing a compensation strategy. The convergence found tangible expression at the December 1998 St Malo summit.

The role of the Kosovo crisis

Although the Kosovo crisis was not, therefore, decisive – or even very important – in reviving their interest in what French leaders liked to call 'Defence Europe', it did provide highly useful ammunition against those who argued that France envisaged this developing in opposition to, or with a view to weakening, NATO. Since 1998 there has been a distinct exemplary dimension to the French approach. In other words, French leaders have consistently and deliberately sought to allay fears and suspicions, in the US and elsewhere, that they are motivated at bottom by an anti-NATO agenda. They have endeavoured to do this not by words alone but by deeds also; and the Kosovo crisis provided important opportunities in this respect.

In an address in Paris in November 1999, then Defence Minister Alain Richard referred to this approach. He spoke of:

> The change in France ... which has put to rest the myth that France was seeking to promote Defence Europe in order to weaken NATO. The way we took on our political and military responsibilities, within the Alliance, during the crises in the Balkans, particularly our command of the Extraction Force in November 1998, is obviously contributing to this change in attitude.[49]

On initial deployment XFOR consisted of troops from France, the UK, the FRG and Italy. The US was only minimally involved and contributed no front-line forces.[50] France had volunteered to be the 'framework nation' for XFOR. This meant that, in exchange for contributing the single largest contingent of troops, the French would command the force in the field. Overall command, however, was vested in SACEUR. Thus, the French had undertaken the lead role in an operational deployment *within the NATO integrated command structures.*

It was not the first time that this had happened since de Gaulle's era, as French forces had been operating under NATO command in Bosnia since 1992. However, the pivotal French role in XFOR was clearly intended to send an important political message, as Richard's subsequent remarks indicated. The signal was twofold. First, the French role in XFOR reinforced the point made in Bosnia that France was prepared to contribute fully to NATO-led operations, even without becoming fully re-integrated into NATO's military structures. In doing so, the French could claim to be acting in good faith within NATO.[51] Second, XFOR was intended to demonstrate that Europeans could manage a significant military mission themselves, with the US sitting 'on the horizon', as Javier Solana put it.[52]

The French government's political signals did have at least a partially positive impact on its most important target audience – the US. In a widely cited press article published in December 1998 – which was in effect the Clinton administration's public response to

the St Malo summit decisions – Madeleine Albright noted with
approval that:

> The Kosovo crisis shows how practical European defence capabilities can
> help fulfil NATO missions. Thanks to the initiative of the French and the
> contributions of the Germans, British, Italians and other allies, NATO is
> deploying an all-European 'extraction force' for the monitors of the
> Organisation for Security and Co-operation in Europe who are being sent
> to the troubled province. This force is under NATO command, and is
> based on solid European capabilities. It shows how European forces can
> work within NATO to great effect in the real world.[53]

Given the tenor of these comments it can fairly be argued that the
deployment of XFOR did play a role in persuading the Clinton administration to offer conditional support,[54] rather than outright opposition
or hostility, to the St Malo agreements.

Matters did not end with the deployment of XFOR. Apart from
the US, France made the most significant contribution to *Operation
Allied Force* in 1999. Again, there was an exemplary dimension to this
and French leaders were eager to remind others – often in detail – of
the scale of their contribution. Richard spent some time detailing the
French contribution before an American audience in February 2000,
for instance:

> French participation in Allied Force was, as you know, quite significant.
> No other country, apart from the United States, was able to deploy so
> wide a range of Air Force, Navy and Army military means, notably in areas
> where few NATO members have any useful capacities, such as intelli-
> gence-gathering tools or Search and Rescue capabilities. France deployed
> 68 combat aircraft (7% of the coalition total), including 51 strike aircraft
> (8.8%). The total number of sorties of French aircraft put us second only
> to the United States, and makes our air contribution by and large the
> leading European one. In particular, French aircraft flew 16.6% of all close
> air support sorties, 13.8% of all reconnaissance sorties, 11.2% of all elec-
> tronic intelligence sorties. France was the only European country to
> deploy a conventional aircraft carrier in the theatre.[55]

Following the Kosovo settlement, the French government
suggested that the command element of the 'Eurocorps'[56] take charge
of KFOR. This was agreed by the NAC in December 1999 and the
Eurocorps commander took over on a six-month tour of duty in April
of the following year. Criticisms were made of both the nature and
extent of the Eurocorps' actual contribution in Kosovo. Some of these
seemed motivated more by crude anti-Europeanism than reasoned
analysis.[57] On the other hand, it was fairly pointed out that the

Eurocorps was only able to contribute some 350 officers to the total KFOR headquarters staff complement of 1,200 during its tour of duty; suggesting that its role was substantially symbolic. But the symbolism mattered. A report published by the NATO Parliamentary Assembly in the autumn of 2000 argued that 'the [deployment] decision marked an important stepping stone, demonstrating European readiness to take more responsibility in a crisis management operation. Indeed, it is the first time that a European multinational headquarters is deployed for a peacekeeping operation'.[58]

The French government concurred with this assessment and seemed happy that important facts on the ground had been established. In a speech to the WEU Parliamentary Assembly in May 2000, Chirac stated that:

> When, nearly a year ago, I first proposed that the general staff of the European Corps should take over the command of KFOR in Kosovo from NATO, the idea seemed presumptuous and even premature. Yet, this is what has come to pass, thanks to the determination of the five members of the European Corps and thanks to German-French co-operation. The European Corps is becoming a Rapid Reaction Corps and its general staff, headed by a Spanish officer, has provided exemplary command of KFOR for several weeks now.[59]

In summary it can be stated that the influence and impact of the Kosovo crisis on the evolution of the ESDP was somewhat more significant for the French government than for the British. It was certainly not a decisive factor in *initiating* French interest. That interest was, as we have seen, already long-established. The importance of the crisis lay, rather, in the opportunity that it afforded the French government to demonstrate that the development of an EU military component was a natural and non-threatening (to NATO and the transatlantic link) development. France attempted to demonstrate this by its own exemplary participation in the NATO-led operations occasioned by the Kosovo crisis and also by creating precedents for missions and operations undertaken with European countries in the lead and reduced or minimal reliance on the United States.

Conclusions

The *direct* impact of the Kosovo crisis on the evolution of the ESDP has been relatively limited. Attempts to develop it would almost certainly have been made anyway, given the agendas of the two pivotal

European governments whose policies and approaches have been discussed in this chapter.

Kosovo did, however, provide an important part of the 'atmospherics'; i.e. the backdrop against which moves towards creating the ESDP were set in train. The crisis undoubtedly did help to strengthen the hand of the ESDP's proponents. It drew attention to EU members' embarrassing lack of operational military capacity when compared to the United States. It also provided the French government with the opportunity to demonstrate that 'more Europe' did not have to mean 'less NATO'. This has helped to save the ESDP from becoming the target of resolute US hostility and opposition under either the Clinton or Bush administrations to date.

In September 2000, a report published by the WEU Institute for Security Studies warned against the consequences of 'the petering out of the 'Kosovo factor''. It added that 'as the memory of that episode begins to recede, it is unlikely that public and political opinion will be willing to go through the very real trauma of defence reform without a relatively clear understanding of what it is for and what it entails'.[60] Although it was not decisive in initiating moves towards the ESDP, receding memories of the crisis may yet contribute to its losing momentum or stalling as European leaders focus their interests and energies elsewhere in the absence of a perceived pressing security threat in their own backyard.

Notes

1 I. Daalder and M. O'Hanlon, 'Unlearning the lessons of Kosovo', *Foreign Policy*, 116 (1999), 138.

2 See, *inter alia*, 'Consequences of Kosovo', *The Economist* (6 February 1999), 20–1; E. Pond, 'Kosovo: catalyst for Europe', *Washington Quarterly*, 22:4 (1999), 77–92; M. V. Rasmussen, 'The Phantom Menace: the strategic objectives of the EU's Rapid Reaction Force'. Paper presented to the annual conference of the British International Studies Association, Bradford, December 2000.

3 *Consolidated Version of the Treaty Establishing the European Community*. Website reference http://europa.eu.int/eur-lex/en/treaties/dat/ec_cons_treaty_en/pdf.

4 France, the FRG, Italy, Belgium, the Netherlands and Luxembourg.

5 On the proposed EDC see, *inter alia*, 'Collective defence', *The Economist* (4 November 1950), 679–80; 'An army in embryo', *The Economist* (22 September 1951), 665–6; 'The Six Power Army', *The Economist* (22 December 1951), 1531–2; 'The Six Power Army', *The Economist* (5 January 1952), 2–4; 'The European Defence Community', *The World*

Today, VIII:6 (1952), 236-48; H. F. Armstrong, 'Postscript to EDC', *Foreign Affairs*, 33:1 (1954), 17–27.

6 The first step had been the creation of the European Coal and Steel Community in 1952.

7 Quoted in A. Sampson, *The New Europeans* (London, Hodder and Stoughton, 1968), p. 192.

8 The UK, France and the Benelux countries.

9 Text reprinted in *The Reactivation of WEU: Statements and Communiques 1984 to 1987* (London, WEU Secretariat, 1988), p. 37.

10 The EEC had become the European Community upon ratification of the Single European Act in 1987.

11 D. Usborne, 'Rome says EC should consider forming its own "army for defence"', *Independent* (19 September 1990).

12 *European Defence and Security in the 1990s* (London, Foreign and Commonwealth Office, 1990).

13 By then the FRG, Italy, Spain, Portugal and Greece had joined the five founder members.

14 K. Booth and N. Wheeler, 'Contending philosophies about security in Europe', in C. McInnes (ed.), *Security and Strategy in the New Europe* (London, Routledge, 1992), p. 28.

15 *Declaration on European Security and Defence* (London, Foreign and Commonwealth Office, 1991), p. 2.

16 *Treaty on European Union* Article J.4 . Website reference http://europa. eu.int/abc/obj/treaties/en/entr2f.htm#Article_J.4.

17 These were outlined in *The Petersberg Declaration*. Website reference www.weu.int/eng/comm/92-petersberg.htm.

18 See, *inter alia*, A. Savill, 'The games that statesmen play', *Independent* (8 July 1992); J. Dempsey, 'WEU armada "aimed at the wrong target"', *Financial Times* (11/12 July 1992); 'When Europeans unravel', *The Economist* (1 August 1992), 30.

19 There is an extensive literature on France-NATO relations during this period. See, *inter alia*, M. Blunden, 'France after the Cold War: inching closer to the Alliance', *Defense Analysis*, 9:3 (1993), 259–70; M. Meimeth, 'France gets closer to NATO', *The World Today*, 50:5 (1994), 84–6; A. Menon, 'From independence to cooperation: France, NATO and European security', *International Affairs*, 71:1 (1995), 19–34; C. Millon, 'France and the renewal of the Atlantic Alliance', *NATO Review*, 44:3 (1996), 13–16; B. Schmitt, 'France's Alliance policy in a changing world', *Aussenpolitik*, IV (1996), 348–58.

20 *Declaration of the Heads of State and Government*. Website reference www.nato.int/docu/comm/49-95/c940111a.htm.

21 R. Mauthner, 'WEU urged to intervene in Bosnia conflict', *Financial Times* (9 December 1992).

22 C. Masters, 'France calls for Europe to act over Rwanda', *Daily Telegraph* (18 June 1994).

23 *A European Defence Policy* (Paris, WEU Assembly, 1994), pp. 23–6.

24 *Press Communiqué M-NAC-1(96)63* (Brussels, NATO Press Service, 1996).

25 For a flavour of the press coverage in the UK see 'NATO acquires a European identity', *The Economist* (8 June 1996), 43; I. Karacs and M. Dejevsky, 'Shedding of US ties satisfies NATO members', *Independent* (4 June 1996); A. Gimson, 'Independent Euro role woos France back to NATO', *Daily Telegraph* (4 June 1996).

26 P. Cornish, 'European security: the end of architecture and the new NATO', *International Affairs*, 72:4 (1996), 751–69; P. Gordon, 'Does the WEU have a role?', *Washington Quarterly*, 20:1 (1997), 125–40; J. Ruggie, 'Consolidating the European pillar: the key to NATO's future', *Washington Quarterly*, 20:1 (1997), 109–24.

27 Fabius and Quiles: M. Rogers, 'Task force accord opens a new chapter for NATO', *Jane's Defence Weekly* (12 June 1996), 3. Robin: *Defining Moments: Alliance Developments 1996.* North Atlantic Assembly. Website reference www.naa.be/docu/1996/an244pc.html.

28 J. Lewis, 'France cools off on full NATO reintegration', *Jane's Defence Weekly* (9 July 1997), 3.

29 See *Consolidated Version of the Treaty on European Union.* Website reference http://europa.eu.int/eur-lex/en/treaties/dat/eu_cons_treaty_en.pdf.

30 Blair: *The Future of NATO: The Washington Summit. Report and Proceedings of the Committee with Minutes of Evidence and Appendices,* House of Commons Select Committee on Defence, Third Report, Session 1998-99, para. 63. Website reference http://parliament.the-stationery-office.co.uk/pa/cm199899/cmselect/cmdfence/39/3915.htm; Robertson: M. Prescott, 'British forces to bear EU stars insignia', *Sunday Times* (19 November 2000); Cook: T. Helm and C. Lockwood, 'EU may be given power over defence', *Daily Telegraph* (3 October 1998).

31 See the extracts from the transcript of the press conference, reprinted in M. Rutten, *From St-Malo to Nice: European Defence Core Documents (Chaillot Paper 47)* (Paris, WEU Institute for Security Studies, 2001), p. 2.

32 *Ibid.*, p. 2.

33 S. Sloan, *The United States and European Defence (Chaillot Paper 39)* (Paris, WEU Institute for Security Studies, 2000). Website reference www.weu.int/institute/index2.html.

34 Text reprinted in Rutten, *From St-Malo to Nice*, pp. 8–9.

35 Meeting of the French Ambassadors – Speech by M. Jacques Chirac, President of the Republic. Website reference www.ambafrance.org.uk/db.phtml?id=1590anda=1.

36 Text of the treaty reprinted in *Western European Union Brussels Treaty* (London, WEU Secretariat, 1969), p. 9.

37 See *Public Perception of WEU's Contribution to Stabilising Democracy in Albania.* WEU Assembly. Website reference www.weu.int/assembly/eng/reports/1650e.html.

38 T. Butcher, 'Britain leads call for EU defence shake-up', *Daily Telegraph* (5 November 1998).

39 *European Security and Defence*, House of Commons Select Committee on Defence, Eighth Report, Session 1999–2000, Minutes of Evidence

para.17. Website reference www.parliament.the-stationery-office.co.uk/
pa/cm199900/cmselect/cmdfence/264/0021602.htm.

40 *Ibid.*, Report para. 25.

41 See, *inter alia*, P. Gordon, 'Their own army?', *Foreign Affairs*, 79:4 (2000), 14 and R. Whitman, *Amsterdam's unfinished business? (Occasional Paper 7)* (Paris, WEU Institute for Security Studies, 1999), pp. 7–8.

42 *Federal Republic of Yugoslavia/Kosovo/Adoption of a common position (6892/98)* (Brussels, Council of the European Union, 1998).

43 *Kosovo: Intense fighting – Ethnic cleansing (9246/98)* (Brussels, Council of the European Union, 1998). The reference is to Chapter VII of the United Nations Charter. This deals with action that the international community can take with regard to threats to or breaches of international peace and security. In effect therefore, the EU statement was signalling that a military response to the Kosovo crisis should not be ruled out, whilst conceding the EU's own inability to organise one.

44 *US Ambassador to NATO on US, NATO, Europe Partnership* (London, Office of Public Affairs US Embassy, 2000), p. 3.

45 Europe's Political Future – speech by the Prime Minister, Tony Blair, to the Polish Stock Exchange, Warsaw, Friday 6 October 2000. Website reference www.fco.gov.uk/news/speechtext.asp?4913.

46 The decision by the EU as a whole to go ahead was taken at the Cologne summit in June 1999 and confirmed at the Helsinki summit six months later. In Helsinki EU members agreed on a 'headline goal' with four components: to develop an EU military capacity by 2003, capable of deploying up to a corps size force within sixty days and sustainable in the field for at least a year. See *Helsinki European Council 10 and 11 December 1999: Presidency Conclusions.* Website reference http://europa.eu.int/council/off/conclu/dec99/dec99_en.htm.

47 Kosovo – Joint press conference given by M. Jacques Chirac, President of the Republic, and M. Lionel Jospin, Prime Minister, following the Cologne European Council. Website reference www.ambafrance.org.uk/db.phtml?id=2861anda=1.

48 NATO – Special meeting of the North Atlantic Council – Speech by M. Jacques Chirac, President of the Republic. Website reference www.ambafrance.org.uk/db.phtml?id=5007.

49 European defence – Speech by M. Alain Richard, Minister of Defence, at the Institute of Higher National Defence Studies. Website reference www.ambafrance.org.uk/db.phtml?id=3455anda=1.

50 According to a subsequent report in the *Financial Times*, XFOR 'included only six Americans'. See D. Buchan, 'Forward march for Europe', *Financial Times* (25 November 1999).

51 On this see *The Future of NATO: The Washington Summit*, para. 72.

52 Quoted in G. Seigle, 'NATO's Kosovo rescue force set for deployment', *Jane's Defence Weekly* (2 December 1998), 4.

53 M. Albright, 'The right balance will secure NATO's future', *Financial Times* (7 December 1998).

54 The conditions being Albright's famous 'Three Ds': no decoupling from, duplication of, or discrimination within NATO.

55 French Defence, NATO and Europe – Introductory remarks by M. Alain Richard, Minister of Defence, at the CSIS. Website reference www.ambafrance.org.uk/db.phtml?id=3744anda=1.

56 The Eurocorps grew out of a Franco-German brigade established in 1987. Designated as being available for both NATO and WEU/EU tasking, five EU member states have assigned troops to the Eurocorps: France, the FRG, Spain, Belgium and Luxembourg. The UK has expressed interest in contributing to the corps' headquarters element. The KFOR assignment was the Eurocorps' first operational deployment.

57 P. Sherwell and C. Hart, 'Eurocorps: neither rapid, reactive nor a force', *Sunday Telegraph* (26 November 2000).

58 *Interim Report: Building European Defence – NATO's ESDI and the European Union's ESDP* (Brussels, NATO Parliamentary Assembly, 2000), para. 69.

59 Europe/Defence – Speech by M. Jacques Chirac, President of the Republic, to the Presidential Committee of the WEU Parliamentary Assembly and the Visiting Fellows from the IHEDN. Website reference www.ambafrance.org.uk/db.phtml?id=4048anda=1.

60 F. Heisbourg *et al.*, *European Defence: Making it Work (Chaillot Paper 42)*. WEU Institute for Security Studies. Website reference www.weu.int/institute/chaillot/chai42e.html.

Chapter 6

The evolution of the 'Atlantic Community'

Transatlantic relations have been a core issue in European – especially West European – security since the end of the Second World War. The first section of this chapter examines the nature of the transatlantic relationship and its Cold War evolution. Attention then moves, in the second section, to considering its development during the years since 1989. It will then be argued, in the third and final section, that the crises in Bosnia and Kosovo have played a key role in helping to refine and reshape the nature and basis of the relationship during the period since the Cold War ended.

Origins of the transatlantic relationship

The 'transatlantic relationship' was essentially a product of the Second World War. Prior to American involvement in that conflict – informally from 1940 and officially from December 1941 – the United States had, with one exception, chosen to remain aloof from European security affairs. The exception had been US involvement in the latter stages of the First World War. Even then, however, there was a distinct undercurrent of ambiguity about the American stance. US participation was as an 'associated power' rather than a full ally of France and Great Britain. In addition, as is well known, President Woodrow Wilson subsequently failed in his efforts to persuade the Senate to ratify US participation in the post-war League of Nations.

The introspective stance was by no means uncontroversial inside the US in the period between the two world wars. These years were characterised by a 'great debate' between so-called 'isolationists' on the one hand and 'internationalists' on the other. In addition this period, especially during the 1920s, saw the emergence of the US as the pivotal player in the world financial system and also as a leading global commercial power.[1] The extent of American influence was graphically demonstrated by the impact on European economies of the Wall Street Crash of 1929.

Thus, there was an important, if not necessarily politically close, relationship between the US and major European states even before the outbreak of the Second World War. However the label 'transatlantic relationship' was seldom used to describe it. This term denotes something more profound and positive than the usual economic and political intercourse between states in the international system. Two core elements characterised the emerging relationship from the 1940s. They were: close co-operation in the military arena, and the perception that a 'community of values' bound states in Western Europe together with the US.

The military co-operation was an obvious product of participation in the common struggle against Germany, Italy and Japan during the first half of the 1940s. There was, from the beginning, a sense that this co-operation was motivated by something more than simple military expediency. This was particularly apparent in relations between the US and the UK. Even before the formal entry of the US into the war, Prime Minister Winston Churchill had been working to maximise American support for the UK's war effort, in large part on the basis of an ideological appeal to President Franklin Roosevelt. This found its most tangible expression in the Atlantic Charter, which the two leaders signed in August 1941. To be sure, the main objective of the exercise for the British government had been to shore up practical American support for its war effort. Nevertheless, as the underlying basis of the Atlantic Charter there were declared to be 'certain common principles ... for a better future for the world'. Chief among those listed were opposition to territorial aggrandisement and 'the abandonment of the use of force'.[2]

Anglo-American co-operation was, therefore, being premised upon a concept of shared views about the nature of international relations and the ways in which countries should conduct themselves. The Atlantic Charter marked out relations between the US and UK as being qualitatively distinct from those which they held with other countries – even allied ones. In this context it is instructive to note that the Soviet Union, which was in the early desperate stages of its defence against Nazi aggression in August 1941, was not a party to the Charter and was mentioned only in passing in its preamble. Other 'free governments in exile' in London, such as the French and Poles, were not mentioned at all.

The Atlantic Charter represents the starting point of what was to become the distinctive transatlantic relationship.[3] In 1966 Harold van B. Cleveland rightly asserted that:

> The change [from traditional patterns of international relations] came in World War II when the Western democracies found themselves allied against a regime which sought not merely territorial aggrandizement or other national advantage, but rather the imposition on Europe of a totalitarian and imperialist new order. The idea of a Western community united not simply by a common military threat but by a common devotion to democratic freedoms was born of that struggle.[4]

Transatlantic relations during the Cold War

The onset of the Cold War had the effect of both extending and institutionalising the military-ideological relationship that had developed between the US and the UK since 1941. As Cleveland has argued, the ideological component 'was perfected and strengthened when the Nazi threat was replaced by that of Communist Russia, whose thrust was even more explicitly directed at the foundations of Western political and economic order'.[5] An extension and institutionalisation of the wartime relationship beyond its Anglo-American core was carried through via the negotiation and signing of the Washington Treaty in 1949 and the subsequent construction of the institution (NATO) which supported it.

Nine West European countries and one other North American one joined the Americans and British as founder members of NATO.[6] Most of these had been allied with the two core powers against the Axis in the Second World War. However it is noteworthy that the boundaries of NATO were deliberately set wider than this; bringing in Portugal, which had been neutral in the war, and more particularly Italy. The decision to admit a former Axis state was the subject of considerable debate. That it was made reflects the extent to which the ideological threat from Communism was keenly felt, especially in the United States, during the late 1940s. The concern was not so much about a direct Soviet attack on Italy, but rather the internal threat of a Communist take-over given that the local Communist Party was strong and enjoyed significant popular support.[7]

The notion of shared fundamental values was written into the
Washington Treaty. The preamble is clear on this score, stating that the
signatories 'are determined to safeguard the freedom, common
heritage and civilisation of their peoples, founded on the principles of
democracy, individual liberty and the rule of law'. Article 2 states that
signatories:

> will contribute toward the further development of peaceful and friendly
> international relations by strengthening their free institutions, by bringing
> about a better understanding of the principles upon which these institu-
> tions are founded, and by promoting conditions of stability and well-
> being. They will seek to eliminate conflict in their international economic
> policies and will encourage economic collaboration between any or all
> of them.[8]

The early years of NATO were dominated by concerns connected with
the need to organise an effective deterrence and defence effort against
the perceived threat of Soviet attack. Although present in the treaty,
'common values' thinking had only a limited operational impact.
NATO included countries where democracy was shaky (such as Italy or
France under the Fourth Republic) or even non-existent (such as
Portugal). This called into question the extent to which the alleged
'common heritage' of democracy really mattered, at least when set
against the pragmatic feeling that 'my enemy's enemy is my friend'.[9]

Discussions during the first half of the 1950s centred on the
proposed creation of the EDC and the concurrent issue of the potential rearmament of the FRG. At this time there was an expectation in
some influential quarters in the US, up to and including President
Eisenhower, that the successful creation of an EDC would facilitate an
American military withdrawal from Western Europe.[10] It was never
clear what, if any, real strength a continuing American *political*
commitment to the Washington Treaty would have had if this had, in
fact, come about.

The emerging 'Atlantic Community'

The idea that a perceptible 'Atlantic Community' was coming into
being, or else should be created, began to surface in the mid-1950s.
During the Cold War era it went through three formative phases in its
evolution. The first was apparent in 1955–56, the second during 1957
and the third from 1961–63.

In its first phase, the idea had two points of origin. First, the collapse of the EDC project in 1954 strongly suggested that a substantial US commitment to the defence of Western Europe would be necessary into the indefinite future. Second, following the death of Stalin in 1953, a slow but increasingly perceptible 'thaw' set into East–West relations. Great store was set by many in a meeting of the leaders of the US, UK, France and the Soviet Union 'at the summit' in Geneva in July 1955. Although the Geneva summit achieved no real breakthroughs, the 'spirit of Geneva' was, nevertheless, evoked for months and years afterwards to denote hopes and expectations of better times ahead in East–West relations.

By the mid-1950s some felt that a rethinking of NATO was required in order to safeguard its future against any charges that improving East–West relations made it less important or even unnecessary. Developing the idea that NATO was the institutional embodiment of a broad Atlantic Community seemed to be the best means of waylaying this negative possibility.

One of the first arguments along these lines appeared in *The Economist* in February 1955. Its editorial comments offered an early definition of what actually constituted the community:

> It is a group of countries that share certain ideas of what is important in western civilisation, and are prepared to organise themselves to see that these ideas survive. It is an organisation which, although based on the concept that Luxembourg and Iceland have as much right to be heard in its councils as the United States, has gone a long way towards recognising the economic and military facts of life. It is a partnership in which each country pulls its own weight and in which each carries the weight to which it is entitled.[11]

The Economist's editorial writers were clearly making the assumption that the Atlantic Community equated to the membership of NATO and that NATO was its organisational manifestation. NATO was not, therefore, simply a military alliance. It was more fundamentally, a sharing of enduring values amongst a group of western countries. This would exist *whether or not there was a Soviet threat.*

This did not mean that an operational Atlantic Community was already in being. Canadian Foreign Minister Lester Pearson argued shortly after the Geneva summit that:

> NATO cannot live on fear alone. It cannot become the source of a real Atlantic community if it remains organized to deal only with the military threat which first brought it into being. A renewed emphasis on the

nonmilitary side of NATO's development would also be the best answer
to the Soviet charge that it is an aggressive, exclusively military agency,
aimed against Moscow.[12]

Pearson's views are important because he was the NATO leader who,
more than any other at the time, concerned himself with the issue of
developing the community. He believed that the existence of shared
values in itself was not enough to keep NATO going at a time of apparently lessening military threat. What was needed was for member states
effectively to operationalise the community by engaging in regular and
extensive multilateral consultations across a range of issues.

A May 1956 NAC meeting affirmed the importance of developing
the institution's non-military side. US Secretary of State John Foster
Dulles suggested that the best way to make progress, and to satisfy
the reformists that something was being done, was to ask those
same reformists to produce a report setting out their views and
making recommendations for improvements. Pearson was given the
job of drafting, together with two colleagues – Gaetano Martino of
Italy and Halvard Lange of Norway. The media dubbed them the
'three wise men'.

The Suez crisis in the autumn of 1956 posed a serious political
threat to NATO. The French and British had deliberately kept their
allies completely in the dark about their preparations for military intervention in the Middle East. Once the interventions were launched
the Eisenhower administration took the view that, because the French
and British had disregarded any sense of political obligation to consult,
neither did it feel bound. As a result the US in effect threatened
economic warfare in order to force France and the UK to cease military operations and withdraw their forces from the Suez Canal zone.[13]

The fallout from the Suez crisis arguably helped save the wise
mens' report from being effectively filed and forgotten. Pearson and
his colleagues presented it to the NAC in December 1956. The main
thrust of the report was to entrench norms of consultation amongst
the member states so that, as a contemporary report in *The Economist*
put it, 'henceforth, a country's failure to consult becomes a sin of
commission, and not just of omission as in the past'. This account
correctly identified the paragraphs on enhanced political consultation
as being the report's most significant feature, adding that 'the NATO
treaty would not originally have been signed if these provisions had
been included'.[14]

Lester Pearson and his fellow wise men sought explicitly to establish a fully fledged consultative and behavioural regime amongst the

NATO membership. The basic principles were set out in paragraph 42 of their report:

> Consultation within an alliance means more than exchange of information, though that is necessary. It means more than letting the NATO Council know about national decisions that have already been taken; or trying to enlist support for those decisions. It means the discussion of problems collectively, in the early stages of policy formation, and before national positions become fixed. At best, this will result in collective decisions on matters of common interest affecting the Alliance. At the least, it will ensure that no action is taken by one member without a knowledge of the views of the others.[15]

All this was fine as far as it went. Consultation within NATO arguably did improve after 1956.[16] Yet the wider and more general broadening-out that Pearson had originally wanted did not happen.

The impact of Suez did, however, help to ensure that interest in the Atlantic Community concept was maintained. The second phase of interest – during 1957 – followed on directly. 1957 saw the publication of the first significant academic contribution to the debate. This was *Political Community and the North Atlantic Area* – the results of a study by a group of scholars working at Princeton University. The most important feature of this study was that it introduced the concept of 'security community' into the debate. This term was used to describe a situation where 'there is real assurance that the members of that community will not fight each other physically, but will settle their disputes in some other way'.[17]

Contrary to subsequent received wisdom, the Princeton scholars did *not* conclude that a security community already existed amongst NATO members as a whole. They argued that war *had* become inconceivable between certain countries (such as Canada and the US and the US and UK) but that there were still concerns about the FRG – at that time a NATO member of just three years' standing.[18] Rather, the authors suggested, the North Atlantic Area (which they defined as embracing not just the NATO members but also Cold War neutrals in Europe) was a less demanding 'political community' in 1957. This they defined as a 'social group with a process of political communication, some machinery for enforcement, and some popular habits of compliance', although 'a political community is not necessarily able to prevent war within the area it covers'.[19]

The Princeton study helped to make the concept of Atlantic Community respectable in serious academic and policy-making circles. Its publication dovetailed with an evident desire amongst NATO members, most especially the core Anglo-American partners, to ensure that efforts to patch up the serious breach in NATO cohesion opened by the Suez affair were consolidated and strengthened. To this end, a NATO summit meeting was proposed – the first such gathering in the institution's history. It took place in Paris in December 1957.

In Paris the term 'interdependence' was introduced into political discourse for the first time. NATO leaders declared that 'our Alliance … must organize its political and economic strength on the principle of interdependence'. They stated further that 'we have agreed to co-operate closely to enable us to carry the necessary burden of defence without sacrificing the individual liberties or the welfare of our peoples. We shall reach this goal only by recognizing our interdependence and by combining our efforts and skills in order to make better use of our resources'.[20] As used by the NATO leaders, therefore, the idea of inter-dependence appeared to denote a more sustained effort at defence burden sharing, with the elimination of wasteful duplicative and purely national efforts.

Some, however, argued that wider political equality should be part of the package as well. This was based on an instinctive feeling that terms such as 'community' and 'interdependence' denote relations based upon broad equality. In NATO, however, this was never the case. There was one clearly pre-eminent power amongst the member-ship and in military security terms Western Europe was a dependent on, rather than being genuinely interdependent with, the United States. This was reportedly the source of some discord at the Paris summit, with complaints from the French, among others.[21] In London *The Economist* was moved to declare, in commenting on the Paris summit, that 'till economic integration cements the European nations, including Britain, together, and enables them to talk to the Americans on a more equal level of achievement, the NATO "community" will remain an embryo'.[22]

Thus, for some the construction of the Atlantic Community remained an unfulfilled aspiration. It certainly continued to be so in the years immediately following the first NATO summit. This was mainly because western leaders had more pressing concerns to attend to; chiefly the protracted Berlin crisis which dominated the period 1958–61. Closer to home, the United States also had the fallout from the 1959 Cuban revolution to contend with. There was in conse-quence a lull in discussion about the development of the Atlantic Community until the early 1960s.

The topic returned to the agenda from 1961. This was mainly in consequence of the coming to power in the US of the Kennedy administration. A number of suggestions were put forward by serving or recently retired high officials for developing a stronger and more comprehensive Atlantic Community, based upon but not restricted to NATO.[23] But it was not until President Kennedy expressed his personal interest in the subject that decisive progress seemed possible. He did so most clearly in his famous Independence Day address in July 1962. This speech represented, in effect, the first official response of the United States to the process of European integration, which had been underway in the EEC since 1957–58.

Kennedy sounded positive. He declared that 'the United States looks on this vast new enterprise [i.e. European integration] with hope and admiration. We do not regard a strong and united Europe as a rival but as a partner'. He proceeded to offer EEC leaders an implicit deal: a greater say in transatlantic and NATO decision-making in return for more effective military burden sharing within NATO. He stated that 'we see in … Europe a partner with whom we can deal on a basis of full equality in all the great and burdensome tasks of building and defending a community of free nations'. Coming to the crux of his speech, the President asserted:

> I will say here and now, on this Day of Independence, that the United States will be ready for a Declaration of Interdependence, that we will be prepared to discuss with a united Europe the ways and means of forming a concrete Atlantic partnership, a mutually beneficial partnership between the new union now emerging in Europe and the old American Union founded here 175 years ago.[24]

In retrospect, this speech represented the high-water mark of official interest in the development of a more profound Atlantic Community during the Cold War years. It was never followed through; for a variety of reasons. Kennedy himself was, of course, removed from the scene less than eighteen months later. For its part the EEC, as noted in Chapter 5, stayed clear of defence and military issues in any guise right up until the end of the Cold War. Also, Kennedy's 1962 vision appeared predicated upon the development of 'federal institutions' for the EEC. Serious progress in this direction was blocked by President de Gaulle later in the 1960s. Some doubted whether the whole idea of what came to be called the 'dumbbell' view of the Atlantic Alliance, with a united Europe standing co-equal with the United States, could work productively in any event.[25]

For the remainder of the Cold War period, the notion of trying to build a viable Atlantic Community lost salience amongst leaders in NATO member states. To be sure, variations on the theme continued to surface in official NATO statements from time to time, but these appeared increasingly ritualistic.[26] In 1966, Cleveland argued that such a community as did exist was essentially 'defensive and reactive', a '[military] coalition and not a political community'.[27] By 1989 the concept seemed all but dead and buried.

The Atlantic Community since the Cold War

Since the Cold War ended, there have been those who have denigrated the idea that any underlying sense of community could continue to exist *sans* the Soviet threat. John Holmes, a former US diplomat, has echoed Cleveland's views of the 1960s in claiming that 'the [NATO] alliance has remained an alliance, a convenience rather than an emotional reality'.[28] Stephen Walt has argued, starting from a similar standpoint, that 'the high-water mark of transatlantic security cooperation is past'. He points to transatlantic disputes and disagreements in a number of areas during the 1990s. He also notes, in common with others, the apparently rising importance of Asia as a factor in US security, economic and commercial policies.[29] Christopher Layne, meanwhile, has baldly asserted that 'Atlantic Community' is 'a term that is a code phrase for overall American leadership' rather than anything more profound or genuinely multilateral.[30]

In assessing these views, it is helpful to distinguish between the idea of a *security community* as defined by the Princeton Study Group in 1957 and what Michael Brenner has more recently called a '*civic community*'. The main distinction between the two is that the latter is based more fundamentally and explicitly on shared norms and values whereas the former, as Brenner puts it, can reflect 'merely the calculated preference of states'.[31] The discussions here will now consider each in turn.

The Atlantic security community

For a security community to exist, war should, ideally, be both *structurally* and *conceptually* inconceivable. Countries within a security community should, therefore, first be incapable of mounting military operations against one another; the so-called 'structural incapacity to attack'. Second, their leaders should share an unwritten but general understanding that war would never be considered against other countries within the security community, however serious and protracted disputes with them may become.

The first benchmark, that of structural incapacity for offensive operations, could in theory be attained in two ways. One would be to integrate the armed forces of the NATO member states so comprehensively that it would become physically impossible for any national leader to detach 'their' forces for separate operations either against neighbours and allies or anywhere else. This indeed was the kind of root-and-branch military integration envisaged in the EDC plans in *European Defence Community* the early 1950s. Had these been adopted they would likely have led to the appointment of a European Defence Minister and to the establishing of a common budget.

A second, and perhaps more realistic, way in which a structural incapacity to attack could be entrenched would involve NATO member states adopting proposals which were in vogue during the 1980s for what was then called 'Non Offensive Defence' (NOD). As its name suggested, NOD thinking boiled down to support for the proposition that participating countries should eschew both weapons systems and military concepts and tactics which gave them the option to attack and conduct offensive military operations beyond their own borders. Such ideas were highly controversial during the Cold War period and were criticised by some who argued that adoption of such a posture would dangerously constrain NATO's options for responding to a Soviet attack without necessarily increasing its ability to deter such an attack. Others argued that it was, in any event, not easy to define and agree on either types of weaponry or military tactics which were exclusively defensive and would be accepted as such by all relevant governments.[32]

Neither of these two structural alternatives has ever been adopted in the transatlantic area. *Limited* military integration has developed within NATO since the 1950s but this has fallen short of the kind of integration envisaged under the EDC and necessary to guarantee the structural incapacity to attack. The vast bulk of members' fighting forces remain under national control in peacetime and there is no legal obligation on any member state (except, historically, the pre-1990 FRG) to actually release NATO-assigned forces to multinational control even in a crisis. In operational situations, national control is ultimately maintained, via the red card system discussed in Chapter 2.

A structural incapacity to attack does not exist today amongst all members of the supposed Atlantic security community. In terms of the size and capabilities of their armed forces, the US and, to a lesser extent, France and the UK can certainly mount significant offensive operations if they want to do so. In certain respects the FRG could too, though here the picture is somewhat more complicated because of historical and, until relatively recently, constitutional constraints. In structural terms, therefore, the existence of an Atlantic security community does not look quite as assured as is sometimes assumed.

What can be said about the state of affairs in the conceptual arena? Is it credible to believe that leaders would ever seriously consider going to war against a fellow NATO (or EU) member or, conversely, feel threatened by the prospect of military attack by their allies? Here the case for stating that a developed security community exists does seem stronger. After all, the bottom line is that no NATO or EU member has gone to war with another member since 1949 and 1957 respectively, nor, discounting for a moment the Greece-Turkish fringe in NATO, ever seriously threatened to do so. How can this be explained?

One of the most popular explanatory theories focuses on the so-called 'democratic peace'. Democratic peace theory draws heavily upon West European and North American experiences – especially relations amongst member states of the EU – for empirical support of its basic proposition that mature democracies never go to war with each other.[33] One might expect greater support for this view with reference to the EU than to NATO given that, as noted earlier, the latter has never insisted *de facto* that all its member states be mature democracies. Thus, tensions between Greece and Turkey can be ascribed to the persisting failure to establish a mature democracy in the latter.

Another popular explanation for the absence of war amongst NATO/EU members since 1945 emphasises the role of increasing interdependence amongst them. According to this view in its simplest form the greater the network of ties and contacts between countries, especially in the economic and commercial arenas, the lower the risk of war. This is because these countries will have come to depend increasingly on one another for supplies of vital materials and for export markets and will not wish to see their access to these disrupted.

Although the connection between interdependence and peace might thus appear to be self-evident it should not be accepted at face value. As John Lewis Gaddis has reminded us, there is very little historical support for the assertion that relations of apparent interdependence *automatically* promote international peace. Gaddis makes his point by citing the specific examples of economic interdependence that existed amongst the major powers in Europe on the eve of the First World War, and he also notes that the US was Japan's largest trading partner in 1941.[34]

During the 1970s, Robert Keohane and Joseph Nye developed the concept of *complex* interdependence. They argued that in a few regions of the world (Western Europe and North America) relations of interdependence were marked by a web of connections, links and relations which provided contact and communication not only between governments but also between a range of other interest groups within wider societies. The role of international institutions was important in providing forums for communication and co-operation. Keohane and Nye argued that, because the web joining states and societies together had become so dense, distinctions between military, economic and political issues were becoming increasingly blurred. As a consequence, military power was no longer seen as the final arbiter of disputes and disagreements in regions where complex interdependence exists.[35]

Jaap de Wilde has argued that the mere existence of interdependence, of whatever form, neither presumes nor leads to equality between states and, as a result, the potential for conflict remains and may even increase as two or more unequal states are drawn ever closer together. What really matter, in de Wilde's view, are *perceptions*. As he puts it, 'the existence of economic and ideological interdependence by itself [is] not enough; it [has] to be recognized'. Citing other writers, de Wilde elaborates on this point:

> Since 1945 the Western democracies seemed to have learned the lesson. Marshall aid was offered and within a few years the enemy states were accepted as equal partners in all kinds of international organizations. Mutual interests outweighed national sentiments. Russett and Starr affirm that this had more to do with the perception of interdependence (the psychological dimension, as they call it) than with the mere facts of interdependence. Much of what is being seen as interdependence is not new, but is just being recognized for the first time. The 'material' facts of interdependence do not necessarily make for peace by themselves; the 'immaterial' facts must be present as well.[36]

The essential foundations of the Atlantic security community today are the perceptions of interdependence which have developed amongst those countries which make it up – the members of NATO and the EU. This has enabled discrepancies in size and relative power to

be overlooked. Most especially, it has facilitated a historic reconciliation between the FRG and its European neighbours. In 1957, it
may be recalled, the Princeton Study Group refrained from describing
the North Atlantic Area as a security community largely on account
of continuing concerns and suspicions about the Germans. Since
that time, however, things have changed. Thus, for example, the
Benelux states appear to have had few problems integrating themselves
further within the European Union alongside the FRG, which by
most objective measurements is the single most powerful state within
the EU.

If not perfect, relations within Western Europe, North America
and between the two regions – collectively labelled here as the 'transatlantic area' – do represent the closest that any group of countries has
yet come to attaining a security community.

For some this community is essentially 'European' rather than
'Atlantic'. In 1997 John Holmes wrote that:

> The idea of Europe as a community has flourished, and the cohabitation
> of the Western European nations within the European Union (EU) has
> reached the point that separation, much less divorce, seems impossible. In
> contrast, could the fifty-year-old relationship between Europe and the
> United States come to an end? Yes, though not immediately, and not
> inevitably.[37]

Holmes thus implied that the US role in the security community
was neither as strong nor as necessary as that of the West European
participants. However, such a view seriously undervalues the United
States' pivotal role as what Josef Joffe has called 'Europe's pacifier'.
During the Cold War, it performed this role by extending a security
guarantee, backed in the final analysis by nuclear weapons, to its
NATO allies and also by taking on the role of NATO's leader. As Joffe
puts it, 'by extending its guarantee, the United States removed the
prime structural cause of conflict among states – the search for an
autonomous defense policy'. Further:

> By sparing the West Europeans the necessity of autonomous choice in
> matters of defense, the United States removed the systemic cause of
> conflict that had underlain so many of Europe's past wars (World War I is
> perhaps the best example.) By protecting Western Europe against others,
> the United States also protected the half-continent against itself. And by
> paving the way from international anarchy to security community the
> United States not only defused ancient rivalries but also built the indis-
> pensable foundation for future cooperation.[38]

The United States continued to play a 'pacifier' role among its allies during the 1990s. This was most clearly seen in the context of relations between Greece and Turkey. In 1996 the US took the lead in defusing heightened tensions between the two, which some had thought might actually lead to war, over disputed islets in the Aegean Sea. Richard Holbrooke, the American mediator, reportedly accused EU members of 'literally sleeping through the night' as the US worked to defuse the crisis.[39] In the following year Madeleine Albright reportedly engaged in 'more than a week of quiet shuttle diplomacy' in order to persuade Greek and Turkish leaders to agree a joint statement at a NATO summit in Madrid.[40]

To imply that the United States is an optional extra in the security community is, therefore, not justified. Whilst its role, arguably, is not quite as fundamental as it was during the Cold War, it is still key – not least because of its continuing role as the leader of NATO. This is one of the two core institutional underpinnings of the contemporary Atlantic security community (the other being the European Union). NATO, by definition, could not exist without the United States.

The Atlantic civic community

The core feature of the Atlantic civic community, as defined above, is the role played by shared fundamental norms and values. Those most often described are individual freedom, political democracy and the rule of law. Where can one best look for evidence for the existence of such a community? There are two main schools of thought. The *broad-sweep* school identifies the existence of common outlooks and shared viewpoints between Europeans and North Americans based, as Christopher Layne has written, on 'the friendship and web of historical, political, and cultural ties' uniting peoples in the two continents.[41] For commentators such as Layne, the existence of particular international institutions, such as NATO, is not necessary for the underlying community of values to be maintained. Layne, indeed, has argued that 'Atlanticism' could survive even if NATO were wound up.

, The second school of thought is *NATO-focused*. Adherents of this view argue that NATO, if not the sole repository of the values of the civic community, does at least represent their most important institutional embodiment. Both Michael Brenner and Thomas Risse-Kappen have developed arguments along these lines. Brenner has called NATO an 'incorporated partnership', explaining the term thus:

> Incorporation has carried the allies beyond policy parallelism or ad hoc collaboration to concert ... Moreover, the articles of incorporation stipulate fixed obligations of the signatory states, establish routine procedures for consultation and joint decision making, and create mechanisms for review and oversight of actions taken. NATO structures are the organizational expression of those undertakings. They provide the staff, the integrated commands, the facilities and resources for carrying out missions. A political culture has evolved around them with a distinct set of norms and expectations. They counter the disposition of member governments to rethink the exceptional commitments that they have made.[42]

Risse-Kappen has argued in similar vein. In his view, NATO is of prime importance because 'as an institution [it] is explicitly built around norms of democratic decision-making, that is, nonhierarchy, frequent consultation implying co-determination, and consensus-building. Its institutional rules and procedures are formulated in such a way as to allow the allies to influence each other'.[43]

The major part of *Cooperation Among Democracies*, Risse-Kappen's key work in this area, is devoted to a series of case studies demonstrating the extent to which the European NATO members were able to influence US foreign policy decision-making through the NATO structures at key junctures during the Cold War. Brenner has also stressed the importance of this factor, writing that 'the culture of multilateralism [within NATO] eases the apprehensions of weaker states about possible domination by the stronger. The consensus rule amplifies the voice of the weaker; it opens opportunity for resisting the will of the stronger – especially that of the United States as the overwhelmingly most powerful and acknowledged leader of the Alliance'.[44]

The existence of an Atlantic civic community remains a contentious issue. On one level it could be argued that, like beauty, it exists in the eye of the beholder. On another level, however, what ultimately matters are the *perceptions* of key leaders and policy makers within the relevant countries. If, in reaching their decisions, their approaches are conditioned by the view that a community of shared norms and values *does* actually exist, then they will operationalise such a belief. They will do this by consulting routinely and, even more significantly, the more powerful will allow the views and agendas of other members of the community to influence their own national policy-making processes before final decisions are reached.

South East Europe:
challenges to the Atlantic Community

The successive crises in Bosnia and Kosovo have, arguably, made the most significant impact on the post-Cold War Atlantic Community as a whole. In this section, their impact, and the ways in which they were dealt with, will be explored in order to determine the extent to which this confirms or undermines the existence of a still viable and significant Atlantic Community now that the Cold War has ended. Because there is little dispute over the existence of a substantial security community, attention will be focused on the more controversial issue of the alleged community of shared norms and values.

Bosnia

During the Cold War period it seemed scarcely conceivable that NATO would become involved in peacekeeping-type military operations. From 1992, however, this situation changed rapidly and fundamentally. Beginning in the spring of that year, when the first tentative contacts were established between the UN Secretary-General and his NATO counterpart (at the initiative of the former), institutional and operational relations between the UN and NATO started to develop. The major catalyst for this was the conflict in Bosnia and the efforts of the international community to bring it under control and, if possible, broker a peace settlement.[45]

Once the first NATO assets and resources had been committed to Bosnia over the course of the second half of 1992, the institution quickly acquired a distinct stake in the success of international operations there and a disincentive to admit failure and withdraw. This was largely a product of concerns about NATO's credibility being on the line, as discussed in Chapter 2. Thus, during the years 1993 and 1994, far from seriously contemplating withdrawal from Bosnia, NATO became progressively more involved. This was particularly evident in the decision, from spring 1993, to offer airpower to support UN humanitarian relief operations and, later, to underpin attempts to declare and maintain certain Bosnian towns and cities as 'safe areas'.

There was, however, a mounting tide of criticism, especially in the United States, of NATO's apparent inability to actually stop the fighting. In a widely cited article published in the summer of 1993, one American analyst went so far as to assert that 'the Western alliance is dead ... it seems likely that history will record the failure of NATO to respond to the Bosnian war with military force as evidence of the demise of an alliance that lasted for half a century'.[46] This was by no means an isolated view.

At the same time, there was little evidence of a desire on the part of either the Clinton administration or in the US Congress to commit American troops to military action in the midst of a brutal civil war. As an alternative, a number of senators, led by Bob Dole, began to argue for a withdrawal of the UN Protection Force (UNPROFOR) and the lifting of the UN arms embargo against the Muslim-dominated Bosnian government.[47] This would have allowed it to import (American) military equipment in order to be able to fight on more equitable terms against the Bosnian Serbs, which the Dole supporters saw as being the main aggressors. Also proposed was the use of NATO airstrikes against the Serbs.

Despite the President having been rhetorically committed to a similar 'lift-and-strike' approach since his successful 1992 election campaign, the Clinton administration had not pushed for this to be adopted during its first twenty-two months in office. This was despite the Senate having passed a bill to terminate US compliance with the UN arms embargo in May 1994.[48] The main reason for the administration's hesitation was the strong opposition of France and the UK, the two NATO members with the largest troop commitments to UNPROFOR. In mid-November 1994, in the wake of crushing Republican victories in mid-term congressional elections, the administration changed its position. It agreed to prohibit US ships – which had been deployed under NATO command in the Adriatic since 1992 to enforce compliance with the embargo – from doing so in the case of cargoes destined for the Bosnian government. The administration tried to play down the significance of the move and stressed that NATO allies had been 'consulted',[49] but the decision nevertheless aroused widespread displeasure amongst the European allies.

By coincidence, most of them were meeting under the auspices of the WEU in the same week that the American decision was announced. The WEU members declared that they:

> take note with regret of the US measures to modify its participation with respect to the enforcement of the arms embargo in the Combined WEU/NATO Operation SHARP GUARD in the Adriatic. In this context, they particularly stress the importance that the US in NATO structures will continue to observe fully the mandatory provisions of all relevant United Nations Security Council Resolutions.[50]

Despite the fact that the language was as diplomatic as could reasonably be expected, this was nevertheless an unprecedented collective public rebuke for the US by its West European allies. To some commentators the American decision and European reaction raised the prospect of a Suez-type breakdown in transatlantic relations.[51]

In fact, as in the 1950s there was a sense of urgency in moving to repair relations and forestall the possibility of NATO being permanently debilitated. Within ten days of the US decision, NATO launched its most significant airstrikes thus far, against Bosnian Serb military positions threatening the town of Bihac. The rationale behind these had at least as much to do with publicly demonstrating NATO's unity and ability to act as with any strategic or humanitarian concerns. The then Secretary-General, Willy Claes, admitted as much when he said that 'this operation ... indicates clearly ... that NATO is not dead at all. This was a multinational operation – Americans, British, French and Dutch pilots ... those who pretend that America is not willing to go on to cooperate are making a serious mistake, I think'.[52]

In the year following the November 1994 controversy, the Clinton administration executed an effective *volte-face* in its Bosnia policy and decided to become much more actively involved in trying to bring about a settlement. The administration's main motivation was the desire to reassert US leadership in European security affairs – with a revitalised NATO as the chosen vehicle through which to do this. In August 1995 NATO, with the US in the vanguard, launched *Operation Deliberate Force*. This, coupled with reverses on the ground, helped convince the Bosnian Serb leadership to accept a ceasefire and engage in the political negotiations that eventually produced the Dayton accords in November.

The most remarkable turnaround in US policy was still to come. Up until 1995, the *sine qua non* of American policy had been a refusal to deploy ground forces in Bosnia. Once the Dayton accords were reached, however, the Clinton administration went on the political offensive to persuade Congress to agree to send 20,000 US troops to be part of the NATO-led IFOR. This appeal was underpinned by frequent reference to NATO's credibility being on the line, as noted in Chapter 2.

The year 1995 was also important in witnessing the emergence of a new 'Clinton Doctrine'. This was almost certainly inspired in large part by the desire of the administration to put the previous year's low point in relations with Europe behind it and reassert the essential importance of the transatlantic link. Back in 1957, it may be recalled, the US had come up with the idea of interdependence as a way of expressing an ideological conviction that transatlantic relations were fundamentally strong. In 1995 the chosen idea, offered as part of the Clinton administration's 'Strategy of Engagement and Enlargement', was that of the United States as a 'European power'.

In June, the Pentagon issued a document on *United States Security Strategy for Europe and NATO*. This declared that 'America has been a European power, it remains a European power, and it will continue to be a European power'. It expanded on this statement thus:

> Europe represents the world's greatest concentration of nations and peoples which share our commitment to democracy and market economies. America's cultural heritage and institutions largely spring from European roots. Our most important multilateral alliance – the North Atlantic Treaty Organization (NATO) – is centered there. The continent is also one of the world's greatest centres of economic power and represents a massive export market for US products. Thus, our continued political, cultural, and economic well-being is inextricably tied to Europe.[53]

For American leaders the European power concept was, this statement suggested, based upon a combination of shared values and strategic and economic interests. It was, argued prominent Americans, the values aspect that really made the relationship distinctive, however. If shared values were not present, the US would, in Ronald Steel's words, 'not [be] a European nation, any more than it is an Asian nation'. Rather, it would be 'an Atlantic power, and a Pacific one, with interests in both continents'.[54]

Joseph Nye, who served as a senior official in the first Clinton administration, subsequently wrote that:

> In a larger sense, the United States shares the values of democracy and human rights more thoroughly with the majority of European countries than with most other states. Values matter in American foreign policy, and the commonality of values between the United States and Europe is an important force keeping the two sides together. The United States is the progeny of a certain island European power, the legacy of which is evident in US political structures, legal mechanisms and civil protections, and language.[55]

The idea of the United States as a European power represented, in effect, a dressing up of the old Atlantic Community concept in different garb. Set against the background of the Bosnian crisis, however, this was something of a *post facto* development. A sense of shared values had *not* been a prominent factor in determining western policy towards Bosnia in the first place. Specifically, the notion of a value-driven humanitarian intervention did not surface in a serious way until the Kosovo crisis began to move centre-stage.

Kosovo

In the spring and early summer of 1999, NATO leaders' public statements stressed repeatedly that *Operation Allied Force* was being fought for values, and not territory or narrow national interests in the traditional sense. Czech President Vaclav Havel, in an address to the Canadian Parliament, said that:

> This is probably the first war ever fought that is not being fought in the name of interests, but in the name of certain principles and values. If it is possible to say about a war that it is ethical, or that it is fought for ethical reasons, it is true of this war. Kosovo has no oil fields whose output might perhaps attract somebody's interest; no member country of the Alliance has any territorial claims there; and, Milosevic is not threatening either the territorial integrity, or any other integrity, of any NATO member. Nevertheless, the Alliance is fighting. It is fighting in the name of human interest for the fate of other human beings ... This war gives human rights precedence over the rights of states.[56]

In similar vein, Alexander Vershbow was quoted as saying that 'NATO is now in the business of defending common values and interests as well as the territory of its members. Our shared values – freedom, democracy, the rule of law, respect for human rights – are themselves every bit as much worth defending as is our territory'.[57]

The quotations above illustrate a key point about the shared values that exist within the transatlantic area in the post-Cold War environment. They are viewed by NATO members as being *available for export* to non-NATO members within the wider Europe. Additionally, any perceived assault upon them is increasingly now viewed as being a strike against the contemporary Atlantic Community and its members.

To argue that NATO's action over Kosovo was not in any way interest-driven is overly simplistic. It would be more accurate to claim that NATO *was* fighting for perceived interests, but that its members interpreted their interests in a different way to the Cold War years. NATO had been formed with the clear objectives, enshrined in Article 5 of its treaty, of deterring and if necessary defending against a *territorial* assault on any of its members. Even then, however, a 'values' element was built into the Washington Treaty. Since the Cold War ended, and particularly as a result of NATO's response to the Kosovo crisis, this latter element has moved increasingly to the fore.

The 'idea of Europe'

During the Kosovo crisis, reference was sometimes made to 'a certain idea of Europe' being under assault. Javier Solana referred to it in a speech in Berlin in June 1999, just before the end of *Operation Allied Force*. His remarks offer useful insights into this strand of NATO thinking:

> What makes NATO so united in this crisis is the fact that in Kosovo our long term interests and our values converge. For behind the plight of the Kosovars there is even more at stake: the future of the project of Europe. The conflict between Belgrade and the rest of the international community is a conflict between two visions of Europe. One vision – Milosevic's vision – is a Europe of ethnically pure states, a Europe of nationalism, authoritarianism and xenophobia. The other vision, upheld by NATO and the European Union and many other countries, is of a Europe of integration, democracy and ethnic pluralism. This is the vision that has turned Europe and North America into the closest, most democratic and prosperous community ever built ... If this positive vision of Europe is to prevail, if Europe is to enter the 21st century as a community of states practicing democracy, pluralism and human rights, we simply cannot tolerate this carnage at its centre.[58]

In understanding how and why member states were motivated by these concerns, it is important to bear in mind the extent to which their concept of NATO's area of responsibility has changed since the end of the Cold War. Before, the term 'NATO area' was specifically defined in the Washington Treaty.[59] It was considered important to be specific because an attack against this area would have triggered an Article 5 collective response.

Since the end of the Cold War, NATO members have adopted a new formulation to describe their wider and broader sphere of interest – the 'Euro-Atlantic Area' (EAA) and they have been willing to conduct 'non-Article 5 operations' within this area. EAA is a label that came into circulation following the creation of NATO's EAPC in 1997. Membership of the EAPC embraces all NATO members, all the former Warsaw Pact states and their successors, the Soviet successor states and most of the countries of South East Europe, with

the important exceptions of the FRY and Bosnia. It defines the parameters of the Euro-Atlantic Area.

When the EAPC was formally established, its founding document
spoke of the commitment of all participants to 'strengthen and extend
peace and stability in the Euro-Atlantic area, on the basis of the shared
values and principles which underlie their co-operation'.[60] These were
identified as 'protection and promotion of fundamental freedoms and
human rights, and safeguarding of freedom, justice, and peace through
democracy'.[61]

NATO's response to the Kosovo crisis suggested to some that a *de
facto* European collective security arrangement might be coming into
being under the auspices of the EAPC. Traditional definitions of
collective security stress the internal policing role of involved countries;
i.e. their obligation to take action against any of their number whose
behaviour violates accepted standards or threatens to disturb order and
security. Yet, Kosovo cannot truly be described as a collective security
action. The FRY was not a member of the EAPC and hence not a part
of the Euro-Atlantic Area. *Operation Allied Force* was, therefore, an act
of *collective defence against outside aggression* – the first such in
NATO's history. It was not, however, an Article 5 operation. What was
being defended, in this instance, was not territory but, rather, the
common values of the Euro-Atlantic community.

In this context the diplomatic and psychological importance of the
EAPC meeting which took place on the margins of the NATO
Washington summit in April 1999 should not be underestimated.
Although EAPC members failed explicitly to endorse NATO's air
attacks on the FRY they nevertheless 'expressed support for the
demands of the international community' and 'emphasized their
abhorrence of the policies of violence, repression and ethnic cleansing
being carried out by the FRY authorities in Kosovo'.[62] NATO officials
subsequently acknowledged the value – for reasons of legitimisation –
of this endorsement from the only multilateral body that brings
together NATO and its European partner states.[63]

Conclusions

The Atlantic Community is, arguably, at least as strong today as before
1989. To recall, Karl Deutsch *et al.* did not think that a transatlantic
security community existed, beyond a few bilateral relationships, when
first discussing the concept in the late 1950s. Apart from the special

case of Greece–Turkey relations, few would question its existence today. In terms of the civic community – or 'community of values' – between the US and its European allies, this has become if anything more overt, if not stronger, since the Cold War's end.

During the 1990s, NATO expanded in the obvious, narrow, sense of taking in more members. More profoundly, the members' understanding of what constituted their area of responsibility was broadened significantly with the adoption of the concept of the Euro-Atlantic Area. This is not simply a geographical entity. Nor is it institutionally defined. Only a minority of EAA states are members of NATO, and some have made clear that they do not wish to join. Rather, the Euro-Atlantic Area is best described as being a community of shared norms and values.

The NATO response to the crisis in Kosovo demonstrated that threats to shared values were sufficient to bring about a robust transatlantic response, even though there had been no direct threat to any member of the Atlantic Community, or the EAA, in a traditional, territorial sense.

Notes

1 For a brief discussion see P. Kennedy, *The Rise and Fall of the Great Powers* (London, Fontana, 1989), pp. 423–30.
2 Declaration of Principles issued by the President of the United States and the Prime Minister of the United Kingdom. Website reference www.nato. int/docu/basictxt/b41081a.htm.
3 In this context it is worth noting that NATO officially regards the Charter as being one of the principal 'antecedents of the Alliance' and it is referred to as such in NATO publications and on the institution's website.
4 H. vB. Cleveland, *The Atlantic Idea and Its European Rivals* (New York, McGraw-Hill, 1966), p. 151.
5 *Ibid.*, p. 151.
6 The nine were France, Italy, the Benelux states, Iceland, Denmark, Norway and Portugal. The other North American country was Canada.
7 For in-depth analysis of the decision to admit Italy as a founder member of NATO see E. T. Smith, *The United States, Italy and NATO, 1947–52* (Basingstoke, Macmillan, 1991).
8 Quotations taken from the text of the treaty reprinted in *The North Atlantic Treaty Organisation: Facts and Figures* (Brussels, NATO, 1989), p. 376.
9 The presence of non-democracies in NATO's ranks remained a bone of contention. See 'Heirs of Pericles' in 'Knights in shining armour? – A survey of NATO', *The Economist* (24 April 1999), 10.

10 Cleveland, *The Atlantic Idea*, p. 127. See also C. Layne, *Death Knell for NATO? (Policy Analysis 394)* (Washington DC, Cato Institute, 2001), pp. 10–11.
11 'NATO's Next Five Years', *The Economist* (5 February 1955), 438.
12 L. Pearson, 'After Geneva: a greater task for NATO', *Foreign Affairs*, 34:1 (1955), 18.
13 For a good discussion of the Suez crisis in these terms see T. Risse-Kappen, *Cooperation Among Democracies: The European Influence on US Foreign Policy* (Princeton, Princeton University Press, 1995), ch. 4.
14 'NATO's watershed', *The Economist* (22 December 1956), 1057.
15 *NATO Facts and Figures*, pp. 389–90.
16 This is a key theme for discussion in M. A. Smith, *NATO in the First Decade after the Cold War* (Dordrecht, Kluwer, 2000).
17 K. Deutsch *et al.*, *Political Community and the North Atlantic Area* (Princeton, Princeton University Press, 1957), p. 5.
18 *Ibid.*, p. 118.
19 *Ibid.*, p. 5.
20 1957 NATO summit statements. Website reference www.nato.int/docu/comm/49-95/c571219a.htm.
21 'Liberty, fraternity, interdependence', *The Economist* (21 December 1957), 1057.
22 *Ibid.*, p. 1058.
23 See, *inter alia*, J. W. Fulbright, 'For a concert of free nations', *Foreign Affairs*, 40:1 (1961), 1–18 and C. Herter, 'Atlantica', *Foreign Affairs*, 41:2 (1963), 299–309.
24 Address at Independence Hall, President John F. Kennedy, Philadelphia, July 4, 1962. Website reference www.cs.umb.edu/jfklibrary/jfk-independencehall-1962.html.
25 Cleveland, *The Atlantic Idea*, pp. 159–63.
26 See, for example, the *Declaration on Atlantic Relations*, which was adopted at NATO's 25th anniversary summit in June 1974. Website reference www.nato.int/docu/comm/49-95/c740618b.htm.
27 Cleveland, *The Atlantic Idea*, pp. 152–3.
28 J. Holmes, *The United States and Europe after the Cold War: A New Alliance?* (Columbia, University of South Carolina Press, 1997), p. 1.
29 S. Walt, 'The ties that fray: why Europe and America are drifting apart', *The National Interest*, 54 (1998/99), 3–11.
30 Layne, *Death Knell for NATO?*, p. 4.
31 M. Brenner, 'Multilateralism and European security', *Survival*, 35:2 (1993), 141.
32 On NOD see B. Møller, *Common Security and Nonoffensive Defence: A Neorealist Perspective* (Boulder, Lynne Rienner, 1992).
33 See, *inter alia*, C. Layne, 'Kant or Cant: the myth of the democratic peace', *International Security*, 19:2 (1994), 5–49 and J. Owen, 'How liberalism produces democratic peace', *International Security*, 19:2 (1994), 87–125.
34 J. L. Gaddis, 'The long peace: elements of stability in the postwar international system', *International Security*, 10:4 (1986), 111–12.

35 R. Keohane and J. Nye, *Power and Interdependence (second edition)* (Boston, Scott, Foresman, 1989).

36 J. de Wilde, 'Promises of interdependence: risks and opportunities', *Bulletin of Peace Proposals*, 19:2 (1988), 163.

37 Holmes, *The United States and Europe after the Cold War*, pp. 1–2.

38 J. Joffe, 'Europe's American pacifier', *Foreign Policy*, 54 (1984), 68–9.

39 M. Sheridan, 'Holbrooke Aegean jibe angers Foreign Office', *Independent* (10 February 1996).

40 B. Clark, 'Breakthrough in Greek–Turk relations', *Financial Times* (9 July 1997).

41 C. Layne, 'Atlanticism without NATO', *Foreign Policy*, 67 (1987), 24.

42 M. Brenner, *Terms of Engagement: The United States and the European Security Identity* (Westport, Praeger, 1998), p. 63.

43 Risse-Kappen, *Cooperation Among Democracies*, p. 36.

44 Brenner, *Terms of Engagement*, p. 63.

45 For background see M. A. Smith, *On Rocky Foundations: NATO, the United Nations and Peace Operations in the Post-Cold War Era* (Bradford, University Department of Peace Studies, 1996).

46 J. Chace, 'Present at the destruction', *World Policy Journal*, X:2 (1993), 89. See also C. Bertram, 'NATO on track for the 21st century?', *Security Dialogue*, 26:1 (1995), 65–71.

47 The embargo, passed in 1992, was being enforced against all parties to the Bosnian conflict.

48 *An Act to remove the United States arms embargo of the Government of Bosnia and Herzegovina (S.2042)*, One Hundred Third Congress, Second Session. Website reference http://frwebgate.access.gpo.gov/cgi-bin/useftp. cgi?IPaddress=162.140.64..../103_cong_bill.

49 See the transcript of the State Department's Daily Briefing for journalists on 14 November 1994. Website reference http://dosfan.lib.uic.edu/ERC/briefing/daily_briefings/1994/941114db.html.

50 *Noordwijk Declaration*. Website reference http://www.weu.int/eng/comm/94-noordwijk.htm.

51 See, *inter alia*, I. Davidson, 'Conflict of interest', *Financial Times* (16 November 1994); 'In need of fastening', *The Economist* (27 May 1995), 15–16.

52 *NATO: Meeting New Challenges*. Bureau of Public Affairs, US State Department. Website reference http://dosfan.lib.uic.edu/ERC/briefing/dossec/1994/9411/941121dossec.html.

53 *United States Security Strategy for Europe and NATO* (Washington DC, Office of International Security Affairs, Department of Defense, 1995), p. 1. See also R. Holbrooke, 'America, A European Power', *Foreign Affairs*, 74:2 (1995), 38–51.

54 R. Steel, *Temptations of a Superpower* (Cambridge, Mass., Harvard University Press, 1995), p. 80. Steel makes clear that he does not subscribe to the view that the US is a European power in the sense discussed here.

55 J. Nye, 'The US and Europe: continental drift?', *International Affairs*, 76:1 (2000), 55.

56 Address by Vaclav Havel President of the Czech Republic to the Senate and the House of Commons of the Parliament of Canada 29 April 1999. Website reference www.hrad.cz/president/Havel/speeches/1999/2904 _uk.html.

57 Quoted in M. Walker, 'Variable geography: America's mental maps of a Greater Europe', *International Affairs*, 76:3 (2000), 467.

58 NATO as a Community of Values. Manfred Wörner Memorial Lecture by the Secretary General of NATO, Dr Javier Solana. Website reference www.nato.int/docu/speech/1999/s990602a.htm.

59 It was, according to Article 6, 'the territory of any of the Parties in Europe or North America' and 'the forces, vessels or aircraft of any of the Parties, when in or over these territories … or the Mediterranean Sea or the North Atlantic area north of the Tropic of Cancer'. See *NATO Facts and Figures*, p. 377.

60 *Basic Document of the Euro-Atlantic Partnership Council (Press Release M-NACC-EAPC-1(97)66)* (Brussels, NATO Press Service, 1997), p. 1.

61 *Partnership for Peace: Framework Document (Annex to M-1(94)2)* (Brussels, NATO Press Service, 1994), p. 1.

62 Chairman's summary of the Meeting of the Euro-Atlantic Partnership Council at Summit Level, Washington DC. Website reference www.nato.int/docu/pr/1999/p99-067e.htm.

63 Authors' interviews with NATO officials, November 2001.

Conclusion

The discussions here will briefly revisit the main issues and debates that have been examined in the substantive chapters of this volume in order to assess the ways in which the Kosovo crisis, relative to other factors, has had an impact in shaping them since the late 1990s. Following this, overall conclusions will be drawn as to the extent to which the crisis can be said to have significantly affected the post-Cold War European security landscape.

A 'Kosovo precedent': new wars, new interventions?

When NATO undertook armed action without an explicit mandate from the UNSC, it entered a kind of international no-man's land between upholding the sanctity of state sovereignty and that of human life. While NATO members asserted that the humanitarian and strategic imperatives of saving Kosovar Albanian lives and preventing destabilisation in South East Europe drove the action, states such as Russia and China saw the Kosovo conflict as an unacceptable violation of the FRY's state sovereignty. The result was controversy and debates that simmer on today. These debates raised important issues about how the armed conflict should best be viewed. Was Kosovo a war, a limited war or something else? NATO's military action best met the description of being an *intervention*, but this descriptor itself was full of variations, including the one that has been subject to the widest debate; i.e. *humanitarian* intervention.

As discussed in Chapter 1, the idea of humanitarian intervention can be broadly defined as being forced outside intervention in the affairs of a sovereign state to uphold human rights or save the lives of people threatened by the violent oppression of a regime.[1] This presents the international community with a paradox. Bruce Cronin highlighted the difficulties of humanitarian intervention when he wrote:

> On one hand, international law and diplomatic practice are clearly biased in favor of state autonomy in matters that are considered to be domestic ... On the other hand, multilateral treaties and international institutions have long provided for collective action in situations where governments violate generally accepted norms of behaviour.[2]

This paradox brings into sharp focus the potential for conflict between the long-standing doctrine of non-intervention that buttresses state sovereignty and the increasingly universal norms of the international system on human rights that challenge the sacrosanct view of the sovereignty of the state. The crux of this paradox is the problem of establishing criteria for intervention, and humanitarian intervention in particular.

Determining the ethical basis of intervention and establishing its legitimacy is a core challenge. Kosovo brought into focus this twin problem. As the discussions in Chapter 1 indicate, the ethics of humanitarian intervention are far from being a simple and clear-cut matter. Although some governments, such as in the UK, have made valuable contributions to articulating a set of criteria, there remains no consensus on this matter in the international community as a whole.[3] With the events of 11 September 2001 prompting an international intervention in Afghanistan, albeit for reasons other than humanitarian imperatives, the problem of establishing agreed criteria for any kind of international intervention is unlikely to go away.

On the related issue of legitimacy, Kosovo seemingly saw the UNSC being increasingly sidelined. Closer analysis suggests, however, that far from marking the end of the UN role in conferring legitimacy on international intervention, Kosovo reinforced the need for this global security organisation, as demonstrated by the key role that NATO members have conceded to the UN in overseeing the post-conflict reconstruction of Kosovo. What was confirmed by the Kosovo crisis is that the UN Charter and the security role that derives from it makes the UN an international body that is optimised for dealing with inter-state conflict better than the intra-state kind.

The long-term impact of the Kosovo crisis on debates about intervention in Europe specifically is not likely to be very large. Intervention in Europe, given the strong institutional basis of the security order in this part of the world, is likely to be a case-by-case phenomenon and one undertaken only in extreme circumstances, when all diplomatic options have been exhausted. Kosovo, however, has more general importance when viewed as part of a wider pattern of post-Cold War interventions that seem likely to increase rather than decrease in the wake of the events of 11 September.

The future of NATO: Kosovo and after

The first part of Chapter 2 focused on controversies surrounding the workings of NATO's multilateral political decision-making and military command and control structures during *Operation Allied Force*. The allegedly negative lessons which the US, in particular, had drawn from the Kosovo experience in this respect made headlines once again in the autumn of 2001. This happened as a consequence of the military operations in Afghanistan.

Much of the analysis and commentary surrounding the conduct of these operations focused on the extent to which the Americans ran them on a unilateral basis, with no direct reference to NATO or any other multilateral structures or processes. The Kosovo experience was often cited as a key reason for this approach. As one British commentator put it, 'the frustrations of American commanders with the cumbersome (and, at times, leaky) nature of Nato's collective decision-making during the Kosovo conflict [have] made them wary of too much military involvement now by other countries'.[4] Another argued that, after Kosovo, 'it is unlikely that they [the Americans] will ever again wish to use NATO to manage a serious shooting war'.[5] Extrapolating from this, some drew the conclusion that, in the post-11 September security environment, NATO was becoming obsolete.

Such arguments seem overdone. To begin with, the 'cumbersome nature' of allied decision-making during *Operation Allied Force* should not be overestimated. As discussed in Chapter 2, at a very early stage in the operation, NATO members in effect decided that most of their number would cede day-to-day supervisory authority to a sub-group of the most powerful – the Quints. Within this caucus, the key decisions about target approval were often made by an even smaller grouping of three – the US, UK and France.

What really counted during *Operation Allied Force* were not the formal structures of NATO, which reportedly were soon substantially cast aside when confronted by an actual military crisis. The important thing was the existence of an *informal* network of links, ties and shared habits of co-operation amongst member states. These had been built up over a fifty-year period in the case of many of the states concerned. They represented the main contribution of 'NATO' to the prosecution of the Kosovo campaign and, incidentally, in the 2001–02 Afghan war also. In this latter case, the value of shared habits of co-operation and working together was acknowledged even by the US Department of Defense,[6] popularly assumed to be the chief proponent of a unilateral approach. In reality, the US was far from being the only NATO member engaged in the war on terror in Afghanistan.

Nevertheless, there were discernible differences in the conduct of the Kosovo and Afghan operations. During the former the US had, for all the frustrations, operated throughout substantially within an international chain of command. Afghan operations were run through a US national command chain, with bilateral arrangements being made with other contributing countries.

What accounts for the differences in the US approach to the Kosovo and Afghan campaigns? The key difference is that Kosovo was counted as being *within the NATO area of responsibility*. Afghanistan, on the other hand, was not. As discussed in Chapter 6, the NATO area today is different to that which existed during the Cold War. Then, it was clearly defined to include only the territory of the member states in Europe and North America and the waters surrounding them. Since the end of the Cold War, NATO has officially adopted the notion that it has an interest in security and stability in the wider Euro-Atlantic Area.[7]

Despite American interest in a potential 'global NATO', the contemporary EAA does not extend to countries and regions beyond Europe. Even within its own area, its reach is not as broad and expansive as some at first assume. Officially, Kazakhstan, the Kyrghyz Republic, Tajikistan, Turkmenistan and Uzbekistan are all included within the EAA, on the basis of their participation in PfP. However, as NATO officials have privately admitted, these Central Asian countries have been little more than nominal participants.[8] They have developed no real substantive relationship with NATO – although this may change as a consequence of renewed US interest in Central Asia following 11 September and the campaign in Afghanistan.

South East Europe has become the central region of the new NATO area; a development both reflected and reinforced by NATO's response to the Kosovo crisis. As noted in Chapters 2 and 6 here, NATO members believe that a large amount of the institution's post-Cold War credibility is invested in the region, particularly in making sure that the peace agreements currently in place in Bosnia, Kosovo and Macedonia continue to hold. As Gilles Andréani *et al.* have put it:

> If the Kosovo crisis found [NATO members] united, it was not because events in the region affected both sides of the Atlantic in the same way, or because of any intrinsic strategic value of Balkan territory, but because the governments elevated the crisis into a test for the credibility of an Alliance which they could not allow to collapse. There are not many instances when this is likely to be the case.[9]

There was no serious expectation amongst its member states that NATO would be formally involved in the post-11 September operations in Afghanistan. Its non-involvement should not, therefore, be taken as an indication that it is an institution in decline.

If, on the other hand, NATO members were beginning to disengage from South East Europe then this *would* be a significant indicator that the institution had had its day, given the credibility that it has invested in the region. However, there is currently no real evidence to suggest that such a process of disengagement is underway, even on the part of the United States, as discussed in Chapter 2. By the middle of 2002, the international military presence in Bosnia and Kosovo looked set to continue into the foreseeable future.

A 'Europeanised' future?

In Chapter 5, it was argued that the Kosovo crisis played a smaller and more indirect role in helping initiate the development of the European Union's ESDP than many have assumed. It is, therefore, perhaps not surprising that, since 1999, Kosovo has played a less significant role in shaping its evolution than have other factors.

The events of 11 September seemed to some to have set back the evolution of the ESDP. Marta Dassù and Nicholas Whyte have, for example, written that, since then, 'the idea of a 'common' European defence policy has almost instantly receded and given way to a renewed bilateralism in transatlantic relationships'.[10] There was increased friction within the EU in the period immediately following 11 September, when the major powers (France, the FRG and the UK) began meeting as a threesome to discuss the 'European' response to international terrorism. This caucusing took place to the growing chagrin of the other members. An intended three-power dinner discussion convened by Tony Blair in November 2001 degenerated into near-farce. There was an outcry amongst the smaller EU members, which led Blair to backtrack and invite a number of their leaders along too.[11]

Overall, the impression conveyed was one of disunity, drift and consequent impotence on the part of the European Union collectively. Individual member states – chiefly France and the UK – did make significant military contributions in Afghanistan. These were on the basis of national agreements with the US, however, and there was no role as such for the EU's emerging military dimension. Indeed, in another embarrassing public disagreement, the Belgian government, as the then EU presidency state, had been rebuffed in December 2001 for suggesting that the impending deployment of an international peacekeeping force to Kabul might become the first ESDP operation.[12] In common with other military activities in Afghanistan, the Kabul force was subsequently made up of an *ad hoc* 'coalition of the willing' under the command of a British General.

Despite these reversals, it would be premature, at best, to assume that the ESDP initiative has completely run out of steam. As the discussions in Chapter 5 made clear, leading EU members – the British and French – have had powerful reasons for supporting it and ensuring that it does not die.

The most likely arena for an actual EU military operation is South East Europe. By 2002 the region was coming increasingly to be seen as the key litmus test for the EU's aspirations to be able to act more coherently and effectively on the international stage. EU officials noted that what they called the 'Western Balkans' were absorbing between 50 and 60 per cent of the time and effort of Javier Solana, now the EU's foreign policy supremo.[13]

The EU has the biggest stake and role in Macedonia, rather than in Bosnia or Kosovo. In both of these places, the senior international representative is an appointee of the UN. In Macedonia, meanwhile, an EU Special Representative fills the position. This official's task is to offer 'advice' to the Macedonian authorities across a range of areas.[14] In the spring of 2002, the European Commission published a report setting out a comprehensive range of 'suggestions' to ensure continued stability in Macedonia. It included proposals for reform of the economy and the political and legal systems.[15] Underpinning this was an informal pledge of eventual EU membership providing that the country avoided instability and conflict and maintained its 'European orientation'.[16]

The military forces in Macedonia since August 2001 had, it is true, been organised and commanded within a NATO framework. On the other hand, the personnel were almost exclusively European. In the first such force – 'Task Force Harvest' in August and September 2001 – it was reported that there was 'only one American ... a press officer', although US support assets such as airlift and intelligence gathering were being utilised extensively.[17] By the summer of 2002 there was growing discussion about whether EU members might soon be able and willing to take over the command and control of the military forces in Macedonia from NATO. They had signalled willingness in principle to do so at their Barcelona summit meeting in March.[18]

An expanding Atlantic Community?

The NATO response to the Kosovo crisis confirmed that South East Europe, a geographically adjacent region, is now regarded as being a place in which the basic values of the Atlantic Community are expected to be observed and upheld. The relatively prompt NATO response – just over a year elapsed between the first official expression of concern and the launch of *Operation Allied Force* – contrasted with the division and hesitation which characterised the first three years of the response to the civil war in Bosnia. In the case of Macedonia, the reaction by both NATO and the EU to the threat of civil war was even quicker, and more effectively pre-emptive, during 2001.

It would be premature to argue that the boundaries of either the security or civic communities have yet been extended into much of South East Europe. The states and peoples in the region still tend to be regarded as objects for remedial treatment or action, rather than as full participants in the communities. Nevertheless, there does now exist the prospect that some of them will, ultimately, be fully integrated. This will be done through membership of one or both of the two core community institutions, i.e. NATO and the EU.

At present, South East Europe enjoys a unique status with both NATO and the EU. It is not yet a full part of the western-based communities, and parts of the region may not become so for some considerable time, if ever. It is, on the other hand, considered to be a region of special interest and importance. Both NATO and the EU now regard South East Europe as being within their areas of responsibility. Both also have a greater institutional stake in the future peace, stability and prosperity of this region than of any other in the world.

Russia's role and place in European security affairs

Post-Kosovo relations between Russia and NATO remain dogged by two things – the ambivalence of NATO policy towards Russia and the decline of Russia as both a regional and global power. The former may in fact be a product of the latter. With Russia's ultimate post-Cold War position in European and global security affairs uncertain and changing, NATO has found it difficult to pursue a consistent policy other than vaguely assuming that it is a given that Russia cannot be ignored. Yet, on a number of vital issues, Russian views have not seemed to carry much weight in NATO's decision-making. For example, Russia's objections to enlargement did not ultimately divert NATO from taking in new members between 1997 and 1999, and pledging to do so again from 2002.

As for Russia's economic and military decline, this was clearly evident in the last decade of the twentieth century and the prospects for future Russian recovery remain ultimately uncertain. The scale of Russian decline during the 1990s can be illustrated by the fact that Russia's Gross Domestic Product in 1998 was only 55 per cent of the level registered by the Soviet Union in 1989,[19] although in recent years the Russian economy has shown some signs of revival. The decline in Russia's international influence is undoubtedly linked to its internal problems. The economic decline of Russia underpins the erosion of its military power in terms of both conventional and nuclear forces.

With this decline come inevitable questions regarding Russia's place in the international order. Can Russia be considered a regional power – let alone a superpower – given its palpable inability to prevent NATO from launching *Operation Allied Force* and exert military pressure of its own during the Kosovo crisis? Although Russia's nuclear arsenal, together with its permanent seats on the UNSC and in the G8, still afford it an importance in international affairs, this is a status that is likely to fade unless the domestic problems which have eviscerated Russian power since the late 1980s are overcome.

What the Kosovo crisis appears to have done for Russian leaders is similar to the impact of the Suez crisis of 1956 on the UK's political establishment. The significance of Kosovo is that it drove home to the Russian political and military establishment the limitations on Russian power and influence and persuaded key leaders to pursue policies matching Russia's means rather than memories of its previous status as a great or superpower.

The rise in the perceived threat of international terrorism has provided a common set of interests upon which to build a new Russia–NATO relationship. For NATO, Russia still matters in security terms, but in ways that are different and related to the changes in the international security environment since 11 September. The rapid emergence of the NRC during 2001–02 has provided a new opportunity for Russia and NATO to work together on security matters, both in Europe and further afield. In remains to be seen, however, how far this potential will be realised.

South East European futures: unachievable goals?

The normative bases of the Dayton agreements, UNSC Resolution 1244 and the Stability Pact for South Eastern Europe all promote democracy in conjunction with a civic model of nationalism that is distant, if not alien to, ethnic national identities in South East Europe. On this crucial issue of nationalism, the gulf in understanding between the recipients and givers of norms lies at the crux of the problem of norm transmission and inculcation in the region. With nationalist tension and conflict still existing in parts of Europe, this gulf remains an important issue for European security.

Moreover, with the majority of conflicts around the world being intra-state, with an ethnic or nationalist dimension present in a large number of them, the issue of what concept of nationalism should underpin norms and values is scarcely an irrelevant one. 'Failed states' are a major source of instability and potential base for international terrorists.[20] Thus, how the international community imparts norms in the context of post-conflict peace-building makes an understanding of the problems of nationalism in the post-11 September security environment an important normative element in the war on terror.

As the discussions in Chapter 3 made clear, post-crisis efforts at peace-building in South East Europe have been premised on the belief that the states and societies in the region should base their political, social and legal systems on 'internationally accepted' norms. These are largely modelled on the experiences of the democratic states of North America and Western Europe. To this end, the international community, led by NATO and EU member states, has set up intrusive supervisory apparatus, in Kosovo in particular. According to the House of Commons Select Committee on Foreign Affairs, UNSC Resolution 1244 provides for 'an unprecedented constitutional role for the UN ... to take the place of a government which has abused its own citizens in the way the Milosevic government did in respect of the majority population of Kosovo'.[21] In similar vein, the Independent International Commission on Kosovo has argued that 'Resolution 1244 created a unique institutional hybrid, a UN protectorate with unlimited power' and of potentially unlimited duration.[22] In Bosnia the situation is somewhat different, but the international community nevertheless is able to exercise considerable influence in shaping the normative development of the state. More widely in South East Europe, NATO and the EU, by political influence and economic leverage, have considerable power in shaping the region's development in all aspects.

In Chapter 3, however, it was argued that attempts to impose 'western' norms and values on other states and societies without adapting them to local conditions can potentially have counterproductive consequences. This does not mean that the norms themselves are either flawed or irrelevant. Rather, the international approach might not take sufficiently into account the consequences of a strong sense of ethnic identity amongst peoples in South East Europe. This raises the issue of whether the policy prescriptions chosen are ones that will lead to lasting stability and a winding down of the major commitments of the international community in the region. A better tailoring of international norms to conditions in South East Europe may hold out the prospect of greater and lasting progress towards stability.

Conclusions: lessons of Kosovo?

The immediate aftermath of the Kosovo crisis in 1999 saw considerable debate and discussion about what its 'lessons' might be. This was followed again fairly predictably, by a number of 'revisionist' views suggesting that, perhaps, the impact of the crisis was less significant and profound than many had first believed.

Debates over the vexing issues associated with international intervention were not new. A string of post-Cold War interventions of various kinds, from the Persian Gulf to Somalia, had already generated a series of conundrums and dilemmas that defied the articulation of clear lessons. Kosovo was no exception.

For NATO, the military operations over Kosovo provided confirmation of the Alliance's post-Cold War redefinition of its main area of interest and responsibility. In this respect Kosovo was a key step in a process that had begun with the initial NATO involvement in Bosnia from the summer of 1992.

With the European Union's ESDP, the Kosovo crisis did no more than accelerate trends that were already apparent. Its foreign and security policy wing was not brought into being by the crisis. Nevertheless, Kosovo was important in accelerating a trend towards making South East Europe its principal focal point. The region has since become the main testing ground for the EU's aspirations to be a significant international security actor.

If there are any lessons to be gained from the pattern of Russia-NATO relations during and after the crisis, they warn of the dangers of attempting to draw long-term conclusions about such an unpredictable relationship. It might be argued that the response to the crisis in Kosovo provides lessons about the importance of international efforts at norm transmission, in the face of indigenous nationalism, being enacted with great care and delicacy. Even so, this challenge is not limited to Kosovo or, indeed, to South East Europe.

Judah has offered the opinion that 'there were no particular lessons' to be drawn from the Kosovo crisis.[23] Daalder and O'Hanlon, meanwhile, have argued that 'the overall verdict on Kosovo is less likely to offer new lessons than to affirm old truths'.[24] Overall, it does seem that the Kosovo crisis and the international response reinforced and reflected trends and developments that were already emerging or apparent, rather than giving rise to anything dramatically new. The crisis, therefore, offers us few simple lessons to be learned. On the other hand, the way in which it was tackled tells us much about the nature and evolution of post-Cold War European security.

Notes

1 Conversely, such intervention might also be considered when human suffering is threatened as a consequence of state disintegration and/or civil war.
2 B. Cronin, 'Multilateral intervention and the international community', in M. Keren and D. Sylvan (eds), *International Intervention: Sovereignty versus Responsibility* (London, Frank Cass, 2002), p. 147.
3 See D. Sylvan and J. Pevehouse, 'Deciding whether to intervene', in *ibid.*, pp. 56–74.
4 P. Riddell, 'Britain keeps its walk-on part on the world stage', *The Times* (22 October 2001).
5 C. Grant, 'A more political NATO, a more European Russia', in E. Bannerman *et al.*, *Europe After September 11th* (London, Centre for European Reform, 2001), p. 49.

6 'Special report: The future of NATO', *The Economist* (4 May 2002), 26.
7 See I. Daalder and J. Goldgeier, 'Putting Europe first', *Survival*, 43:1 (2001), 81.
8 Authors' interviews with NATO officials, November 2001.
9 G. Andréani *et al.*, *Europe's Military Revolution* (London, Centre for European Reform, 2001), p. 74.
10 M. Dassù and N. Whyte, 'America's Balkan disengagement?', *Survival*, 43:4 (2001), 133.
11 See Bannerman *et al.*, *Europe After September 11th*, pp. 39–41 and 'Guess who wasn't coming to dinner?', *The Economist* (10 November 2001), 45–6.
12 See M. Fletcher and M. Evans, 'No 10 fury as EU claims Afghan role', *The Times* (15 December 2001).
13 Authors' interviews with EU officials, July 2002.
14 *Strategic Survey 2001/2002* (London, International Institute for Strategic Studies, 2002), p. 154.
15 *Former Yugoslav Republic of Macedonia: Stabilisation and Association Report (Com(2002)163)*. Website reference http://europa.eu.int/comm/external_relations/see/sap/com02-_342.pdf.
16 Authors' interviews with EU officials, July 2002.
17 'Wake up, Europe!', *The Economist* (15 September 2001), 41.
18 *Presidency Conclusions: Barcelona European Council 15 and 16 March 2002* (Brussels, Council of the European Union, 2002), p. 26.
19 *The Russian Economy in June 1999: Net Assessment of the Russian Economy*. Website reference www.csis.org/ruseura/rus_econ.html.
20 See J. Record, 'Collapsed countries, casualty dread, and the new American way of war', *Parameters*, 32:2 (2002), 4–23 and R. Takeyh and N. Gvosdev, 'Do terrorist networks need a home?', *Washington Quarterly*, 25:3 (2002), 98–108.
21 *Kosovo Volume I: Report and Proceedings of the Committee*, House of Commons Select Committee on Foreign Affairs, Fourth Report, Session 1999–2000 (London, The Stationery Office, 2000), p. lxi.
22 Independent International Commission on Kosovo, *Kosovo Report* (Oxford, Oxford University Press, 2000), p. 9.
23 T. Judah, *Kosovo: War and Revenge* (New Haven, Yale University Press, 2000), pp. 307–8.
24 I. Daalder and M. O'Hanlon, 'Unlearning the lessons of Kosovo', *Foreign Policy*, 116 (1999), 129.

Appendix

Key documents

Charter of the United Nations
San Francisco June 1945 (excerpts)

Chapter 1
Purposes and Principles

Article 2

The Organization and its Members, in pursuit of the Purposes stated in Article 1, shall act in accordance with the following Principles.

1. The Organization is based on the principle of the sovereign equality of all its Members ...

4. All Members shall refrain in their international relations from the threat or use of force against the territorial integrity or political independence of any state, or in any other manner inconsistent with the Purposes of the United Nations ...

7. Nothing contained in the present Charter shall authorize the United Nations to intervene in matters which are essentially within the domestic jurisdiction of any state or shall require the Members to submit such matters to settlement under the present Charter; but this principle shall not prejudice the application of enforcement measures under Chapter VII.

Chapter 7
Action with Respect to Threats to the Peace, Breaches of the Peace, and Acts of Aggression

Article 39

The Security Council shall determine the existence of any threat to the peace, breach of the peace, or act of aggression and shall make recommendations, or decide what measures shall be taken in accordance with Articles 41 and 42, to maintain or restore international peace and security ...

Article 41

The Security Council may decide what measures not involving the use of armed force are to be employed to give effect to its decisions, and it may call upon the Members of the United Nations to apply such measures. These may include complete or partial interruption of economic relations and of rail, sea, air, postal, telegraphic, radio, and other means of communication, and the severance of diplomatic relations.

Article 42

Should the Security Council consider that measures provided for in Article 41 would be inadequate or have proved to be inadequate, it may take such action by air, sea, or land forces as may be necessary to maintain or restore international peace and security. Such action may include demonstrations, blockade, and other operations by air, sea, or land forces of Members of the United Nations ...

Article 51

Nothing in the present Charter shall impair the inherent right of individual or collective self-defence if an armed attack occurs against a Member of the United Nations, until the Security Council has taken measures necessary to maintain international peace and security. Measures taken by Members in the exercise of this right of self-defence shall be immediately reported to the Security Council and shall not in any way affect the authority and responsibility of the Security Council under the present Charter to take at any time such action as it deems necessary in order to maintain or restore international peace and security.

Chapter 8
Regional Arrangements

Article 52

Nothing in the present Charter precludes the existence of regional arrangements or agencies for dealing with such matters relating to the maintenance of international peace and security as are appropriate for regional action provided that such arrangements or agencies and their activities are consistent with the Purposes and Principles of the United Nations.

Article 53

The Security Council shall, where appropriate, utilize such regional arrangements or agencies for enforcement action under its authority. But no enforcement action shall be taken under regional arrangements or by regional agencies without the authorization of the Security Council ...

UNSC Resolution 1199 (1998)

Adopted by the Security Council at its 3930th meeting on 23 September 1998

The Security Council,

Recalling its resolution 1160 (1998) of 31 March 1998,

Having considered the reports of the Secretary-General pursuant to that resolution, and in particular his report of 4 September 1998 ...

Noting with appreciation the statement of the Foreign Ministers of France, Germany, Italy, the Russian Federation, the United Kingdom of Great Britain and Northern Ireland and the United States of America (the Contact Group) of 12 June 1998 at the conclusion of the Contact Group's meeting with the Foreign Ministers of Canada and Japan ... and the further statement of the Contact Group made in Bonn on 8 July 1998 ...

Noting also with appreciation the joint statement by the Presidents of the Russian Federation and the Federal Republic of Yugoslavia of 16 June 1998 ...

Noting further the communication by the Prosecutor of the International Tribunal for the Former Yugoslavia to the Contact Group on 7 July 1998, expressing the view that the situation in Kosovo represents an armed conflict within the terms of the mandate of the Tribunal,

Gravely concerned at the recent intense fighting in Kosovo and in particular the excessive and indiscriminate use of force by Serbian security forces and the Yugoslav Army which have resulted in numerous civilian casualties and, according to the estimate of the Secretary-General, the displacement of over 230,000 persons from their homes,

Deeply concerned by the flow of refugees into northern Albania, Bosnia and Herzegovina and other European countries as a result of the use of force in Kosovo, as well as by the increasing numbers of displaced persons within Kosovo, and other parts of the Federal Republic of Yugoslavia, up to 50,000 of whom the United Nations High Commissioner for Refugees has estimated are without shelter and other basic necessities,

Reaffirming the right of all refugees and displaced persons to return to their homes in safety, and *underlining* the responsibility of the Federal Republic of Yugoslavia for creating the conditions which allow them to do so,

Condemning all acts of violence by any party, as well as terrorism in pursuit of political goals by any group or individual, and all external support for such activities in Kosovo, including the supply of arms and training for terrorist activities in Kosovo and *expressing concern* at the reports of continuing violations of the prohibitions imposed by resolution 1160 (1998),

Deeply concerned by the rapid deterioration in the humanitarian situation throughout Kosovo, *alarmed* at the impending humanitarian catastrophe as described in the report of the Secretary-General, and *emphasizing* the need to prevent this from happening,

Deeply concerned also by reports of increasing violations of human rights and of international humanitarian law, and *emphasizing* the need to ensure that the rights of all inhabitants of Kosovo are respected,

Reaffirming the objectives of resolution 1160 (1998), in which the Council expressed support for a peaceful resolution of the Kosovo problem which would include an enhanced status for Kosovo, a substantially greater degree of autonomy, and meaningful self-administration,

Reaffirming also the commitment of all Member States to the sovereignty and territorial integrity of the Federal Republic of Yugoslavia,

Affirming that the deterioration of the situation in Kosovo, Federal Republic of Yugoslavia, constitutes a threat to peace and security in the region,

Acting under Chapter VII of the Charter of the United Nations,

1. *Demands* that all parties, groups and individuals immediately cease hostilities and maintain a ceasefire in Kosovo, Federal Republic of Yugoslavia, which would enhance the prospects for a meaningful dialogue between the authorities of the Federal Republic of Yugoslavia and the Kosovo Albanian leadership and reduce the risks of a humanitarian catastrophe;

2. *Demands also* that the authorities of the Federal Republic of Yugoslavia and the Kosovo Albanian leadership take immediate steps to improve the humanitarian situation and to avert the impending humanitarian catastrophe;

3. *Calls upon* the authorities in the Federal Republic of Yugoslavia and the Kosovo Albanian leadership to enter immediately into a meaningful dialogue without preconditions and with international involvement, and to a clear timetable, leading to an end of the crisis and to a negotiated political solution to the issue of Kosovo, and *welcomes* the current efforts aimed at facilitating such a dialogue;

4. *Demands further* that the Federal Republic of Yugoslavia, in addition to the measures called for under resolution 1160 (1998), implement immediately the following concrete measures towards achieving a political solution to the situation in Kosovo as contained in the Contact Group statement of 12 June 1998:

(a) cease all action by the security forces affecting the civilian population and order the withdrawal of security units used for civilian repression;

(b) enable effective and continuous international monitoring in Kosovo by the European Community Monitoring Mission and diplomatic missions accredited to the Federal Republic of Yugoslavia, including access and complete freedom of movement of such monitors to, from and within Kosovo unimpeded by government authorities, and expeditious issuance of appropriate travel documents to international personnel contributing to the monitoring;

(c) facilitate, in agreement with the UNHCR and the International Committee of the Red Cross (ICRC), the safe return of refugees and displaced persons to their homes and allow free and unimpeded access for humanitarian organizations and supplies to Kosovo;

(d) make rapid progress to a clear timetable, in the dialogue referred to in paragraph 3 with the Kosovo Albanian community called for in resolution 1160 (1998), with the aim of agreeing confidence-building measures and finding a political solution to the problems of Kosovo;

5. *Notes*, in this connection, the commitments of the President of the Federal Republic of Yugoslavia, in his joint statement with the President of the Russian Federation of 16 June 1998:

(a) to resolve existing problems by political means on the basis of equality for all citizens and ethnic communities in Kosovo;

(b) not to carry out any repressive actions against the peaceful population;

(c) to provide full freedom of movement for and ensure that there will be no restrictions on representatives of foreign States and international institutions accredited to the Federal Republic of Yugoslavia monitoring the situation in Kosovo;

(d) to ensure full and unimpeded access for humanitarian organizations, the ICRC and the UNHCR, and delivery of humanitarian supplies;

(e) to facilitate the unimpeded return of refugees and displaced persons under programmes agreed with the UNHCR and the ICRC, providing State aid for the reconstruction of destroyed homes,

and *calls for* the full implementation of these commitments;

6. *Insists* that the Kosovo Albanian leadership condemn all terrorist action, and emphasizes that all elements in the Kosovo Albanian community should pursue their goals by peaceful means only;

7. *Recalls* the obligations of all States to implement fully the prohibitions imposed by resolution 1160 (1998);

8. *Endorses* the steps taken to establish effective international monitoring of the situation in Kosovo, and in this connection welcomes the establishment of the Kosovo Diplomatic Observer Mission;

9. *Urges* States and international organizations represented in the Federal Republic of Yugoslavia to make available personnel to fulfil the

responsibility of carrying out effective and continuous international monitoring in Kosovo until the objectives of this resolution and those of resolution 1160 (1998) are achieved;

10. *Reminds* the Federal Republic of Yugoslavia that it has the primary responsibility for the security of all diplomatic personnel accredited to the Federal Republic of Yugoslavia as well as the safety and security of all international and non-governmental humanitarian personnel in the Federal Republic of Yugoslavia and *calls upon* the authorities of the Federal Republic of Yugoslavia and all others concerned in the Federal Republic of Yugoslavia to take all appropriate steps to ensure that monitoring personnel performing functions under this resolution are not subject to the threat or use of force or interference of any kind;

11. *Requests* States to pursue all means consistent with their domestic legislation and relevant international law to prevent funds collected on their territory being used to contravene resolution 1160 (1998);

12. *Calls upon* Member States and others concerned to provide adequate resources for humanitarian assistance in the region and to respond promptly and generously to the United Nations Consolidated Inter-Agency Appeal for Humanitarian Assistance Related to the Kosovo Crisis;

13. *Calls upon* the authorities of the Federal Republic of Yugoslavia, the leaders of the Kosovo Albanian community and all others concerned to cooperate fully with the Prosecutor of the International Tribunal for the Former Yugoslavia in the investigation of possible violations within the jurisdiction of the Tribunal;

14. *Underlines* also the need for the authorities of the Federal Republic of Yugoslavia to bring to justice those members of the security forces who have been involved in the mistreatment of civilians and the deliberate destruction of property;

15. *Requests* the Secretary-General to provide regular reports to the Council as necessary on his assessment of compliance with this resolution by the authorities of the Federal Republic of Yugoslavia and all elements in the Kosovo Albanian community, including through his regular reports on compliance with resolution 1160 (1998);

16. *Decides*, should the concrete measures demanded in this resolution and resolution 1160 (1998) not be taken, to consider further action and additional measures to maintain or restore peace and stability in the region;

17. *Decides* to remain seized of the matter.

Statement
Issued at the Extraordinary Ministerial Meeting
of the North Atlantic Council
Brussels April 1999

1. The crisis in Kosovo represents a fundamental challenge to the values of democracy, human rights and the rule of law, for which NATO has stood since its foundation. We are united in our determination to overcome this challenge.

2. The Federal Republic of Yugoslavia (FRY) has repeatedly violated United Nations Security Council resolutions. The unrestrained assault by Yugoslav military, police and paramilitary forces, under the direction of President Milosevic, on Kosovar civilians has created a massive humanitarian catastrophe which also threatens to destabilise the surrounding region. Hundreds of thousands of people have been expelled ruthlessly from Kosovo by the FRY authorities. We condemn these appalling violations of human rights and the indiscriminate use of force by the Yugoslav government. These extreme and criminally irresponsible policies, which cannot be defended on any grounds, have made necessary and justify the military action by NATO.

3. NATO's military action against the FRY supports the political aims of the international community: a peaceful, multi-ethnic and democratic Kosovo in which all its people can live in security and enjoy universal human rights and freedoms on an equal basis. In this context, we welcome the statement of the UN Secretary-General of 9th April and the EU Council Conclusions of 8th April.

4. NATO's air strikes will be pursued until President Milosevic accedes to the demands of the international community. President Milosevic knows what he has to do. He must:
- ensure a verifiable stop to all military action and the immediate ending of violence and repression;
- ensure the withdrawal from Kosovo of the military, police and paramilitary forces;
- agree to the stationing in Kosovo of an international military presence;
- agree to the unconditional and safe return of all refugees and displaced persons and unhindered access to them by humanitarian aid organisations;
- provide credible assurance of his willingness to work on the basis of the Rambouillet Accords in the establishment of a

political framework agreement for Kosovo in conformity with international law and the Charter of the United Nations.

5. Responsibility for the present crisis lies with President Milosevic. He has the power to bring a halt to NATO's military action by accepting and implementing irrevocably the legitimate demands of the international community.

6. We underline that NATO is not waging war against the Federal Republic of Yugoslavia. We have no quarrel with the people of the FRY who for too long have been isolated in Europe because of the policies of their government.

7. We are grateful for the strong and material support we have received from our Partners in the region and more widely in the international community in responding to the crisis.

8. The Alliance shares a common interest with Russia in reaching a political solution to the crisis in Kosovo and wants to work constructively with Russia, in the spirit of the Founding Act, to this end.

9. As a result of President Milosevic's sustained policy of ethnic cleansing, hundreds of thousands of Kosovar people are seeking refuge in neighbouring countries, particularly in Albania and the former Yugoslav Republic of Macedonia. Others remain in Kosovo, destitute and beyond the reach of international relief. These people in Kosovo are struggling to survive under conditions of exhaustion, hunger and desperation. We will hold President Milosevic and the Belgrade leadership responsible for the well-being of all civilians in Kosovo.

10. NATO and its members have responded promptly to this emergency. We have activated with our Partners the Euro-Atlantic Disaster Response Coordination Centre. NATO forces in the former Yugoslav Republic of Macedonia have constructed emergency accommodation for refugees and have cared for them. NATO troops are also being deployed to Albania to support the humanitarian efforts there and to assist the Albanian authorities in providing a secure environment for them. We will sustain and intensify our refugee and humanitarian relief operations in cooperation with the UNHCR, the lead agency in this field. NATO-led refugee and humanitarian aid airlift operations for both Albania and the former Yugoslav Republic of Macedonia are already under way and they will increase. The steps being taken by NATO and the efforts of other international organisations and agencies, including the European Union, are complementary and mutually reinforcing.

11. We pay tribute to NATO's servicemen and women whose commitment and skill are ensuring the success of NATO's military and humanitarian operations.

12. Atrocities against the people of Kosovo by FRY military, police and paramilitary forces violate international law. Those who are responsible for the systematic campaign of violence and destruction against innocent Kosovar civilians and for the forced deportation of hundreds of thousands of refugees will be held accountable for their actions. Those indicted must be brought before the International Criminal Tribunal for the former Yugoslavia (ICTY) in The Hague in accordance with international law and the relevant resolutions of the United Nations Security Council. Allies reaffirm there can be no lasting peace without justice.

13. NATO has repeatedly stated that it would be unacceptable if the FRY were to threaten the territorial integrity, political independence and security of Albania and the former Yugoslav Republic of Macedonia. We have consulted closely and at a high level with both countries on their specific concerns. We will respond to any challenges by the FRY to the security of Albania and the former Yugoslav Republic of Macedonia stemming from the presence of NATO forces and their activities on their territory.

14. We are concerned over the situation in the Republic of Montenegro. We reaffirm our support for the democratically elected government of President Milo Djukanovic which has accepted tens of thousands of displaced persons from Kosovo. President Milosevic should be in no doubt that any move against President Djukanovic and his government will have grave consequences.

15. The Kosovo crisis underscores the need for a comprehensive approach to the stabilisation of the crisis region in south-eastern Europe and to the integration of the countries of the region into the Euro-Atlantic community. We welcome the EU initiative for a Stability Pact for South-Eastern Europe under the auspices of the OSCE, as well as other regional efforts including the South Eastern Europe Co-operation initiative. We are strengthening the security dialogue between NATO and countries of the region with a view to building a dynamic partnership with them and have tasked the Council in Permanent Session to develop measures to this end. We look forward to a time when the people of Serbia can re-establish normal relations with all the peoples of the Balkans. We want all the countries of south-eastern Europe to enjoy peace and security.

The Alliance's Strategic Concept
Washington DC April 1999 (excerpts)

Introduction

1. At their Summit meeting in Washington in April 1999, NATO Heads of State and Government approved the Alliance's new Strategic Concept.

2. NATO has successfully ensured the freedom of its members and prevented war in Europe during the 40 years of the Cold War. By combining defence with dialogue, it played an indispensable role in bringing East-West confrontation to a peaceful end. The dramatic changes in the Euro-Atlantic strategic landscape brought by the end of the Cold War were reflected in the Alliance's 1991 Strategic Concept. There have, however, been further profound political and security developments since then.

3. The dangers of the Cold War have given way to more promising, but also challenging prospects, to new opportunities and risks. A new Europe of greater integration is emerging, and a Euro-Atlantic security structure is evolving in which NATO plays a central part. The Alliance has been at the heart of efforts to establish new patterns of cooperation and mutual understanding across the Euro-Atlantic region and has committed itself to essential new activities in the interest of a wider stability. It has shown the depth of that commitment in its efforts to put an end to the immense human suffering created by conflict in the Balkans. The years since the end of the Cold War have also witnessed important developments in arms control, a process to which the Alliance is fully committed. The Alliance's role in these positive developments has been underpinned by the comprehensive adaptation of its approach to security and of its procedures and structures. The last ten years have also seen, however, the appearance of complex new risks to Euro-Atlantic peace and stability, including oppression, ethnic conflict, economic distress, the collapse of political order, and the proliferation of weapons of mass destruction.

4. The Alliance has an indispensable role to play in consolidating and preserving the positive changes of the recent past, and in meeting current and future security challenges. It has, therefore, a demanding agenda. It must safeguard common security interests in an environment of further, often unpredictable change. It must maintain collective defence and reinforce the transatlantic link and ensure a balance

that allows the European Allies to assume greater responsibility. It must deepen its relations with its partners and prepare for the accession of new members. It must, above all, maintain the political will and the military means required by the entire range of its missions.

5. This new Strategic Concept will guide the Alliance as it pursues this agenda. It expresses NATO's enduring purpose and nature and its fundamental security tasks, identifies the central features of the new security environment, specifies the elements of the Alliance's broad approach to security, and provides guidelines for the further adaptation of its military forces.

Part I – The Purpose and Tasks of the Alliance

6. NATO's essential and enduring purpose, set out in the Washington Treaty, is to safeguard the freedom and security of all its members by political and military means. Based on common values of democracy, human rights and the rule of law, the Alliance has striven since its inception to secure a just and lasting peaceful order in Europe. It will continue to do so. The achievement of this aim can be put at risk by crisis and conflict affecting the security of the Euro-Atlantic area. The Alliance therefore not only ensures the defence of its members but contributes to peace and stability in this region.

7. The Alliance embodies the transatlantic link by which the security of North America is permanently tied to the security of Europe. It is the practical expression of effective collective effort among its members in support of their common interests.

8. The fundamental guiding principle by which the Alliance works is that of common commitment and mutual co-operation among sovereign states in support of the indivisibility of security for all of its members. Solidarity and cohesion within the Alliance, through daily cooperation in both the political and military spheres, ensure that no single Ally is forced to rely upon its own national efforts alone in dealing with basic security challenges. Without depriving member states of their right and duty to assume their sovereign responsibilities in the field of defence, the Alliance enables them through collective effort to realise their essential national security objectives.

9. The resulting sense of equal security among the members of the Alliance, regardless of differences in their circumstances or in their national military capabilities, contributes to stability in the Euro-

Atlantic area. The Alliance does not seek these benefits for its members alone, but is committed to the creation of conditions conducive to increased partnership, cooperation, and dialogue with others who share its broad political objectives.

10. To achieve its essential purpose, as an Alliance of nations committed to the Washington Treaty and the United Nations Charter, the Alliance performs the following fundamental security tasks:
Security: To provide one of the indispensable foundations for a stable Euro-Atlantic security environment, based on the growth of democratic institutions and commitment to the peaceful resolution of disputes, in which no country would be able to intimidate or coerce any other through the threat or use of force.
Consultation: To serve, as provided for in Article 4 of the Washington Treaty, as an essential transatlantic forum for Allied consultations on any issues that affect their vital interests, including possible developments posing risks for members' security, and for appropriate co-ordination of their efforts in fields of common concern.
Deterrence and Defence: To deter and defend against any threat of aggression against any NATO member state as provided for in Articles 5 and 6 of the Washington Treaty.
And in order to enhance the security and stability of the Euro-Atlantic area:

- Crisis Management: To stand ready, case-by-case and by consensus, in conformity with Article 7 of the Washington Treaty, to contribute to effective conflict prevention and to engage actively in crisis management, including crisis response operations.
- Partnership: To promote wide-ranging partnership, cooperation, and dialogue with other countries in the Euro-Atlantic area, with the aim of increasing transparency, mutual confidence and the capacity for joint action with the Alliance.

11. In fulfilling its purpose and fundamental security tasks, the Alliance will continue to respect the legitimate security interests of others, and seek the peaceful resolution of disputes as set out in the Charter of the United Nations. The Alliance will promote peaceful and friendly international relations and support democratic institutions. The Alliance does not consider itself to be any country's adversary.

Part II – Strategic Perspectives

The Evolving Strategic Environment

12. The Alliance operates in an environment of continuing change. Developments in recent years have been generally positive, but uncertainties and risks remain which can develop into acute crises. Within this evolving context, NATO has played an essential part in strengthening Euro-Atlantic security since the end of the Cold War. Its growing political role; its increased political and military partnership, cooperation and dialogue with other states, including with Russia, Ukraine and Mediterranean Dialogue countries; its continuing openness to the accession of new members; its collaboration with other international organisations; its commitment, exemplified in the Balkans, to conflict prevention and crisis management, including through peace support operations: all reflect its determination to shape its security environment and enhance the peace and stability of the Euro-Atlantic area.

13. In parallel, NATO has successfully adapted to enhance its ability to contribute to Euro-Atlantic peace and stability. Internal reform has included a new command structure, including the Combined Joint Task Force (CJTF) concept, the creation of arrangements to permit the rapid deployment of forces for the full range of the Alliance's missions, and the building of the European Security and Defence Identity (ESDI) within the Alliance.

14. The United Nations (UN), the Organisation for Security and Cooperation in Europe (OSCE), the European Union (EU), and the Western European Union (WEU) have made distinctive contributions to Euro-Atlantic security and stability. Mutually reinforcing organisations have become a central feature of the security environment.

15. The United Nations Security Council has the primary responsibility for the maintenance of international peace and security and, as such, plays a crucial role in contributing to security and stability in the Euro-Atlantic area.

16. The OSCE, as a regional arrangement, is the most inclusive security organisation in Europe, which also includes Canada and the United States, and plays an essential role in promoting peace and stability, enhancing cooperative security, and advancing democracy and human rights in Europe. The OSCE is particularly active in the fields of preventive diplomacy, conflict prevention, crisis management, and

post-conflict rehabilitation. NATO and the OSCE have developed close practical cooperation, especially with regard to the international effort to bring peace to the former Yugoslavia.

17. The European Union has taken important decisions and given a further impetus to its efforts to strengthen its security and defence dimension. This process will have implications for the entire Alliance, and all European Allies should be involved in it, building on arrangements developed by NATO and the WEU. The development of a common foreign and security policy (CFSP) includes the progressive framing of a common defence policy. Such a policy, as called for in the Amsterdam Treaty, would be compatible with the common security and defence policy established within the framework of the Washington Treaty. Important steps taken in this context include the incorporation of the WEU's Petersberg tasks into the Treaty on European Union and the development of closer institutional relations with the WEU.

18. As stated in the 1994 Summit declaration and reaffirmed in Berlin in 1996, the Alliance fully supports the development of the European Security and Defence Identity within the Alliance by making available its assets and capabilities for WEU-led operations. To this end, the Alliance and the WEU have developed a close relationship and put into place key elements of the ESDI as agreed in Berlin. In order to enhance peace and stability in Europe and more widely, the European Allies are strengthening their capacity for action, including by increasing their military capabilities. The increase of the responsibilities and capacities of the European Allies with respect to security and defence enhances the security environment of the Alliance.

19. The stability, transparency, predictability, lower levels of armaments, and verification which can be provided by arms control and non-proliferation agreements support NATO's political and military efforts to achieve its strategic objectives. The Allies have played a major part in the significant achievements in this field. These include the enhanced stability produced by the CFE Treaty, the deep reductions in nuclear weapons provided for in the START treaties; the signature of the Comprehensive Test Ban Treaty, the indefinite and unconditional extension of the Nuclear Non-Proliferation Treaty, the accession to it of Belarus, Kazakhstan, and Ukraine as non-nuclear weapons states, and the entry into force of the Chemical Weapons Convention. The Ottawa Convention to ban anti-personnel landmines and similar agreements make an important contribution to alleviating human suffering.

There are welcome prospects for further advances in arms control in conventional weapons and with respect to nuclear, chemical, and biological (NBC) weapons ...

Part III – The Approach to Security in the 21st Century

25. The Alliance is committed to a broad approach to security, which recognises the importance of political, economic, social and environmental factors in addition to the indispensable defence dimension. This broad approach forms the basis for the Alliance to accomplish its fundamental security tasks effectively, and its increasing effort to develop effective cooperation with other European and Euro-Atlantic organisations as well as the United Nations. Our collective aim is to build a European security architecture in which the Alliance's contribution to the security and stability of the Euro-Atlantic area and the contribution of these other international organisations are complementary and mutually reinforcing, both in deepening relations among Euro-Atlantic countries and in managing crises. NATO remains the essential forum for consultation among the Allies and the forum for agreement on policies bearing on the security and defence commitments of its members under the Washington Treaty.

26. The Alliance seeks to preserve peace and to reinforce Euro-Atlantic security and stability by: the preservation of the transatlantic link; the maintenance of effective military capabilities sufficient for deterrence and defence and to fulfil the full range of its missions; the development of the European Security and Defence Identity within the Alliance; an overall capability to manage crises successfully; its continued openness to new members; and the continued pursuit of partnership, cooperation, and dialogue with other nations as part of its co-operative approach to Euro-Atlantic security, including in the field of arms control and disarmament.

The Transatlantic Link

27. NATO is committed to a strong and dynamic partnership between Europe and North America in support of the values and interests they share. The security of Europe and that of North America are indivisible. Thus the Alliance's commitment to the indispensable transatlantic link and the collective defence of its members is fundamental to its credibility and to the security and stability of the Euro-Atlantic area.

The Maintenance of Alliance Military Capabilities

28. The maintenance of an adequate military capability and clear preparedness to act collectively in the common defence remain central to the Alliance's security objectives. Such a capability, together with political solidarity, remains at the core of the Alliance's ability to prevent any attempt at coercion or intimidation, and to guarantee that military aggression directed against the Alliance can never be perceived as an option with any prospect of success.

29. Military capabilities effective under the full range of foreseeable circumstances are also the basis of the Alliance's ability to contribute to conflict prevention and crisis management through non-Article 5 crisis response operations. These missions can be highly demanding and can place a premium on the same political and military qualities, such as cohesion, multinational training, and extensive prior planning, that would be essential in an Article 5 situation. Accordingly, while they may pose special requirements, they will be handled through a common set of Alliance structures and procedures.

The European Security and Defence Identity

30. The Alliance, which is the foundation of the collective defence of its members and through which common security objectives will be pursued wherever possible, remains committed to a balanced and dynamic transatlantic partnership. The European Allies have taken decisions to enable them to assume greater responsibilities in the security and defence field in order to enhance the peace and stability of the Euro-Atlantic area and thus the security of all Allies. On the basis of decisions taken by the Alliance, in Berlin in 1996 and subsequently, the European Security and Defence Identity will continue to be developed within NATO. This process will require close cooperation between NATO, the WEU and, if and when appropriate, the European Union. It will enable all European Allies to make a more coherent and effective contribution to the missions and activities of the Alliance as an expression of our shared responsibilities; it will reinforce the transatlantic partnership; and it will assist the European Allies to act by themselves as required through the readiness of the Alliance, on a case-by-case basis and by consensus, to make its assets and capabilities available for operations in which the Alliance is not engaged militarily under the political control and strategic direction either of the WEU or as otherwise agreed, taking into account the full participation of all European Allies if they were so to choose.

Conflict Prevention and Crisis Management

31. In pursuit of its policy of preserving peace, preventing war, and enhancing security and stability and as set out in the fundamental security tasks, NATO will seek, in cooperation with other organisations, to prevent conflict, or, should a crisis arise, to contribute to its effective management, consistent with international law, including through the possibility of conducting non-Article 5 crisis response operations. The Alliance's preparedness to carry out such operations supports the broader objective of reinforcing and extending stability and often involves the participation of NATO's Partners. NATO recalls its offer, made in Brussels in 1994, to support on a case-by-case basis in accordance with its own procedures, peacekeeping and other operations under the authority of the UN Security Council or the responsibility of the OSCE, including by making available Alliance resources and expertise. In this context NATO recalls its subsequent decisions with respect to crisis response operations in the Balkans. Taking into account the necessity for Alliance solidarity and cohesion, participation in any such operation or mission will remain subject to decisions of member states in accordance with national constitutions.

32. NATO will make full use of partnership, cooperation and dialogue and its links to other organisations to contribute to preventing crises and, should they arise, defusing them at an early stage. A coherent approach to crisis management, as in any use of force by the Alliance, will require the Alliance's political authorities to choose and co-ordinate appropriate responses from a range of both political and military measures and to exercise close political control at all stages ...

36. Russia plays a unique role in Euro-Atlantic security. Within the framework of the NATO-Russia Founding Act on Mutual Relations, Cooperation and Security, NATO and Russia have committed themselves to developing their relations on the basis of common interest, reciprocity and transparency to achieve a lasting and inclusive peace in the Euro-Atlantic area based on the principles of democracy and co-operative security. NATO and Russia have agreed to give concrete substance to their shared commitment to build a stable, peaceful and undivided Europe. A strong, stable and enduring partnership between NATO and Russia is essential to achieve lasting stability in the Euro-Atlantic area ...

Enlargement

39. The Alliance remains open to new members under Article 10 of the Washington Treaty. It expects to extend further invitations in coming years to nations willing and able to assume the responsibilities and obligations of membership, and as NATO determines that the inclusion of these nations would serve the overall political and strategic interests of the Alliance, strengthen its effectiveness and cohesion, and enhance overall European security and stability. To this end, NATO has established a programme of activities to assist aspiring countries in their preparations for possible future membership in the context of its wider relationship with them. No European democratic country whose admission would fulfil the objectives of the Treaty will be excluded from consideration ...

Part V – Conclusion

65. As the North Atlantic Alliance enters its sixth decade, it must be ready to meet the challenges and opportunities of a new century. The Strategic Concept reaffirms the enduring purpose of the Alliance and sets out its fundamental security tasks. It enables a transformed NATO to contribute to the evolving security environment, supporting security and stability with the strength of its shared commitment to democracy and the peaceful resolution of disputes. The Strategic Concept will govern the Alliance's security and defence policy, its operational concepts, its conventional and nuclear force posture and its collective defence arrangements, and will be kept under review in the light of the evolving security environment. In an uncertain world the need for effective defence remains, but in reaffirming this commitment the Alliance will also continue making full use of every opportunity to help build an undivided continent by promoting and fostering the vision of a Europe whole and free.

The Treaty on European Union
Maastricht December 1991 (excerpt)

The Union shall define and implement a common foreign and security policy covering all areas of foreign and security policy, the objectives of which shall be:

- To safeguard the common values, fundamental interests, independence and integrity of the Union in conformity with the principles of the United Nations Charter;
- To strengthen the security of the Union in all ways;
- To preserve peace and strengthen international security;
- To promote international cooperation;
- To develop and consolidate democracy and the rule of law, and respect for human rights and fundamental freedoms.

The common foreign and security policy shall include all questions relating to the security of the Union, including the progressive framing of a common defence policy ... which might lead to a common defence, should the European Council so decide ... The Western European Union (WEU) is an integral part of the development of the Union providing the Union with access to an operational capability ...

Western European Union Petersberg Declaration
Bonn June 1992 (excerpt)

Apart from contributing to the common defence ... military units of WEU member States, acting under the authority of WEU, could be employed for:
- Humanitarian and rescue tasks;
- Peacekeeping tasks;
- Tasks of combat forces in crisis management, including peace-making.

A Planning Cell will be established ... The Planning Cell will be responsible for preparing contingency plans for the employment of forces under WEU auspices [and] preparing recommendations for the necessary command, control and communication arrangements ...

Ministerial Meeting of the North Atlantic Council
Berlin June 1996 (excerpt)

The Alliance will support the development of the E[uropean] S[ecurity and] D[efence] I[dentity] within NATO by conducting, at the request of and in coordination with the WEU, military planning and exercises for illustrative WEU missions identified by the WEU.

As an essential element of the development of this identity, we will prepare, with the involvement of NATO and the WEU, for WEU-led operations (including planning and exercising of command elements and forces). Such preparations within the Alliance should take into account the participation, including in European command arrangements, of all European Allies if they were so to choose ...

Joint Declaration issued at the British–French Summit St Malo December 1998 (excerpt)

The European Union needs to be in a position to play its full role on the international stage ... To this end, the Union must have the capacity for autonomous action, backed up by credible military forces, the means to decide to use them, and a readiness to do so, in order to respond to international crises.

In order for the European Union to take decisions and approve military action where the [NATO] Alliance as a whole is not engaged, the Union must be given appropriate structures and a capacity for analysis of situations, sources of intelligence, and a capability for relevant strategic planning, without unnecessary duplication, taking account of the existing assets of the WEU and the evolution of its relations with the EU ...

An Alliance for the 21st Century: [NATO] Washington Summit Communiqué Washington DC April 1999 (excerpt)

We acknowledge the resolve of the European Union to have the capacity for autonomous action so that it can take decisions and approve military action where the Alliance as a whole is not engaged. As this process goes forward, NATO and the EU should ensure the development of effective mutual consultation, cooperation and transparency, building on the mechanisms existing between NATO and the WEU. We therefore stand ready to define and adopt the necessary arrangements for ready access by the European Union to the collective assets and capabilities of the Alliance, for operations in which the Alliance as a whole is not engaged militarily as an Alliance ...

Presidency Conclusions
Cologne European Council
June 1999 (excerpt)

In pursuit of our Common Foreign and Security Policy objectives and
the progressive framing of a common defence policy, we are convinced
that the [European] Council should have the ability to take decisions
on the full range of conflict prevention and crisis management tasks
defined in the Treaty on European Union, the 'Petersberg tasks' ...

We are now determined to launch a new step in the construction
of the European Union. To this end we task the General Affairs
Council to prepare the conditions and the measures necessary to
achieve these objectives, including the definition of the modalities for
the inclusion of those functions of the WEU which will be necessary
for the EU to fulfil its new responsibilities in the area of the Petersberg
tasks ...

Presidency Conclusions
Helsinki European Council
December 1999 (excerpt)

The European Council underlines its determination to develop an
autonomous capacity to take decisions and, where NATO as a whole is
not engaged, to launch and conduct EU-led military operations in
response to international crises. This process will avoid unnecessary
duplication and does not imply the creation of a European army ...

Building on the guidelines established at the Cologne European
Council ... the European Council has agreed in particular the following: cooperating voluntarily in EU-led operations, Member States
must be able, by 2003, to deploy within 60 days and sustain for at least
1 year military forces of up to 50,000–60,000 persons capable of the
full range of Petersberg tasks. New political and military bodies and
structures will be established within the Council to enable the Union
to ensure the necessary political guidance and strategic direction to
such operations ...

NATO–Russia Relations: A New Quality
Russia-NATO Summit
Rome May 2002

At the start of the 21st century we live in a new, closely interrelated world, in which unprecedented new threats and challenges demand increasingly united responses. Consequently, we, the member states of the North Atlantic Treaty Organization and the Russian Federation are today opening a new page in our relations, aimed at enhancing our ability to work together in areas of common interest and to stand together against common threats and risks to our security. As participants of the Founding Act on Mutual Relations, Cooperation and Security, we reaffirm the goals, principles and commitments set forth therein, in particular our determination to build together a lasting and inclusive peace in the Euro-Atlantic area on the principles of democracy and cooperative security and the principle that the security of all states in the Euro-Atlantic community is indivisible. We are convinced that a qualitatively new relationship between NATO and the Russian Federation will constitute an essential contribution in achieving this goal. In this context, we will observe in good faith our obligations under international law, including the UN Charter, provisions and principles contained in the Helsinki Final Act and the OSCE Charter for European Security.

Building on the Founding Act and taking into account the initiative taken by our Foreign Ministers, as reflected in their statement of 7 December 2001, to bring together NATO member states and Russia to identify and pursue opportunities for joint action at twenty, we hereby establish the NATO-Russia Council. In the framework of the NATO-Russia Council, NATO member states and Russia will work as equal partners in areas of common interest. The NATO-Russia Council will provide a mechanism for consultation, consensus-building, cooperation, joint decision, and joint action for the member states of NATO and Russia on a wide spectrum of security issues in the Euro-Atlantic region.

The NATO-Russia Council will serve as the principal structure and venue for advancing the relationship between NATO and Russia. It will operate on the principle of consensus. It will work on the basis of a continuous political dialogue on security issues among its members with a view to early identification of emerging problems, determination of optimal common approaches and the conduct of joint actions, as appropriate. The members of the NATO-Russia Council, acting in their national capacities and in a manner consistent with their respective collective commitments and obligations, will take joint decisions and will bear equal responsibility, individually and jointly, for their implementation. Each member may raise in the NATO-Russia Council issues related to the implementation of joint decisions.

The NATO-Russia Council will be chaired by the Secretary General of NATO. It will meet at the level of Foreign Ministers and at the level of Defence Ministers twice annually, and at the level of Heads of State and Government as appropriate. Meetings of the Council at Ambassadorial level will be held at least once a month, with the possibility of more frequent meetings as needed, including extraordinary meetings, which will take place at the request of any Member or the NATO Secretary General.

To support and prepare the meetings of the Council a Preparatory Committee is established, at the level of the NATO Political Committee, with Russian representation at the appropriate level. The Preparatory Committee will meet twice monthly, or more often if necessary. The NATO-Russia Council may also establish committees or working groups for individual subjects or areas of cooperation on an ad hoc or permanent basis, as appropriate. Such committees and working groups will draw upon the resources of existing NATO committees.

Under the auspices of the Council, military representatives and Chiefs of Staff will also meet. Meetings of Chiefs of Staff will take place no less than twice a year, meetings at military representatives level at least once a month, with the possibility of more frequent meetings as needed. Meetings of military experts may be convened as appropriate.

The NATO-Russia Council, replacing the NATO-Russia Permanent Joint Council, will focus on all areas of mutual interest identified in Section III of the Founding Act, including the provision to add other areas by mutual agreement. The work programmes for 2002 agreed in December 2001 for the PJC and its subordinate bodies will continue to be implemented under the auspices and rules of the NATO-Russia Council. NATO member states and Russia will continue to intensify their cooperation in areas including the struggle against terrorism, crisis management, non-proliferation, arms control and confidence-building measures, theatre missile defence, search and rescue at sea, military-to-military cooperation, and civil emergencies. This cooperation may complement cooperation in other fora. As initial steps in this regard, we have today agreed to pursue the following cooperative efforts:

- *Struggle Against Terrorism*: strengthen cooperation through a multi-faceted approach, including joint assessments of the terrorist threat to the Euro-Atlantic area, focused on specific threats, for example, to Russian and NATO forces, to civilian aircraft, or to critical infrastructure; an initial step will be a joint assessment of the terrorist threat to NATO, Russia and Partner peacekeeping forces in the Balkans.

- *Crisis Management*: strengthen cooperation, including through: regular exchanges of views and information on peacekeeping operations, including continuing cooperation and consultations on the situation in the Balkans; promoting interoperability between national peacekeeping contingents, including through joint or coordinated training initiatives; and further development of a generic concept for joint NATO-Russia peacekeeping operations.

- *Non-Proliferation*: broaden and strengthen cooperation against the proliferation of weapons of mass destruction (WMD) and the means of their delivery, and contribute to strengthening existing non-proliferation arrangements through: a structured exchange of views, leading to a joint assessment of global trends in proliferation of nuclear, biological and chemical agents; and exchange of experience with the goal of exploring opportunities for intensified practical cooperation on protection from nuclear, biological and chemical agents.

- *Arms Control and Confidence-Building Measures*: recalling the contributions of arms control and confidence- and security-building measures (CSBMs) to stability in the Euro-Atlantic area and reaffirming adherence to the Treaty on Conventional Armed Forces in Europe (CFE) as a cornerstone of European security, work cooperatively toward ratification by all the States Parties and entry into force of the Agreement on Adaptation of the CFE Treaty, which would permit accession by non-CFE states; continue consultations on the CFE and Open Skies Treaties; and continue the NATO-Russia nuclear experts consultations.

- *Theatre Missile Defence*: enhance consultations on theatre missile defence (TMD), in particular on TMD concepts, terminology, systems and system capabilities, to analyse and evaluate possible levels of interoperability among respective TMD systems, and explore opportunities for intensified practical cooperation, including joint training and exercises.

- *Search and Rescue at Sea*: monitor the implementation of the NATO-Russia Framework Document on Submarine Crew Rescue, and continue to promote cooperation, transparency and confidence between NATO and Russia in the area of search and rescue at sea.

- *Military-to-Military Cooperation and Defence Reform*: pursue enhanced military-to-military cooperation and interoperability through enhanced joint training and exercises and the conduct of joint demonstrations and tests; explore the possibility of establishing an integrated NATO-Russia military training centre for missions to address the challenges of the 21st century; enhance cooperation on defence reform and its economic aspects, including conversion.
- *Civil Emergencies*: pursue enhanced mechanisms for future NATO-Russia cooperation in responding to civil emergencies. Initial steps will include the exchange of information on recent disasters and the exchange of WMD consequence management information.
- *New Threats and Challenges*: In addition to the areas enumerated above, explore possibilities for confronting new challenges and threats to the Euro-Atlantic area in the framework of the activities of the NATO Committee on Challenges to Modern Society (CCMS); initiate cooperation in the field of civil and military airspace controls; and pursue enhanced scientific cooperation.

The members of the NATO-Russia Council will work with a view to identifying further areas of cooperation.

UNSC Resolution 1244 (1999) (excerpts)

Adopted by the Security Council at its 4011th meeting on 10 June 1999

The Security Council,

Bearing in mind the purposes and principles of the Charter of the United Nations, and the primary responsibility of the Security Council for the maintenance of international peace and security,

Recalling its resolutions 1160 (1998) of 31 March 1998, 1199 (1998) of 23 September 1998, 1203 (1998) of 24 October 1998 and 1239 (1999) of 14 May 1999,

Regretting that there has not been full compliance with the require-ments of these resolutions,

Determined to resolve the grave humanitarian situation in Kosovo, Federal Republic of Yugoslavia, and to provide for the safe and free return of all refugees and displaced persons to their homes,

Condemning all acts of violence against the Kosovo population as well as all terrorist acts by any party,

Recalling the statement made by the Secretary-General on 9 April 1999, expressing concern at the humanitarian tragedy taking place in Kosovo,

Reaffirming the right of all refugees and displaced persons to return to their homes in safety,

Recalling the jurisdiction and the mandate of the International Tribunal for the Former Yugoslavia,

Welcoming the general principles on a political solution to the Kosovo crisis adopted on 6 May 1999 (S/1999/516, annex 1 to this resolu-tion) and welcoming also the acceptance by the Federal Republic of Yugoslavia of the principles set forth in points 1 to 9 of the paper presented in Belgrade on 2 June 1999 (S/1999/649, annex 2 to this resolution), and the Federal Republic of Yugoslavia's agreement to that paper,

Reaffirming the commitment of all Member States to the sovereignty and territorial integrity of the Federal Republic of Yugoslavia and the other States of the region, as set out in the Helsinki Final Act and annex 2,

Reaffirming the call in previous resolutions for substantial autonomy and meaningful self-administration for Kosovo,

Determining that the situation in the region continues to constitute a threat to international peace and security,

Determined to ensure the safety and security of international personnel and the implementation by all concerned of their responsibilities under the present resolution, and *acting* for these purposes under Chapter VII of the Charter of the United Nations,

1. *Decides* that a political solution to the Kosovo crisis shall be based on the general principles in annex 1 and as further elaborated in the principles and other required elements in annex 2;

2. *Welcomes* the acceptance by the Federal Republic of Yugoslavia of the principles and other required elements referred to in paragraph 1

above, and *demands* the full cooperation of the Federal Republic of Yugoslavia in their rapid implementation;

3. *Demands* in particular that the Federal Republic of Yugoslavia put an immediate and verifiable end to violence and repression in Kosovo, and begin and complete verifiable phased withdrawal from Kosovo of all military, police and paramilitary forces according to a rapid timetable, with which the deployment of the international security presence in Kosovo will be synchronized;

4. *Confirms* that after the withdrawal an agreed number of Yugoslav and Serb military and police personnel will be permitted to return to Kosovo to perform the functions in accordance with annex 2;

5. *Decides* on the deployment in Kosovo, under United Nations auspices, of international civil and security presences, with appropriate equipment and personnel as required, and welcomes the agreement of the Federal Republic of Yugoslavia to such presences;

6. *Requests* the Secretary-General to appoint, in consultation with the Security Council, a Special Representative to control the implementation of the international civil presence, and *further requests* the Secretary-General to instruct his Special Representative to coordinate closely with the international security presence to ensure that both presences operate towards the same goals and in a mutually supportive manner;

7. *Authorizes* Member States and relevant international organizations to establish the international security presence in Kosovo as set out in point 4 of annex 2 with all necessary means to fulfil its responsibilities under paragraph 9 below;

8. *Affirms* the need for the rapid early deployment of effective international civil and security presences to Kosovo, and *demands* that the parties cooperate fully in their deployment;

9. *Decides* that the responsibilities of the international security presence to be deployed and acting in Kosovo will include:

(a) Deterring renewed hostilities, maintaining and where necessary enforcing a ceasefire, and ensuring the withdrawal and preventing the return into Kosovo of Federal and Republic military, police and paramilitary forces, except as provided in point 6 of annex 2;

(b) Demilitarizing the Kosovo Liberation Army (KLA) and other armed Kosovo Albanian groups as required in paragraph 15 below;

(c) Establishing a secure environment in which refugees and displaced persons can return home in safety, the international civil presence can operate, a transitional administration can be established, and humanitarian aid can be delivered;

(d) Ensuring public safety and order until the international civil presence can take responsibility for this task;

(e) Supervising demining until the international civil presence can, as appropriate, take over responsibility for this task;

(f) Supporting, as appropriate, and coordinating closely with the work of the international civil presence;

(g) Conducting border monitoring duties as required;

(h) Ensuring the protection and freedom of movement of itself, the international civil presence, and other international organizations;

10. *Authorizes* the Secretary-General, with the assistance of relevant international organizations, to establish an international civil presence in Kosovo in order to provide an interim administration for Kosovo under which the people of Kosovo can enjoy substantial autonomy within the Federal Republic of Yugoslavia, and which will provide transitional administration while establishing and overseeing the development of provisional democratic self-governing institutions to ensure conditions for a peaceful and normal life for all inhabitants of Kosovo;

11. *Decides* that the main responsibilities of the international civil presence will include:

(a) Promoting the establishment, pending a final settlement, of substantial autonomy and self-government in Kosovo, taking full account of annex 2 and of the Rambouillet accords ...

(b) Performing basic civilian administrative functions where and as long as required;

(c) Organizing and overseeing the development of provisional institutions for democratic and autonomous self-government pending a political settlement, including the holding of elections;

(d) Transferring, as these institutions are established, its administrative responsibilities while overseeing and supporting the consolidation of Kosovo's local provisional institutions and other peace-building activities;

(e) Facilitating a political process designed to determine Kosovo's future status, taking into account the Rambouillet accords ...

(f) In a final stage, overseeing the transfer of authority from Kosovo's provisional institutions to institutions established under a political settlement;

(g) Supporting the reconstruction of key infrastructure and other economic reconstruction;

(h) Supporting, in coordination with international humanitarian organizations, humanitarian and disaster relief aid;

(i) Maintaining civil law and order, including establishing local police forces and meanwhile through the deployment of international police personnel to serve in Kosovo;

(j) Protecting and promoting human rights;

(k) Assuring the safe and unimpeded return of all refugees and displaced persons to their homes in Kosovo;

12. *Emphasizes* the need for coordinated humanitarian relief operations, and for the Federal Republic of Yugoslavia to allow unimpeded access to Kosovo by humanitarian aid organizations and to cooperate with such organizations so as to ensure the fast and effective delivery of international aid;

13. *Encourages* all Member States and international organizations to contribute to economic and social reconstruction as well as to the safe return of refugees and displaced persons, and *emphasizes* in this context the importance of convening an international donors' conference, particularly for the purposes set out in paragraph 11 (g) above, at the earliest possible date;

14. *Demands* full cooperation by all concerned, including the international security presence, with the International Tribunal for the Former Yugoslavia;

15. *Demands* that the KLA and other armed Kosovo Albanian groups end immediately all offensive actions and comply with the requirements for demilitarization as laid down by the head of the international security presence in consultation with the Special Representative of the Secretary-General;

16. *Decides* that the prohibitions imposed by paragraph 8 of resolution 1160 (1998) shall not apply to arms and related *matériel* for the use of the international civil and security presences;

17. *Welcomes* the work in hand in the European Union and other international organizations to develop a comprehensive approach to the economic development and stabilization of the region affected by the Kosovo crisis, including the implementation of a Stability Pact for South Eastern Europe with broad international participation in order to further the promotion of democracy, economic prosperity, stability and regional cooperation;

18. *Demands* that all States in the region cooperate fully in the implementation of all aspects of this resolution;

19. *Decides* that the international civil and security presences are established for an initial period of 12 months, to continue thereafter unless the Security Council decides otherwise;

20. *Requests* the Secretary-General to report to the Council at regular intervals on the implementation of this resolution, including reports from the leaderships of the international civil and security presences, the first reports to be submitted within 30 days of the adoption of this resolution;

21. *Decides* to remain actively seized of the matter.

Stability Pact for South Eastern Europe
Cologne June 1999 (excerpts)

II Principles and Norms

5. We solemnly reaffirm our commitment to all the principles and norms enshrined in the UN Charter, the Helsinki Final Act, the Charter of Paris, the 1990 Copenhagen Document and other OSCE documents, and, as applicable, to the full implementation of relevant UN Security Council Resolutions, the relevant conventions of the Council of Europe and the General Framework Agreement for Peace in Bosnia and Herzegovina, with a view to promoting good neighbourly relations.

6. In our endeavours, we will build upon bilateral and multilateral agreements on good neighbourly relations concluded by States in the region participating in the Pact, and will seek the conclusion of such agreements where they do not exist. They will form an essential element of the Stability Pact.

7. We reaffirm that we are accountable to our citizens and responsible to one another for respect for OSCE norms and principles and for the implementation of our commitments. We also reaffirm that commitments with respect to the human dimension undertaken through our membership in the OSCE are matters of direct and legitimate concern to all States participating in the Stability Pact, and do not belong exclusively to the internal affairs of the State concerned. Respect for these commitments constitutes one of the foundations of international order, to which we intend to make a substantial contribution.

8. We take note that countries in the region participating in the Stability Pact commit themselves to continued democratic and

economic reforms, as elaborated in paragraph 10, as well as bilateral and regional cooperation amongst themselves to advance their integration, on an individual basis, into Euro-Atlantic structures. The EU Member States and other participating countries and international organisations and institutions commit themselves to making every effort to assist them to make speedy and measurable progress along this road. We reaffirm the inherent right of each and every participating State to be free to choose or change its security arrangements, including treaties of alliance as they evolve. Each participating State will respect the rights of all others in this regard. They will not strengthen their security at the expense of the security of other States.

III Objectives

9. The Stability Pact aims at strengthening countries in South Eastern Europe in their efforts to foster peace, democracy, respect for human rights and economic prosperity, in order to achieve stability in the whole region. Those countries in the region who seek integration into Euro-Atlantic structures, alongside a number of other participants in the Pact, strongly believe that the implementation of this process will facilitate their objective.

10. To that end we pledge to cooperate towards:
- preventing and putting an end to tensions and crises as a prerequisite for lasting stability. This includes concluding and implementing among ourselves multilateral and bilateral agreements and taking domestic measures to overcome the existing potential for conflict;
- bringing about mature democratic political processes, based on free and fair elections, grounded in the rule of law and full respect for human rights and fundamental freedoms, including the rights of persons belonging to national minorities, the right to free and independent media, legislative branches accountable to their constituents, independent judiciaries, combating corruption, deepening and strengthening of civil society;
- creating peaceful and good-neighbourly relations in the region through strict observance of the principles of the Helsinki Final Act, confidence building and reconciliation, encouraging work in the OSCE and other fora on regional confidence building measures and mechanisms for security cooperation;

- preserving the multinational and multiethnic diversity of countries in the region, and protecting minorities;
- creating vibrant market economies based on sound macro policies, markets open to greatly expanded foreign trade and private sector investment, effective and transparent customs and commercial/ regulatory regimes, developing strong capital markets and diversified ownership, including privatisation, leading to a widening circle of prosperity for all our citizens;
- fostering economic cooperation in the region and between the region and the rest of Europe and the world, including free trade areas;
- promoting unimpeded contacts among citizens;
- combatting organised crime, corruption and terrorism and all criminal and illegal activities;
- preventing forced population displacement caused by war, persecution and civil strife as well as migration generated by poverty;
- ensuring the safe and free return of all refugees and displaced persons to their homes, while assisting the countries in the region by sharing the burden imposed upon them;
- creating the conditions, for countries of South Eastern Europe, for full integration into political, economic and security structures of their choice ...

Select bibliography

Document collections

Auerswald, P. and Auerswald, D., *The Kosovo Conflict: A Diplomatic History Through Documents* (Cambridge, Kluwer Law International, 2000).

Weller, M., *The Crisis in Kosovo 1989–1999: International Documents and Analysis, Volume 1* (Cambridge, Documents and Analysis Publishing, 1999).

Official reports

Les enseignement du Kosovo, French Ministry of Defence, November 1999. Website reference www.defence.gouv.fr/actualites/dossier/d36/index. html.

Kosovo: Vols I–II, House of Commons Select Committee on Foreign Affairs (London, The Stationery Office, 2000).

Kosovo: Lessons from the Crisis, UK Ministry of Defence (London, The Stationery Office, 2000).

Report to Congress: Kosovo/Operation Allied Force After-Action Report, US Department of Defense (Washington DC, US Government Printing Office, 2000).

Lessons of Kosovo: Vols I–II, House of Commons Select Committee on Defence (London, The Stationery Office, 2000).

Lord Robertson of Port Ellen, *Kosovo: An Account of the Crisis*, UK Ministry of Defence, October 1999. Website reference www.mod.uk/news/ kosovo/account/intro.htm.

Lord Robertson of Port Ellen, *Kosovo One Year On: Achievement and Challenge*, NATO, March 2000. Website reference www.nato.int/ kosovo/repo2000/index.htm.

Secondary academic sources

The nature of armed conflict

Baylis, J. *et al.*, *Contemporary Strategy: Theories and Concepts* (London, Croom Helm, 1987).

Black, J., *War: Past, Present and Future* (New York, St. Martin's Press, 2000).

Freedman, L., *The Revolution in Strategic Affairs (Adelphi Paper 318)* (Oxford, Oxford University Press, 1998).

Freedman, L. (ed.), *Strategic Coercion: Concepts and Cases* (Oxford, Oxford University Press, 1998).

Gacek, C., *The Logic of Force: The Dilemma of Limited War in American Foreign Policy* (New York, Columbia University Press, 1994).

Handel, M., *Masters of War: Classical Strategic Thought (3rd edition)* (London, Frank Cass, 2001).

Ignatieff, M., *Virtual War: Kosovo and Beyond* (London, Chatto and Windus, 2000).

Osgood, R., *Limited War: The Challenge to American Strategy* (Chicago, University of Chicago Press, 1957).

Conflict in South East Europe

Anzulovic, B., *Heavenly Serbia: From Myth to Genocide* (London, Hurst and Co., 1999).

Bokovoy, M. *et al.* (eds), *State–Society Relations in Yugoslavia 1945–1992* (Basingstoke, Macmillan, 1997).

Cohen, L., *Broken Bonds: Yugoslavia's Disintegration and Balkan Politics in Transition* (Boulder, Westview, 1995).

Crampton, R., *The Balkans since the Second World War* (London, Longman, 2002).

Crampton, R., *Eastern Europe in the Twentieth Century* (London, Routledge, 1994).

Dyker, D. and Vejvoda, I. (eds), *Yugoslavia and After: A Study in Fragmentation, Despair and Rebirth* (London, Longman, 1996).

Glenny, M., *The Balkans 1804–1999: Nationalism, War and the Great Powers* (London, Granta, 1999).

Holbrooke, R., *To End a War* (New York, The Modern Library, 1999).

Jelavich, B., *History of the Balkans: Twentieth Century* (Cambridge, Cambridge University Press, 1985).

Judah, T., *The Serbs: History, Myth and the Destruction of Yugoslavia* (New Haven, Yale University Press, 1997).

Larrabee, F. S. (ed.), *The Volatile Powder Keg: Balkan Security after the Cold War* (Washington DC, The American University Press, 1994).

Lukic, R. and Lynch, A., *Europe from the Balkans to the Urals: The Disintegration of Yugoslavia and the Soviet Union* (Oxford, Oxford University Press, 1996).

Magas, B. and Zanic, I., *The War in Croatia and Bosnia-Herzegovina 1991–1995* (London, Frank Cass, 2001).

Owen, D., *Balkan Odyssey* (London, Victor Gollancz, 1995).

Ramet, S., *Balkan Babel: The Disintegration of Yugoslavia from the Death of Tito to the War for Kosovo* (Boulder, Westview, 1999).

Schöpflin, G., *Politics in Eastern Europe 1945–1992* (Oxford, Blackwell, 1993).

Simms, B., *Unfinest Hour: Britain and the Destruction of Bosnia* (London, Penguin, 2001).

Woodward, S., *Balkan Tragedy: Chaos and Dissolution After the Cold War* (Washington DC, Brookings Institution, 1995).

The Kosovo conflict

After Milosevic: A Practical Agenda for Lasting Balkans Peace (Brussels, International Crisis Group, 2001).

Ali, T. (ed.), *Masters of the Universe? NATO's Balkan Crusade* (London, Verso, 2000).

Allin, D. *et al.*, *What Status for Kosovo? (Chaillot Paper 50)* (Paris, Institute for Security Studies, Western European Union, 2001).

Booth, K. (ed.), *The Kosovo Tragedy: The Human Rights Dimensions* (London, Frank Cass, 2001).

Buckley, M. and Cummings, S., *Kosovo: Perceptions of War and Its Aftermath* (London, Continuum, 2001).

Buckley, W. (ed.), *Kosovo: Contending Voices on Balkan Interventions* (Grand Rapids MI, William B. Eerdmans Publishing Co., 2000).

Daalder, I. and O'Hanlon, M., *Winning Ugly: NATO's War to Save Kosovo* (Washington DC, Brookings Institution, 2000).

Duijzings, G., *Religion and the Politics of Identity in Kosovo* (London, Hurst and Co., 2000).

Hammond, P. and Herman, E. (eds), *Degraded Capability: The Media and the Kosovo Crisis* (London, Pluto, 2000).

Humanitarian Law Violations in Kosovo (New York, Human Rights Watch, 1998).

Judah, T., *Kosovo: War and Revenge* (New Haven, Yale University Press, 2000).

Kosovo: The Evidence (London, Amnesty International, 1998).

The Kosovo Report: Conflict, International Response, Lessons Learned (Oxford, Oxford University Press, 2000).

Leurdijk, D. and Zandee, D., *Kosovo: From Crisis to Crisis* (Aldershot, Ashgate, 2001).

Martin, P. and Brawley, M. (eds), *Alliance Politics, Kosovo, and NATO's War: Allied Force or Forced Allies?* (Basingstoke, Palgrave, 2000).

Malcolm, N., *Kosovo: A Short History* (Basingstoke, Papermac, 1998).

Mertus, J., *Kosovo: How Myths and Truths Started a War* (Berkeley, University of California Press, 1999).

Prifti, P., *Confrontation in Kosova: The Albanian–Serb Struggle, 1969–1999* (New York, Columbia University Press, 1999).

Rezun, M., *Europe's Nightmare: The Struggle for Kosovo* (Westport, Praeger, 2001).

Roberts, A., 'NATO's "humanitarian war" over Kosovo', *Survival*, 41:3 (1999), 102–23.

Schnabel, A. and Thakur, R. (eds), *Kosovo and the Challenge of Humanitarian Intervention: Selective Indignation, Collective Action, and International Citizenship* (Tokyo, United Nations University Press, 2000).

Schwartz, S., *Kosovo: Background to a War* (London, Anthem Press, 2000).

Spillman, K. and Krause, J. (eds), *Kosovo: Lessons Learned for International Cooperative Security* (Bern, Peter Lang, 2000).

Thomas, R., *Serbia under Milosevic: Politics in the 1990s* (London, Hurst and Co., 1999).

Vickers, M., *Between Serb and Albanian: A History of Kosovo* (London, Hurst and Co., 1998).

Waller, M. *et al.* (eds), *Kosovo: The Politics of Delusion* (London, Frank Cass, 2001).

Weymouth, T. and Henig, S. (eds), *The Kosovo Crisis: The Last American War in Europe?* (London, Reuters, 2001).

Security

Buzan, B., *People, States and Fear: An Agenda for International Security Studies in the Post-Cold War Era* (New York, Harvester Wheatsheaf, 1991).

Buzan, B. *et al.*, *Security: A New Framework for Analysis* (Boulder, Lynne Rienner, 1998).

Freedman, L., 'International security: changing targets', *Foreign Policy*, 110 (1998), 48–65.

Terry, S., '"Deepening" and "widening": an analysis of security definitions in the 1990s', *Journal of Military and Strategic Studies*, (Autumn 1999). Website reference www.stratnet.ucalgary.ca/journal/.

Intervention, sovereignty and 'stateness'

Abiew, F., *The Evolution of the Doctrine and Practice of Humanitarian Intervention* (The Hague, Kluwer Law International, 1999).

Bull, H. (ed.), *Intervention in World Politics* (Oxford, Clarendon Press, 1984).

Chesterman, S., *Just War or Just Peace? Humanitarian Intervention and International Law* (Oxford, Oxford University Press, 2001).

Chomsky, N., *A New Generation Draws the Line: Kosovo, East Timor and the Standards of the West* (London, Verso, 2000).

Chomsky, N., *The New Military Humanism: Lessons from Kosovo* (London, Pluto, 1999).

Coker, C. (ed.), *The United States, Western Europe and Military Intervention Overseas* (London, Macmillan, 1987).

Connaughton, R., *Military Intervention and Peacekeeping: The Reality* (Aldershot, Ashgate, 2001).

Connaughton, R., *Military Intervention in the 1990s: A New Logic of War* (London, Routledge, 1992).

Dorman, A. and Otte, T., *Military Intervention: From Gunboat Diplomacy to Humanitarian Intervention* (Aldershot, Dartmouth, 1995).

Ero, C. and Long, S., 'Humanitarian intervention: a new role for the United Nations?', *International Peacekeeping*, 2:2 (1995), 140–56.

Fowler, M. and Bunck, J., 'What constitutes the sovereign state?', *Review of International Studies*, 22:4 (1996), 381–404.

Freedman, L. (ed.), *Military Intervention in European Conflicts* (Oxford, Blackwell, 1994).

Glennon, M., *Limits of Law, Prerogatives of Power: Interventionism After Kosovo* (London, Palgrave, 2001).

Guicherd, C., 'International law and the war in Kosovo', *Survival*, 41:2 (1999), 19–34.

Keren, M. and Sylvan, D. (eds), *International Intervention: Sovereignty versus Responsibility* (London, Frank Cass, 2002).

Levite, A., *et al.* (eds), *Foreign Military Intervention: The Dynamics of Protracted Conflict* (New York, Columbia University Press, 1992).

Littman, M., *Kosovo: Law and Diplomacy* (London, Centre for Policy Studies, 1999).

Lyons, G. and Mastanduno, M. (eds), *Beyond Westphalia? State Sovereignty and International Intervention* (Baltimore, The Johns Hopkins University Press, 1995).

Mazarr, M., 'The military dilemmas of humanitarian intervention', *Security Dialogue*, 24:2 (1993), 151–62.

Mayall, J. (ed.), *The New Interventionism 1991–1994: United Nations Experience in Cambodia, former Yugoslavia and Somalia* (Cambridge, Cambridge University Press, 1996).

Morgenthau, H., 'To intervene or not to intervene', *Foreign Affairs*, 45:3 (1967), 425–36.

Mott, W., 'The paradoxes of intervention', *Defence Analysis*, 12:2 (1996), 189–204.

Murphy, S., *Humanitarian Intervention: The United Nations in an Evolving World Order* (Philadelphia, University of Pennsylvania Press, 1996).

Ortega, M., *Military Intervention and the European Union (Chaillot Paper 45)* (Paris, Institute for Security Studies, Western European Union, March 2001).

Ramsbotham, O. and Woodhouse, T., *Humanitarian Intervention in Contemporary Conflict: A Reconceptualization* (Cambridge, Polity Press, 1996).

The Responsibility to Protect (Ottawa, International Commission on Intervention and State Sovereignty, December 2001).

The Responsibility to Protect: Research, Bibliography and Background (Ottawa, International Commission on Intervention and State Sovereignty, December 2001).

Reus-Smit, C., 'Human rights and the social construction of sovereignty', *Review of International Studies*, 27:4 (2001), 519–38.

Stern, E. (ed.), *The Limits of Military Intervention* (Beverly Hills, Sage, 1977).

Tomes, R., 'Operation Allied Force and the legal basis for humanitarian interventions', *Parameters*, 30:1 (2000), 8–50.

Tomuschat, C. (ed.), *Kosovo and the International Community* (The Hague, Kluwer Law International, 2002).

Walter, B. and Snyder, J. (eds), *Civil Wars, Insecurity, and Intervention* (New York, Columbia University Press, 1999).

Weber, C., 'Reconsidering statehood: examining the sovereignty/intervention boundary', *Review of International Studies*, 18:3 (1992), 199–216.

Weiss, T., *Military-Civilian Interactions: Intervening in Humanitarian Crises* (Lanham, Rowman and Littlefield, 1999).

Wheeler, N., *Saving Strangers: Humanitarian Intervention in International Society* (Oxford, Oxford University Press, 2000).

Ethics of intervention

Carment, D. and Harvey, F., *Using Force to Prevent Ethnic Violence: An Evaluation of Theory and Evidence* (Westport, Praeger, 2001).

Coates, A., *The Ethics of War* (Manchester, Manchester University Press, 1997).

Forbes, I. and Hoffman, M. (eds), *Political Theory, International Relations and the Ethics of Intervention* (Basingstoke, St. Martin's Press, 1993).

Heidenrich, J., *How to Prevent Genocide: A Guide for Policymakers, Scholars, and the Concerned Citizen* (Westport, Praeger, 2001).

Hoffman, S., *et al.*, *The Ethics and Politics of Humanitarian Intervention* (Notre Dame IN, University of Notre Dame Press, 1996).

Liotta, P., 'Towards a bad end: the ethics of intervention in the former Yugoslavia', *European Security*, 7:4 (1998), 33–68.

Phillips, R. and Cady, D., *Humanitarian Intervention: Just War vs. Pacifism* (London, Rowman and Littlefield, 1996).

Regan, R., *Just War: Principles and Cases* (Washington DC, The Catholic University Press of America, 1996).

Rodley, N. (ed.), *To Loose the Bands of Wickedness: International Intervention in Defence of Human Rights* (London, Brassey's, 1992).

Smith, K. and Light, M. (eds), *Ethics and Foreign Policy* (Cambridge, Cambridge University Press, 2001).

Nationalism, self-determination and ethnic conflict

Bell-Fialkoff, A., *Ethnic Cleansing* (Basingstoke, Macmillan, 1996).

Bose, S., *Bosnia after Dayton: Nationalist Partition and International Intervention* (London, Hurst and Co., 2002).

Bugajski, J., *Nations in Turmoil: Conflict and Cooperation in Eastern Europe* (Boulder, Westview, 1993).

Denitch, B., *Ethnic Nationalism: The Tragic Death of Yugoslavia* (Minneapolis, University of Minnesota Press, 1994).

Guibernau, M., *Nationalisms: The Nation-State and Nationalism in the Twentieth Century* (London, Polity Press, 1996).

Gurr, T. R. and Harff, B., *Ethnic Conflict in World Politics* (Boulder, Westview, 1994).

Hobsbawm, E. J., *Nations and Nationalism since 1780: Programme, Myth and Reality* (Cambridge, Cambridge University Press, 1992).

Huntington, S. P., *The Clash of Civilizations and the Remaking of World Order* (London, Touchstone Books, 1997).

Hutchinson, J. and Smith, A. D. (eds), *Ethnicity* (Oxford, Oxford University Press, 1996).

Hutchinson, J. and Smith, A. D. (eds), *Nationalism* (Oxford, Oxford University Press, 1994).

Ignatieff, M., *The Warrior's Honor: Ethnic War and the Modern Conscience* (London, Vintage, 1999).

Kumar, R., *Divide and Fall? Bosnia in the Annals of Partition* (London, Verso, 1999).

Latawski, P. (ed.), *Contemporary Nationalism in East Central Europe* (Basingstoke, Macmillan, 1995).

Opello, W. and Rosow, S., *The Nation-State and Global Order: A Historical Introduction to Contemporary Politics* (Boulder, Lynne Rienner, 1999).

Pavkovic, A., *The Fragmentation of Yugoslavia: Nationalism in a Multi-national State* (Basingstoke, Macmillan, 1997).

Poulton, H., *The Balkans: Minorities and States in Conflict* (London, Minority Rights Publications, 1991).

Seton-Watson, H., *Nations and States: An Enquiry into the Origins of Nations and the Politics of Nationalism* (London, Methuen, 1977).

Shehadi, K., *Ethnic Self-Determination and the Break-up of States (Adelphi Paper 283)* (Oxford, Oxford University Press, 1993).

Smith, A. D., *The Nation in History: Historiographical Debates About Ethnicity and Nationalism* (London, Polity Press, 2000).

Smith, A. D., *Nations and Nationalism in a Global Era* (London, Polity Press, 1995).

Snow, D., *Uncivil Wars: International Security and the New Internal Conflicts* (Boulder, Lynne Rienner, 1996).

Stack, J. and Hebron, L. (eds), *The Ethnic Entanglement: Conflict and Intervention in World Politics* (Westport, Praeger, 1999).

Stavenhagen, R., *Ethnic Conflicts and the Nation-State* (Basingstoke, Macmillan, 1996).

Sugar, P. and Lederer, I. (eds), *Nationalism in Eastern Europe* (Seattle, University of Washington Press, 1971).

Democracy and peace-building

Brown, M. *et al.* (eds), *Debating the Democratic Peace* (Cambridge, Mass, The MIT Press, 1996).

Burg, S., *War or Peace? Nationalism, Democracy, and American Foreign Policy in Post-Communist Europe* (New York, New York University Press, 1996).

Cordell, K. (ed), *Ethnicity and Democratisation in the New Europe* (London, Routledge, 1999).

Dunne, M. and Bonazzi, T. (eds), *Citizenship and Rights in Multicultural Societies* (Keele, Keele University Press, 1995).

Liebich, A. *et al.* (eds), *Citizenship East and West* (London, Kegan Paul International, 1995).

MacMillan, J., *On Liberal Peace: Democracy, War and the International Order* (London, Tauris, 1998).

Post-Cold War NATO and European security

Bronstone, A., *European Security into the Twenty-First Century* (Aldershot, Ashgate, 2000).

Carr, F. and Ifantis, K., *NATO in the New European Security Order* (Basingstoke, Macmillan, 1996).

David, C-P. and Levesque, J. (eds), *The Future of NATO: Enlargement, Russia, and European Security* (Quebec City, McGill-Queen's University Press, 1999).

Dutkiewicz, P. and Jackson, R., *NATO Looks East* (Westport, Praeger, 1998).

Gordon, P. (ed.), *NATO's Transformation: The Changing Shape of the Atlantic Alliance* (Lanham, Rowman and Littlefield, 1997).

Grayson, G., *Strange Bedfellows: NATO Marches East* (Lanham, University Press of America, 1999).

Hodge, C. (ed.), *Redefining European Security* (New York, Garland Publishing, 1999).

Kay, S., *NATO and the Future of European Security* (Lanham, Rowman and Littlefield, 1998).

Michta, A. (ed.), *America's New Allies: Poland, Hungary, and the Czech Republic in NATO* (Seattle, University of Washington Press, 1999).

Papacosma, S. V. *et al.*, *NATO after Fifty Years* (Wilmington, SR Books, 2001).

Park, W. and Rees, G. W. (eds), *Rethinking Security in Post-Cold War Europe* (London, Longman, 1998).

Sandler, T., *The Political Economy of NATO: Past, Present, and into the 21st Century* (Cambridge, Cambridge University Press, 1999).

Thompson, K. (ed.), *NATO and the Changing World Order* (Lanham, University Press of America, 1996).

Wyllie, J., *European Security in the New Political Environment* (London, Longman, 1997).

European security identity and transatlantic relations

Brenner, M., *Terms of Engagement: The United States and the European Security Identity* (Westport, Praeger, 1998).

Cornish, P., *Partnership in Crisis: The US, Europe and the Fall and Rise of NATO* (London, Pinter, 1997).

Duke, S., *The Elusive Quest for European Security: From EDC to CFSP* (Basingstoke, Macmillan, 2000).

Eliassen, K. (ed.), *Foreign and Security Policy in the European Union* (London, Sage, 1998).

Kupchan, C. (ed.), *Atlantic Security: Contending Visions* (Washington DC, Council on Foreign Relations, 1998).

Vanhoonacker, S., *The Bush Administration (1989–1993) and the Development of a European Security Identity* (Aldershot, Ashgate, 2001).

Russia and NATO

Adomeit, H., 'Russia as a "great power" in world affairs: images and reality', *International Affairs*, 71:1 (1995), 35–68.

Antonenko, O., 'Russia, NATO and European security after Kosovo', *Survival*, 41:4 (1999-2000), 124–44.

Arbatov, A. *et al.* (eds), *Russia and the West: The 21st Century Security Environment* (London, M. E. Sharpe, 1999).

Baranovsky, V. (ed.), *Russia and Europe: The Emerging Security Agenda* (Oxford, Oxford University Press, 1997).

Braithwaite, R., 'Russian realities and western policy', *Survival*, 36:3 (1994), 11–27.

Buszynski, L., *Russian Foreign Policy after the Cold War* (Westport, Praeger, 1996).

Cimbala, S. (ed.), *The Russian Military into the Twenty-First Century* (London, Frank Cass, 2001).

Dick, C. J., *How Far Can the West Afford to Ignore Russia?* (Camberley, Conflict Studies Research Centre, 1999).

Goodby, J. (ed.), *Regional Conflicts: The Challenge to US-Russian Co-operation* (Oxford, Oxford University Press, 1995).

Levitin, O., 'Inside Moscow's Kosovo muddle', *Survival*, 42:1 (2000), 130–40.

Sherr, J. and Main, S., *Russian and Ukrainian Perceptions of Events in Yugoslavia* (Camberley, Conflict Studies Research Centre, 1999).

Smith, M. A., *Russian Thinking on European Security After Kosovo* (Camberley, Conflict Studies Research Centre, 1999).

Tikhomirov, V. (ed.), *Russia After Yeltsin* (Aldershot, Ashgate, 2001).

Index